CREATING a COACHING CULTURE

for Professional Learning Communities

JANE A. G. KISE • BETH RUSSELL

Solution Tree | Press

a division of
Solution Tree

Published by Solution Tree Press

555 North Morton Street
Bloomington, IN 47404

800.733.6786 (toll free) / 812.336.7700
FAX: 812.336.7790

email: info@solution-tree.com
solution-tree.com

Visit **go.solution-tree.com/PLCbooks** to download the reproducibles in this book.

Printed in the United States of America

14 13 12 11 10   1 2 3 4 5

FSC
Mixed Sources
Product group from well-managed
forests and other controlled sources
Cert no. SW-COC-002283
www.fsc.org
© 1996 Forest Stewardship Council

Library of Congress Cataloging-in-Publication Data

Kise, Jane A. G.
    Creating a coaching culture for professional learning communities / Jane A.G. Kise, Beth Russell.
        p. cm.
    Includes bibliographical references and index.
    ISBN 978-1-935249-41-2 (perfect bound) -- ISBN 978-1-935249-42-9 (library binding) 1. Teachers--In-service training--United States. 2. Teachers--Professional relationships--United States. 3. Professional learning communities--United States. I. Russell, Beth (Beth Ross-Shannon) II. Title.
    LB1731.K55 2010
    370.71'55--dc22
                            2010010117

Solution Tree
Jeffrey C. Jones, CEO & President

Solution Tree Press
President: Douglas M. Rife
Publisher: Robert D. Clouse
Vice President of Production: Gretchen Knapp
Managing Production Editor: Caroline Wise
Senior Production Editor: Suzanne Kraszewski
Copy Editor: Rachel Rosolina
Proofreader: Elisabeth Abrams
Text and Cover Designer: Orlando Angel

Acknowledgments

Our ideas for coaching professional learning communities were honed and enhanced through the leadership teams with which we have worked. We would especially like to thank teacher leaders Kate Andrews, Sara Wernimont, Chris Wernimont, and Joe Chan, who constantly helped us step into the shoes of teachers as we worked together to plan professional development and articulate school strategies.

Beth would like to specifically acknowledge Carol Markham Cousins who kept a constant focus on student learning while processing ideas around professional learning communities. And Jane would like to thank Carol Shumate for her insights and dedication as they worked together to coach professional learning communities.

Solution Tree Press would like to thank the following reviewers:

David Adelizi
Director of Staff Development
Williamsville Central School District
East Amherst, New York

Lisa Maltezos
Principal
Claywell Elementary School
Tampa, Florida

Sue Beach
Professional Development Consultant
Prairie Lakes Area Education Agency 8
Fort Dodge, Iowa

Dorothy Muna
Resource Teacher
Albuquerque Public Schools
Albuquerque, New Mexico

Beverly Ginther
Staff Development Coordinator
Minnetonka Public Schools
Minnetonka, Minnesota

Rosetta Riddle
Professional Learning Coordinator
Henry County Schools
McDonough, Georgia

Sheryle Kuhnley
Math Content Coach
Albuquerque Public Schools
Albuquerque, New Mexico

Winsome Waite
Senior Program Associate
Learning Point Associates
Washington, DC

Visit **go.solution-tree.com/PLCbooks** to download the reproducibles in this book.

Table of Contents

4 Differentiating the PLC Structure 65

5 Coaching for Genuine Community 83

6 Coaching a Group Into a Collaborative Team 103

About the Authors

Jane A. G. Kise, EdD, is an educational consultant specializing in teambuilding, coaching, and school staff development while partnering with schools and districts on in-depth change projects. She is also the coauthor of more than twenty books, including *Differentiated Coaching: A Framework for Helping Teachers Change; Differentiation Through Personality Types: A Framework for Instruction, Assessment, and Classroom Management; Introduction to Type and Coaching; LifeKeys: Discover Who You Are;* and *Work It Out: Using Personality Type to Improve Team Performance.* She holds an MBA in finance from the Carlson School of Management and a doctorate in educational leadership from the University of St. Thomas.

Kise has worked with diverse organizations, including Minneapolis Public Schools and various public and private schools, the Bush Foundation, Twin Cities Public Television, and numerous other institutions. She is a frequent workshop speaker and has presented at National Staff Development Council (NSDC), National Council of Teachers of Mathematics (NCTM), World Futures, and Association for Psychological Type International (APTi) conferences. She has taught writing at the university level. She is a faculty member of the Center for Applications of Psychological Type and past president of APTi. She also volunteers as a reviewer for NCTM. In 2005, she won the Isabel Briggs Myers Memorial Research Award for Outstanding Research in the Field of Psychological Type.

Beth Russell, EdD, is principal of South View Middle School in a suburb of Minneapolis. She holds a BS in child development and family relations from Colorado State University, a master's degree in social work from the University of Minnesota, and a doctorate in educational policy and administration from the University of Minnesota.

Russell has worked in both urban and suburban school systems introducing type. Coauthor of *Differentiated School Leadership: Effective Collaboration, Communication, and Change Through Personality Type* and several articles for education publications, she views type theory as a vehicle for helping students self-advocate for how they learn best and helping teachers identify new strategies so that all students can learn. She has presented at NSDC, World Futures, Association for Supervision and Curriculum Development, and National Urban Alliance conferences. She has participated in the National Institute for School Leadership, trained at the Institute for Learning at the University of Pittsburgh, and directed the

Minneapolis Public Schools in implementing a comprehensive framework for teaching and learning. Russell volunteers as an assessor for the University of St. Thomas Principal Assessment Center and provides peer reviews for educational books for Free Spirit Publishing.

Introduction: Why Use These Pages?

The first and most brutal fact that must be confronted in creating PLCs is that the task is not merely challenging: it is daunting. It is disingenuous to suggest that the transformation will be easy or to present it with a rosy optimism that obscures the inevitable turmoil ahead.

—DuFour, DuFour, Eaker, & Many, 2006

When we googled "professional learning community," we got more than seventy-eight million results. There is no doubt that the concept of teachers coming together in teams to work collaboratively on goals designed to improve student achievement has gained momentum. Other excellent books lay out the essential characteristics and driving mission of professional learning communities (PLCs), such as *Learning by Doing: A Handbook for Professional Learning Communities at Work*™ (DuFour et al., 2006). We assume you are familiar with the framework; perhaps you've even established your PLCs or are a year or more into the process.

So why add another book to the abundance of material out there? Because the evidence is in: researchers agree that launching PLCs may be easy, but turning them into productive, sustainable teams that improve adult and student learning is difficult. Researchers concur that developing effective PLCs takes years, even with extensive support (DuFour, DuFour, & Eaker, 2008; Grossman, Wineburg, & Woolworth, 2001; Hargreaves, 2007; Hord, 2004; Kruse & Louis, 2007). Bruce Joyce (2004) points out that educators have tried—and failed—to build collaborative teams in the past, under guises such as team teaching, the middle school reform model, whole-school action research, and other school improvement efforts. His concern is that without care, the PLC movement will similarly fade away. The following paragraphs highlight some of the most insightful quotes from research on creating PLCs.

Shirley Hord reflects on an extensive project she undertook to implement effective PLCs that included significant outside support and professional development:

> Despite the enthusiastic embrace of PLC principles in many schools in this study, despite the efforts of co-developers and [Southwest Educational Development Laboratory] staff, and despite various levels of success in each of the other four PLC dimensions, the powerful, multiple, and entrenched barriers to shared personal practice remained virtually unmoved after 3 years of effort . . . teachers did not visit one another's classrooms, collaboratively review student work, or engage in significant critical feedback with their colleagues. (2004, p. 152)

Andy Hargreaves (2007), in the concluding essay of a book about research and PLCs, describes his concerns about shallow implementation of PLCs:

> From their promising early beginnings, so-called professional learning communities are increasingly turning into something else. Instead of being intelligently informed by evidence in deep and demanding cultures of trusted relationships that press for success, PLCs are turning into add-on teams that are driven by data in cultures of fear that demand instant results. Data-driven instruction ends up driving educators to distraction—away from the passion and enthusiasm for rich processes of teaching and learning in classrooms and enriched relationships with children, into a tunnel-vision focus on manipulating and improving test scores in literacy and mathematics by any quick fix available—more test preparation here, after-school classes there, concentrating on cells of children who fall just below the line somewhere else. All this does nothing to enhance the actual quality of teaching and learning. (p. 183)

Grossman et al. (2001) analyze their experiences after two-and-a-half years of professional development work with a teacher community:

> In contrast to the idealistic visions sketched in the advocacy literature on teacher community, bringing teachers together can hurt as well as help, especially when norms for interacting in a public sphere are ill defined. Reducing isolation can unleash workplace conflicts that were, ironically, kept in check by the very isolation in which teachers work. To assume that teachers, just because they have experience in creating social organizations among children, can spontaneously organize themselves into congenial social units reflects a romanticism that misrepresents the realities of group dynamics in complex settings such as schools. (p. 991)

Gunn and King (2003) express similar reservations as a result of their efforts with an interdisciplinary team. They state, "Our analysis reveals the complex and often-contradictory work of teacher teams. Hierarchies can emerge, individualistic tendencies can persist, genuine consensus can be elusive, and members can be silenced" (p. 191).

Achinstein (2002) examined the micropolitics of teacher communities and the enormous conflicts that arise when teachers discuss beliefs and practices. She concludes, "Policy makers should reconsider naïve initiatives that put teachers in groups and expect them to learn and grow, disregarding the complexity of the collaborative process and the time needed to navigate differences" (p. 450).

While some PLCs are indeed able to move quickly to deep collaboration, different groups may be at different stages even within the same school. As one professional development coach put it, "We are in our third year of PLCs. While some groups are functioning well and data/assessment gathered is driving instruction, other groups are still spending their time spinning the same old wheels over the same old topics." This book is designed to help you stop the spinning—or help you launch PLCs with as little spinning as possible—by providing tools that help you collaborate efficiently and effectively as you focus on student learning.

Focusing on Student Learning and Adult Learning

Some may think that PLCs should wait to begin focusing on student learning until the adults unanimously agree that they are ready to do so. This is not the case. DuFour et al. (2006) rightly warn that "schools that take the plunge and actually begin *doing* the work of a PLC develop their capacity to help all students learn at high levels far more effectively than schools that spend years *preparing* to become PLCs through reading or even training" (p. 8). However, when taking the plunge, PLCs can easily make one of the following two mistakes:

1. Groups stall, as DuFour et al. (2006) warn against, by completely focusing on adult learning—without taking action—until they figure out how to work together, how to look at data, how to set goals, and so on. If teachers don't apply what they are learning to their own students, nothing will change in classrooms.

2. Groups assume that people can automatically work in teams and jump right into the work of PLCs without any attention to adult learning. You might be lucky. Your group may have the necessary collaborative skills and trust. However, researchers point out that many, if not most, PLCs never develop into effective, sustainable teams.

Creating a Coaching Culture for Professional Learning Communities is carefully designed to help you build a collaborative coaching culture that ensures all adults are learning through activities that keep the team focused on student learning. The coaching framework focuses on both adult learning *and* student learning within PLCs and lets you:

- Coach yourself as a PLC leader

- Coach each individual into a team player

- Create a culture in which peer coaching is both welcomed and effective

- Coach a PLC in efficient ways to meet the needs of all students

These pages aren't a recipe for you to follow. Instead, each chapter tailors information and exercises to fit your leadership style, the learning styles of each teacher, and the particular needs of your school to ensure that your hard work produces results: improved student learning.

While each chapter is useful at every level of PLC leadership, the guiding questions in table I.1 (pages 4–5) should help you get the most out of these pages.

Table I.1: Role-Based Guiding Questions

If your role is . . .	Appropriate guiding questions might be . . .
District leadership	Chapter 2: How can this framework provide synergy among various initiatives? What is the overall culture of our district; which personality preferences do we honor? Do we have biases toward what we consider the "right" way to lead, teach, and learn? Chapter 3: What essential leadership roles do we underplay or ignore in planning? How do our strengths help and hinder in setting vision, mission, values, or goals? Do we provide support for all three stages of PLC development? Are we forming effective leadership teams in each school?
Building leadership	Chapter 3: How can my leadership team and I cover all roles? Which roles need emphasis to move our PLCs to the next stage? Chapter 4: Do professional development efforts and PLC structures meet the needs of all teachers? Why might some PLCs be "stuck"? Chapter 5: What professional development activities might help PLCs improve in making constructive use of their differences? Chapter 6: For which specific PLC activities (for example, data analysis, unit planning, learning progressions, SMART [specific, measurable, achievable, results oriented, and time-bound] goals) do teachers need more training? Chapter 7: As we focus on student learning, which students might we be leaving out? What whole-school efforts might result in fewer students needing interventions *and* meet the needs of students who grasp concepts quickly (for example, choices, assignment menus, student-centered discussions, project-based learning)?
PLC leadership	Chapter 4: What strengths and biases does our PLC have? How can we best support each other's learning? What norms will best support collaboration and communication for this particular group? Chapter 5: How can we team up most effectively to reach all students? How can we develop deep trust for conversations about curriculum, assessment, and interventions? How can we hold each other accountable without becoming judgmental?

If your role is . . .	Appropriate guiding questions might be . . .
PLC leadership *(continued)*	**Chapter 6:** Are we making progress on each of the eight markers of deep collaboration? What adult learning goals do we need now to improve student achievement? **Chapter 7:** What information might we gather to determine whether we habitually leave out some learning styles? What activity might help us understand how to reach students very different from ourselves?
Instructional coach	**Chapter 4:** What is the primary style of this PLC, and how can I use that information to best meet teachers' needs? How might I differentiate the support that teachers need for various efforts? **Chapter 5:** In what ways can I assist in building consensus or resolving conflict? **Chapter 6:** What protocols for looking at data, student work, or assessments best meet the style of this group? How can I help this team make balanced decisions? **Chapter 7:** What are this team's blind spots in regard to student learning needs?
PLC member	**Chapter 3:** Which roles could I play that would move our PLC to the next stage? In what areas does this PLC need more leadership or support? **Chapter 4:** How can I help make this PLC the best part of everyone's job? How can I advocate for my own needs while balancing the needs of others? **Chapter 6:** Where am I comfortable sharing my own work? Samples of student work? Assessments? Lesson plans? Classroom observations? What skills do I need to develop to help all students learn? **Chapter 7:** What are my own biases regarding teaching and learning? Student behavior? What first steps could I take in giving choices or in the other differentiation techniques mentioned?

Chapter 1, "Understanding Why PLCs Need a Coaching Culture," lays out how a coaching model can ensure that your multiyear effort results in effective, sustainable PLCs and how the different elements of the model help overcome specific barriers to PLC effectiveness identified in research.

Chapter 2, "Describing a Framework for Coaching, Teaching, and Learning," describes a framework for making constructive use of differences in collaborative work and decision making with regard to teaching learning. More than sixty years of research and more than ten thousand citations establish the theory of personality type, popularized through the Myers-Briggs Type Indicator® (MBTI), as an effective tool for the following:

- Collaboration

- Communication

- Avoidance of "group think"

- Balanced decision making and problem solving

- Conflict resolution

- Balanced short-term and long-term strategic planning

- Achievement of adult and student learning goals

Through examples and exercises, chapter 2 carefully ties the elements of the framework to how adults and students learn.

Chapter 3, "Coaching Yourself as a Leader," discusses the leadership roles needed to move PLCs through three developmental stages toward effectiveness and sustainability. The chapter is designed to help leaders understand the roles they naturally emphasize and where sharing leadership may be beneficial.

Chapter 4, "Differentiating the PLC Structure," synthesizes the framework of differentiated coaching with the PLC model, examining the emphases, activities, data sources, and atmospheres within teams that will appeal to teachers with different learning styles.

Chapter 5, "Coaching for Genuine Community," provides tools and activities that turn a group of individuals into a team with deep trust and a common vision that listens to and values each member.

Chapter 6, "Coaching a Group Into a Collaborative Team," provides eight markers as to whether PLCs are making progress toward effectiveness and sustainability, as well as tools for developing best practices in each of the eight areas.

Chapter 7, "Coaching for Optimal Student Engagement and Achievement," demonstrates the usefulness of a framework such as personality type for educational decision making. Working through the critical tasks of PLCs, the chapter provides information and tools that help teams avoid biased decisions.

We are not suggesting that every PLC needs to use every activity in this book. Rather, this resource provides activities designed to meet a wide variety of needs so that you can choose the ones that best fit the developmental and learning style needs of the PLCs with which you work, all the while keeping the focus on student learning. For those of you familiar with the three big ideas framework of PLCs (DuFour, DuFour, & Eaker, 2008), you can use table I.2 to guide your choices as you help your PLCs focus on learning, build a collaborative culture, and focus on results. The purpose of a professional *learning* community is to foster an environment in which the adults are learning so that they can better help students learn. We hope that these pages will make your journey to effective collaboration as smooth, as swift, and as satisfying as possible.

Table I.2: Creating a Coaching Culture Within the Three Big Ideas of a PLC

	Relevant Chapters, Activities, and Tools	Page	Goals
First Big Idea: Focus on Learning			
	Activity 5.2, "Evidence-Based Discussions"	92–93	Forming a common belief that effort, not aptitude, creates ability
	Activity 5.3, "A Vision for PLCs"	94–95	Coming to consensus on PLC vision and mission
First critical question: What do our students need to learn?	Activity 6.2, "What Is Rigor?"	107	Developing a common definition of rigor, free from bias
	Activity 6.3, "Evaluating the Rigor of Tasks"	108	Building consensus regarding what makes an academic task rigorous
	Activity 6.9, "Building a Learning Progression"	119–120	Identifying and sequencing concepts and skills for knowledge mastery
	Activity 6.10, "Collaborative Unit Planning"	121–123	Creating deep collaboration on backward planning of curriculum
	Activity 7.1, "Essential Facts for Our Content Area"	138	Collaborating to identify "power standards"
Second critical question: How will we know if they have learned it?	Activity 6.4, "Looking at Assessments"	110–111	Building trust and skills at developing assessments
	Activity 7.3, "Differentiated Formative Assessments"	143	Broadening types of assessments
	Activity 7.4, "Discussion Model for Looking at Student Work"	144–145	Building trust and skills at unbiased review of student work

continued on next page →

	Relevant Chapters, Activities, and Tools	Page	Goals
Third critical question: What will we do if they don't learn it?	Chapter 7, "The Case for Type as an Education Framework," and "'What Will We Do If They Don't Get It?' and Type"	130, 145	Tailoring interventions to meet the needs of diverse students
	Activity 7.2, "Differentiated Lesson Planning"	140	Lesson planning to ensure more students "get it"
	Chapter 7, "Using Type to Evaluate Student Experiences"	141	Evaluating classroom experiences of students needing interventions
Fourth critical question: How will we extend the learning of those who are already proficient or who reach mastery?	Chapter 7, "'How Will We Extend Learning?' and Type"	147	Decreasing the number of students needing interventions

Second Big Idea: Build a Collaborative Culture

Collaborative Teams Focused on Learning

	Relevant Chapters, Activities, and Tools	Page	Goals
PLC norms	Activity 4.1, "Evaluating Your PLC Atmosphere"	66	Understanding the learning needs of each team member
	Activity 4.2, "Understanding the PLC Styles"	68	Tuning PLC activities to meet member needs
	Activity 5.1, "Group Norms and Collaboration Cues"	90	Setting norms that meet the needs of a particular group
Consensus and conflict	Chapter 5, "Process 1: Assessing the Quality of Relationships"	84	Identifying existing relationship difficulties that could hinder PLC effectiveness
	Activity 6.8, "Productive Conflict"	117–118	Meeting different needs during conflict
	Chapter 6, "Markers of a Coaching Culture for PLCs"	104	Strategizing for and evaluating improvement of PLC collaboration depth
	Appendix B, "Problem-Solving Model"	173	Improving PLC ability to make good decisions

	Relevant Chapters, Activities, and Tools	Page	Goals
Commitment to Continuous Improvement			
	Chapter 3, "Coaching Yourself as a Leader"	47	Distributing leadership roles crucial to PLC sustainability
Action Orientation and Experimentation, Collective Inquiry			
	Chapter 4, "Differentiating the PLC Structure"	65	Improving PLC activities and coaching to ensure implementation and action
	Activity 6.5, "Observing Each Other's Classrooms"	112	Building trust for peer coaching, lesson study, and strategy implementation
	Activity 6.7, "Deciding Our Data Direction"	115	Improving selection of data for action research and goals
Third Big Idea: Focus on Results			
SMART goals	Activity 6.6, "Setting PLC Goals"	113–114	Setting clear, measurable goals tied to overall school goals and student learning via adult learning
	Chapter 3, "Coaching Yourself as a Leader"	47	Evaluating clarity and communication of overall PLC vision, mission, values, goals
Using relevant information to improve results	Activity 4.3, "Using Data in PLCs"	73	Understanding a wide variety of data sources and how each type views data
	Activity 4.4, "PLC Inventory"	73–74	Improving the balance of data used and how it is used

Understanding Why PLCs Need a Coaching Culture

Before you begin reading this chapter, take a moment to reflect on the following questions:

- What barriers might you encounter in implementing PLCs in your district or school?

- What reservations do you have regarding PLCs?

Educators who belong to effective, collaborative PLCs *know* that these are very different from mere teams or task forces. When PLCs establish a coaching culture, members feel valued in the same way that they deeply value every other member. We asked teacher leaders from various schools around the country who we've worked with to describe what is different about belonging to or coaching such a PLC.

[A coaching culture] helps open people's minds to solutions, especially in a profession where people are so likely to isolate themselves.

Knowing the talents and strengths of more of my colleagues helps me to refer a teacher in need of assistance to precisely the right person. I now understand that I am not equipped to help everyone personally and have started to utilize the talents of others more regularly. I am more likely to be able to gather resources and information they will need to overcome obstacles.

While I want the same end results, I understand that people's methods will vary and am not so critical when they are different from my own.

Instead of placing blame on things like curriculum, administration, and students, I have found that teachers are more likely to [ask for help] with a personal struggle that is conflicting with their work in the classroom.

Where before I would see teachers as "old-fashioned," "creative," "organized," "strict," I can now understand the way they act and why. All of this only leads to better communication.

I have the vocabulary I need to talk to and about other teachers on common ground . . . in a constructive way. Instead of strengths and weaknesses, [a coaching culture] has allowed me to be able to talk about teachers in relation to our common framework.

> The basic idea is this: you can't talk to everyone the same way because people are different. This sounds obvious, but I think this notion is often forgotten . . . it has given me language to better articulate the difference in people when [coaching] teachers and when talking with teachers about students.

> I've seen more enthusiasm [from teachers]. I've seen their lessons evolve from once a simple lecture to a collaborative chain of ideas throughout the class.

These teachers understand their colleagues' strengths, beliefs, and struggles with teaching and learning. They have a common language for discussion. And they acknowledge that there is no one-size-fits-all PLC model; teachers' needs are as different as those of students in any classroom.

Professional learning communities are, after all, to be places of learning for adults, even as teams focus on student learning. However, as discussed throughout this chapter, a myriad of factors can keep PLCs from becoming both effective and sustainable. A coaching culture helps address these factors before they can undermine the essential work of the learning community. Employing a differentiated coaching model (Kise, 2006) ensures that every adult is learning in ways that translate into enthusiastic teaching. As can be seen in the teacher quotes that began this section, a differentiated coaching culture has the following six key elements:

1. A common framework for unbiased discussions of education

2. A deep understanding of teacher strengths and beliefs

3. Concrete evidence that influences beliefs and shows that change will be worth the effort

4. Communication and assistance (coaching) in ways that meet each teacher's learning style and needs

5. A focus on problems that concern the teachers

6. Deep collaboration that involves examining beliefs and practices about teaching and learning (Kise, 2006, pp. 71–72)

The next section lays out some of the main research findings on barriers to PLC development and how a coaching culture based on these six key elements can overcome them, tailoring the process for each individual, team, and school so that educators willingly engage in their learning communities.

Element 1: A Common, Unbiased Framework

Without a common framework for discussing teaching and learning, reaching consensus becomes difficult, if not impossible. This element of differentiated coaching provides a consistent tool for fruitful inquiry, reflection, and collaboration. DuFour et al. (2008) point out the need for a common language for PLCs to work effectively. Gunn and King (2003), in their work on micropolitical conflicts, report that "the absence of a shared educational orientation among staff members exacerbated these internal micro-political conflicts at the same time these conflicts made it more difficult to develop a shared pedagogical orientation" (p. 176). How much easier would it be to begin the work of PLCs if members shared a common framework from the start?

Throughout these pages, we use the theory of personality type, as explained in chapter 2, to foster unbiased discussions of education. An overall philosophy such as Montessori education is another example of an overarching framework that provides common language. Other frameworks can be used if they:

- Describe teaching and learning in nonjudgmental ways. No one should feel labeled
- Are strengths-based, emphasizing how each person teaches and learns rather than suggesting limits on what they can do
- Describe which learning styles a practice will reach
- Apply across cultures and to both adults and students
- Provide bridges among varying staff development efforts (Kise, 2006, p. 74)

The common framework brings a welcoming of diversity as members realize that different perspectives enrich solutions. Stoll and Louis (2007) see the welcoming of diversity as a key element of PLCs:

> This principle does not speak to a tolerance of difference. Instead, it positions difference as a core value of the school. People celebrate difference because it serves as the spark for new learning, growth, and development. When diverse teaching styles and knowledge bases are highlighted and encouraged in the school, it pushes people into avenues of growth that had never before been contemplated, thereby stretching the professional repertoire beyond usual, habitual, or comfortable practice. (p. 33)

Such a framework helps groups work through the following barriers to collaboration.

Teacher Biases

Who we are is how we teach and lead—we use our own strengths and favorite activities. However, those strengths often drive our beliefs about learning, and those beliefs can be so tightly wired to our own personalities that we may view them as essential truths, unaware of our own biases (Kise, 2007; Murphy, 1992; Payne & VanSant, 2009). A common, nonjudgmental framework allows PLCs to turn discussions from "right" and "wrong" to "Which students will this practice reach?"

For example, we used our common framework to help a teacher who resisted using some of the tools for increasing critical thinking that her PLC had chosen. She finally grasped how she emphasized relationships in her classroom at the expense of academic rigor as she read about this tendency in teachers like herself. She then asked for coaching.

Content Area Biases

As we explore the theory of personality type, you will see that teachers with similar personalities tend to cluster in different content areas (Hammer, 1996). Think about it. Does your mind conjure different images at the thought of *math teacher*, *physical education teacher*, or *English teacher*? While these natural clusterings simply reflect people choosing careers that fit their strengths, they also mean that PLCs within a content area can work to reinforce biases against students whose personalities are very different from the norm of the teachers in that area.

For example, a mathematics team planned to drill students on procedures for solving a few key problem sets, believing that at least some of the kids would remember the procedures and get a few extra points on the accountability tests. When the teachers learned that they all shared the same learning style, and that learning style naturally tends to rely on procedures, they decided they needed to look harder at other learning techniques that had a better chance of producing content mastery for more students.

Leadership Biases

In chapter 3, "Coaching Yourself as a Leader," we look at the PLC leadership tasks at each stage of PLC development and discuss which tasks are most natural for leaders with different personalities. As with teachers and content areas, certain personalities tend to cluster into school leadership, which means that policies and plans may reflect biases and overlook the needs of teachers and students who are very different from the norm for school administrators.

Each chapter also provides reflection material for using a common framework to explore biases, improve problem solving, or share leadership roles.

Element 2: A Deep Understanding of Teacher Strengths and Beliefs

For coaching to work, one has to understand why teachers do what they do. Why does one teacher quickly implement a chosen strategy for improving student learning while another substitutes a different strategy or refuses to change at all? This element of differentiated coaching can help PLCs overcome the following barriers.

Different Belief Systems

Hargreaves (1994) identified teacher frustration with coaches and peers due to different beliefs about how students learn. In a coaching culture, members can challenge each other's beliefs because of the trust the group has nurtured and the neutral framework members use to discuss teaching and learning. The following list includes some sample beliefs that blocked change until unearthed and addressed:

- "If I put students in groups, I won't have control over what they learn." Conversations with this teacher revealed that she believed a quiet atmosphere fostered student learning; groups represented chaos to her. Once her colleagues understood, they shared methods they used for structuring group activities to ensure that learning goals were met.

- "If I give zeros on late work, these students will learn through natural consequences." This teacher believed a no-tolerance grading policy reflected high standards. One colleague shared Reeves' (2006) work on how giving no points for late work resulted in lowering grade averages so much that many students stopped working altogether. The PLC then examined alternative systems. (Activity 2.3, on page 33, contains a reading that PLCs can use to explore this issue.)

Unproductive Opinions of Colleagues' Practices

School staff members may already hold opinions that interfere with the atmosphere of trust needed for effective PLCs (Grossman et al., 2001; Hargreaves, 2002). These opinions range from "That is wrong" to "I could never do that and therefore shouldn't try." A coaching culture turns such judgments into constructive examination of practices.

Balancing Classroom Strategies and Content Mastery

Too often, with a focus on data, PLCs concentrate on quick-fix strategies rather than examining weaknesses in their own content mastery that might be blocking student learning (Hargreaves & Shirley, 2009; McLaughlin & Talbert, 2006). Teacher strengths and beliefs often lead to emphasizing either strategies or content mastery, as happened for the procedures-oriented math team mentioned previously. Awareness of these natural tendencies helps PLCs balance short-term teaching strategies and long-term mastery for themselves and for their students.

Element 3: Concrete Evidence That Influences Beliefs

While many resources on PLCs emphasize data-driven decisions, test data are not the only evidence worthy of driving educational decisions—not even test data from teacher-created formative assessments. Classroom observations, student work, research, student input from interviews or written reflections, behavior data, and many other information sources might be just as important—and might be far more influential in changing the practices of some teachers even if overall decisions reflect test data.

Why? Teachers value different kinds of information. Think of teachers you know who might respond as follows to a research-based strategy:

- "That won't be helpful for the lessons I'm teaching tomorrow. Give me something useful."

- "Maybe it worked for the students in the studies, but I bet they're nothing like my students. Don't make me experiment."

- "It seems one-size-fits-all. I don't want to stifle imaginations. Can I change it?"

- "How does it fit with the education theories on which I base my teaching? Can you show me the synthesis?"

Leaders need to design the work of PLCs so that the evidence they produce convinces teachers with various informational needs of the effectiveness of strategies or norms the school will emphasize. Doing so can help PLCs overcome the following barriers.

Closed System of Opinion

With all of the time pressures on schools, PLCs can quickly become closed systems of opinion rather than an avenue for continued intellectual development in both content area and the latest educational research (Grossman et al., 2001).

When PLC leaders understand the beliefs that drive classroom practices as well as the evidence needed to change those beliefs, they can target professional development activities to make those changes. Chapter 6, "Coaching a Group Into a Collaborative Team," introduces protocols that help teachers identify when their schools may have become a closed system. Chapter 7, "Coaching for Optimal Student Engagement and Achievement," introduces methods of looking at student work or student experiences to help teachers realize when they need outside input or expertise to further their learning.

Conflict

A coaching culture helps PLCs work through conflicts. Peck (1987) describes a community as "a group that can fight gracefully" (p. 71). Achinstein (2002) found that "conflict is not only central to community, but how teachers manage conflicts, whether they suppress or embrace their differences, defines the community borders and ultimately the potential for organizational learning and change" (p. 421). Chapter 5, "Coaching for Genuine Community," introduces a conflict model that helps teachers use their differences to create the best learning environment for teachers and students.

Element 4: Communication and Coaching That Meet Each Teacher's Needs

In a coaching culture, the group works together to develop discussion techniques, information sharing, observation protocols, lesson plan formats, and other tools that can be differentiated to meet each teacher's needs. The group can also use this information to determine which group member might benefit most from outside training, coaching, or other opportunities. Thinking about how members coach each other can help PLCs overcome the following barriers.

Balancing Student Learning and Adult Professional Development

Often, either student learning or adult professional development is lost at the expense of the other. A coaching culture recognizes that adult learning is as important as student learning. Stoll and Louis (2007) point out:

> Our understanding of a *professional* learning community is that teachers, too, are learners who are taught important and interesting lessons by their students, by the broader community, by each other, and by the parents of their students. We have noticed that teachers who are active learners have new and exciting ideas to share, and the excitement of their professional learning breathes life and energy into their classrooms. We have also observed teachers who perpetuate standard practices, who bring few new ideas or practices into their instruction. These classrooms lack the spontaneity, excitement, and enthusiasm of the classrooms where teachers share their own learning with their students. This is perhaps the most important concept of a learning community: that all members of the community are energized by learning from and with one another. (p. 31)

Learning to Reflect and to Take Action

Teachers are often new to the work of inquiry and reflection that is essential to PLCs. This work is demonstrated by:

1. Identifying what students need to learn

2. Determining how teachers know if the students learned it

3. Planning what to do when students did not learn it

4. Planning what to do if some students mastered the material (DuFour, Eaker, & DuFour, 2005)

In a coaching culture, PLCs ensure that members collect and reflect on the evidence needed to motivate teachers to take action.

Element 5: A Focus on Problems That Concern the Teachers

One of the key elements of effective PLC development that surfaces through research is shared leadership (Hord & Sommers, 2008; Jackson & Temperley, 2007; McLaughlin & Talbert, 2006). Hord (2004) recaps the difficulty of establishing shared leadership in a traditional school:

> The notion of collegiality between teacher and principal generally causes uncertainty among teachers because they naturally think in terms of hierarchy. As with many supervisor-employee relationships, the teachers expect to carry out decisions made above them in the organizational structure rather than to be part of making those decisions. To enter into a mutual relationship with the principal, they must let go of such former habits as criticizing the principal with other teachers and instead learn to openly discuss questions and concerns in the presence of the principal. (p. 24)

Inherent in shared leadership is that teachers should have a say in the focus of their PLC work. For a coaching culture, this doesn't mean that school leaders let PLCs choose *any* focus, but rather that leaders work to tie the teachers' areas of most concern back to school initiatives. Teacher concerns then become avenues for fostering the changes leadership wants to see. Consider it as creating buy-in—solving whatever problem or issue a teacher has locked onto, while at the same time tying that focus back to school priorities.

This element of differentiated coaching is especially important in overcoming a key barrier to successful PLCs: a lack of urgency. A school needs more than vision, values, and protocols to convince teachers that PLCs are worth the effort. Teachers need a sense of urgency and a compelling reason to change. Hord (2004) found that the reasons for change are generally external: motivators she uncovered include new testing accountability that highlights problems, a change in leadership or curricular expectations, or structural difficulties or changes. Tying the problems teachers want to solve back to the vision and values of the school can simultaneously provide the evidence teachers need for change and move the school toward the long-term goals.

Consider a PLC that Jane worked with at a high-poverty middle school. The teachers reported that only about 25 percent of their students engaged in class work; most sat passively, daydreaming or doodling. Less than 10 percent had scored at a proficient level on the state accountability tests. The school vision was to engage all students in critical thinking, providing them access to a rigorous curriculum. The teachers said, "These students don't care if they do well or not. How do we get them to care?"

Rather than starting with rigor as the stated PLC focus, Jane worked with the teachers to explore why students didn't care. An exercise in the math classroom revealed that students cared, but believed they were incapable of learning math. Students wrote statements like, "I can't do math. I watch." "Good students are fast. Every problem takes me so long." "I listen. I don't learn." In response, the PLC changed the problem definition to, "How do we engage students in tasks that build their academic confidence?" With that definition, the PLC began exploring rigorous, authentic learning tasks that engaged students.

Note that in this case, sharing leadership by allowing teachers to choose their focus while ensuring they saw evidence that changed their beliefs meant that the PLC moved toward the school goals of critical thinking and academic rigor. Chapter 3 explores the leadership strengths needed for shared leadership, while chapter 6 provides group processes for identifying problems.

Element 6: Deep "Level III" Collaboration

The traditional culture of autonomy in many schools, often a factor that attracted teachers to the field, means that educators have not developed group process techniques (Little, 1990). The Level III collaboration called for in the differentiated coaching model (Kise, 2006) is the sought-after deep collaboration that marks effective PLCs and makes them worth the three to five years of formation efforts.

At Level I, teachers team up for administrative tasks such as planning field trips, coordinating interventions for specific students, or ensuring that they build relationships with each student. While these tasks are important, they do not focus on improving instructional practices.

At Level II, teachers collaborate in segmented ways. For example, elementary teachers might swap students for math and reading, drawing on each other's expertise. A middle school science teacher might agree to reinforce certain graphing skills at the request of the math department. Or a team might agree on certain disciplinary processes. Again, these segmented collaborations are important, but they do not significantly affect teaching and learning.

Level III collaboration involves deep discussions about teaching and learning. Educators work together to unearth assumptions about teaching and learning, gain from one another's natural strengths, share strategies and ideas, and investigate what is possible in the classroom.

A coaching culture for PLCs has the core purpose of providing insights and tools that foster Level III collaboration, which represents radical change for most schools. Sometimes teachers chose the profession because it allowed them to work alone; Cooper (1988)—in a paper titled "Whose Culture Is It Anyway?"—wonders if reformers understand that school culture belongs to the teachers. If teachers do not see the merit of deep collaboration, why would they change that culture? Yet Grossman et al. (2001) emphasize:

> Of all the habits of mind modeled in schools, the habit of working to understand others, of striving to make sense of differences, of extending to others the assumption of good faith, of working towards the enlarged understanding of the group—in short, the *pursuit of community*—may be the most important. In an era of narrow academic standards and accountability, it is all too easy to forget that the ultimate accountability of schools is to the sustenance of a thoughtful, engaged, and vigorous democratic society. (p. 1000)

The collaborative efforts fostered through differentiated coaching work to overcome the following barriers.

The Difficulty of Moving From Isolation to Shared Practice

Establishing a coaching culture sets up discussions that, from the start, encourage teachers to share practice, often the most intimidating element of PLC membership for teachers used to classroom autonomy. Sharing unpopular points of view may be just as difficult. Chapter 6 provides tools and discussion guides for helping develop the trust and skills to share classroom practices and results in ways that lead to new understandings for the entire PLC.

Lack of Group Processing Skills and Social Trust

The culture of many schools promotes conflict avoidance, often resulting in pseudocommunities in which discussions remain shallow but harmonious since nothing of substance is discussed (Stein, Smith, Henningsen, & Silver, 2009). Chapter 4, "Differentiating the PLC Structure," which can be used to help teachers think deeply about their own agendas, shows how to avoid the barriers to community Peck (1987) identifies:

- Expectations and preconceptions
- Prejudices, ideologies, and precommitment to solutions
- The need to heal, convert, fix, or solve
- The need to control

Does this list sound familiar? Like a recap of attitudes you have seen around the table when educators sit down to discuss curriculum, teaching strategies, or strategic plans? A coaching culture helps people understand which of these traps they most need to avoid in order to be productive group members.

Informal Power Structures

School leaders may be unaware of alliances or past conflicts that might undermine collaboration or the usefulness of PLC structures, protocols, and norms (Gunn & King, 2003). The coaching culture emphasis on helping each team member develop collaborative skills can help leaders identify and overcome these difficulties.

Essentials of PLCs

In essence, creating a coaching culture sets up an environment in which key components for effective PLCs, listed in handout 1.1 (page 22), are possible. Educators must keep at least twelve key components in mind when planning the work of creating effective, sustainable professional learning communities. While this chapter lays out the challenge, the rest of the book provides two frameworks that together can help PLCs succeed:

1. A common framework for discussing teaching and learning, illustrated through the use of personality type

2. The six elements of differentiated coaching as a tool for ensuring that every teacher agrees that the effort to create effective, sustainable PLCs is worth the preparation and hard work—so every student learns

Reflection

1. PLCs take a tremendous amount of effort, but the reward is improved learning for adults and students. Take a moment to do a quickwrite—jot down your thoughts about this chapter. What difficulties in PLC formation were familiar to you? Which were new?

2. Copy the following bullets on a card to use as a bookmark. Keep them in mind as you begin to coach your PLC:

    + Change is hard work

    + Systemic change takes three to five years

    + Shortchanging the process shortchanges results

    + Focus on long-term results, not short-term gains

    + Balance adult and student needs

    + Shared leadership toward shared goals fosters shared success

3. Consider handout 1.2, "Markers of a Coaching Culture" (page 23). Comparing the markers side-by-side, which ones best describe your current PLC culture? Use your answers to draft three top priorities in moving toward a coaching culture. Refer to these priorities as you evaluate which of the activities in *Creating a Coaching Culture* will most benefit your team.

    a.

    b.

    c.

Handout 1.1

Key Components of Effective PLCs

DuFour et al. (2006) list the following six key components of effective PLCs:

1. A focus on learning

2. A collaborative culture, including shared beliefs, values, and vision, and an atmosphere of trust and respect

3. Collective inquiry into best practices

4. An action orientation

5. A commitment to continuous improvement

6. A results orientation

Hord and Sommers (2008) expand on collaboration, adding the following three key components:

1. Shared and supportive leadership involving administrators and teachers

2. Supportive conditions, including adequate time, suitable spaces, and access to needed resources

3. Shared personal practice in which community members give and receive feedback to improve individually and collectively

Stoll and Louis (2007) add the final three key components:

1. Collective responsibility by all staff members for all children, which nudges teachers to truly collaborate, to stay involved and informed about the children with whom they interact, and to stay actively involved in school functions

2. Appreciation of diversity

3. Positive role modeling; encouraging administrators and teachers to model learning for students

Handout 1.2

Markers of a Coaching Culture

The following table contrasts markers (or characteristics) of PLCs that lack a coaching culture—and, therefore, fail to become effective and sustainable—with those PLCs that establish a coaching culture that leads to deep, sustainable collaboration and improved student achievement. Chapter 6 provides tools to help PLCs develop the markers of a coaching culture.

Markers of a Noncoaching Culture	Markers of a Coaching Culture
Every PLC in the school continually completes the same activities. Classrooms are expected to look the same.	Members welcome diversity as a tool for making better decisions and use a framework such as type to communicate more clearly and understand other viewpoints.
The PLC focus is on student test gains with no consideration for professional development effectiveness. Data are limited to test results and behavior.	Members can ask questions, share beliefs, challenge ideas, and disagree with each other as part of their mutual commitment to adult learning and improved student achievement.
PLC activities are restricted to reading, study, and discussion with no accountability for classroom implementation.	Sharing examples of what did not go well in classrooms becomes as natural as sharing what went well.
Educators seldom reflect upon, document, or revisit decisions.	The team takes time to debate and define problems before deciding how to solve them. Team members know how to reach consensus.
Teachers share superficially and avoid questioning each other's practices.	Conflict becomes a source of renewal—members know how to handle it and use it as a context for learning and for exchanging opinions for knowledge.
PLC time consists of sharing of opinions without outside resources such as books, expert information, research results, or the actions of other teams.	Members are willing to admit when they do not know the answers—only then can PLCs recognize when they need outside assistance to help all students achieve.
Attendance is sporadic. Teachers either do not find the meetings valuable, or they lack trust.	Members welcome being held accountable to use what they learned and share student results with the team.
No one can articulate the goals or purpose of the PLC.	Members recognize and respect that there may be many paths to the same end, but they are willing to sacrifice individuality if it interferes with the needs of the group.

Describing a Framework for Coaching, Teaching, and Learning

Before you begin reading this chapter, take a moment to reflect on the following questions:

- Describe an incident in which your supervisor (school principal or district personnel) praised the way a colleague implemented a strategy or solved an instructional dilemma. Did you feel expected to implement the strategy or solution in exactly the same way? Or did you feel free to implement a practice that provided the same outcome for students, but in a very different way?

- Think of a discussion with content-alike staff during which you looked at strategies for deepening student content knowledge. Were you ever hesitant to disagree for fear of being judged? What strategy did you dislike? Why?

Imagine a team in which two teachers actually think the other's classroom is harmful to students. Or perhaps you don't have to use your imagination. We've certainly seen it time and again. The following descriptions came from conversations Jane had with two teachers on the same grade-level team.

Teacher 1: Teacher 2 marches those little dears through the halls and the curriculum like they're marionettes. They still need nurturing, and playtime, and chances to do whatever they want to do. I mean, keeping primary grade students in from recess if they forget homework? What she's really teaching them is to hate school already!

Teacher 2: Teacher 1 claims her students aren't ready for parts of the curriculum. She hasn't even unpacked some of the books. I know; I checked. Instead, she hauls her class outside for what she calls "learning." I pity their teachers next year when their classes are filled with students from both of our classrooms. What a mess!

Actually, Teachers 1 and 2 are both great teachers, but they are so entrenched in their own teaching styles that they cannot imagine how children in the other's classroom can possibly be learning. How do you build trust between these teachers? Engage them in positive dialogue that fosters a desire to collaborate and learn from each other? Develop agreement on curriculum needed for classrooms next year? In this case, the framework of personality type proved invaluable in overcoming the differences that were blocking these teachers from working together. Let's look at that framework first and then return to "The Case of the Critical Colleagues."

Note: This chapter has multiple uses. Leaders and coaches can read it reflectively and self-select their preferences. Handouts and activities are available for leaders to use with PLCs so that members can both identify their own styles and learn about each other's strengths. Or members can read the chapter on their own, self-select their preferences, and then share selectively with the group through protocols that help to establish trust (introduced in chapter 4).

Constructive Use of Differences

The theory of psychological type, originating in the work of Carl Jung and popularized through the mother-daughter team Katharine Briggs and Isabel Myers and their Myers-Briggs Type Indicator, describes normal differences in normal people regarding how they do the following:

- Gain energy
- Take in information
- Make decisions
- Approach work and life

All of these differences impact how people lead, teach, and learn, and therefore enlighten any discussion of education.

For each of these factors, people show a preferred psychological behavior, referred to as a *preference*. The preferences are neither good nor bad, just different from one another. The Association for Psychological Type International (www.aptinternational.org) has "constructive use of differences" as part of its mission statement. Their perception of this phrase goes far beyond tolerance, which sets as a goal, "I understand that we are different, and I will allow that difference to exist." Instead, constructive use of differences has as a goal, "I understand that we are different, and I look forward to working with you on efforts that will benefit from our diverse ways of looking at the world." It is this understanding that propels PLCs toward effectiveness.

To better understand the idea of psychological preferences, think for a moment about our many physical preferences. For example, in the following space, sign your name with your nonpreferred hand—the one that seldom holds your pen:

_____

People often describe writing with their nonpreferred hand as awkward, slow, or frustrating. They sometimes have to think about which way the letters form.

Now, switch hands and sign your name again:

_____

People often describe writing with their preferred hand as smooth, comfortable, or natural. They don't have to think about it. Nor did most people ever think about whether they would be right-handed or left-handed; it just happened.

Type theory accounts for eight mental preferences. For each mental preference pair, normal people can use both, but prefer one over the other. Compare this to how basketball players have a preferred hand, a physical preference, for shooting layups. However, good coaches insist that players develop skills with the other hand as well. The same is true of type preferences. As people mature, they develop skills with each of the preferences, but still prefer one over the other.

Finding your true preferences provides an avenue for benefiting from how others who share your preferences have coached themselves to excellence in many aspects of life. Within these pages, we use type theory to understand leadership styles, collaboration and communication styles, possible pitfalls for working within a PLC, and other applications. First, though, let's focus on the essential nature of each preference.

Extraversion and Introversion: What Is Your Source of Energy?

Leading, teaching, learning, and collaborating take energy—lots of it. Type theory holds that people gain energy through one of the following two preferences:

- *Extraversion*—gaining energy through action and interaction
- *Introversion*—gaining energy through solitude and reflection

While people often think of Extraversion in terms of who has the most friends or attends the most parties, note that the word is spelled differently than *extroversion*. People with both preferences need interactions with people as well as solitude. However, interactions energize people who prefer Extraversion; they walk away from conversations, activities, and exchanges with more energy than when they began. People who prefer Introversion may enjoy those conversations just as much, but start to feel their energy drain away unless they have a chance for some down time. Consider the following example:

A social studies teacher joined a mathematics PLC meeting to discuss a student group-work protocol that both content areas planned to use. She asked, "Should we try the protocol ourselves, taking the suggested roles?" More than five seconds passed during which no one said anything. The social studies teacher began laughing, "What are all of you thinking about? My PLC is never this quiet!" The math team, whose members all prefer Introversion, commented that they were thinking about whether they needed to try the activity or just discuss it. The social studies teacher, who preferred Extraversion, said, "Well, I'm not really sure I'll be ready to teach it to students if I haven't actually used the protocol myself. Maybe we should discuss each role here, and I'll try it with my own PLC."

This preference pair has a significant impact on collaboration because of the natural interaction styles of each type. Those who prefer Extraversion often enjoy processing thoughts and ideas aloud. In fact, they find that their ideas take shape as they bounce them off of other people. They often get new ideas when they hear the first one come to life through the sound of their own voices. One of our friends describes it as "talking to think."

Those who prefer Introversion, however, often like to reflect before speaking about an idea. They may strive to formulate viewpoints in their own minds, even thinking through the best way to enter a conversation before saying a word. If discussion is moving particularly thick and fast, they may say nothing until asked.

As a whole, U.S. society honors Extraversion. We give points for class participation, we worry about our quiet children, and we expect up-and-coming leaders to be quick on their feet with ideas and actions. PLCs need to work carefully to honor both preferences if everyone's thoughts and ideas are to be heard.

Using handout 2.1, "Extraversion or Introversion: How Are You Energized?" (page 39), place yourself on each of the continuums. How do you prefer to interact? Remember, mature people develop skills with both preferences; try to reflect on which one is most natural for you and provides the most energy.

ACTIVITY 2.1 Extraversion or Introversion?

Goal: To help PLC members understand and appreciate each other's preferences for Extraversion and Introversion

Materials: Index cards marked with red circles on one side and green circles on the other side; copies of handout 2.1, "Extraversion and Introversion: How Are You Energized?" (page 39)

Directions: Provide each participant with an index card and a copy of handout 2.1. Ask participants to place the index card red side up in front of them where the others can see it. Inform them that the group will have "red-card time," silence, to reflect on the following questions:

- Does Extraversion or Introversion describe you best?

- Are Extraverted or Introverted students more successful in school?

When participants are ready to discuss the questions, they are to turn their cards to the green side. Everyone should remain silent until all cards are green side up.

Usually, two to three minutes pass before all cards are turned over. Sometimes, people realize through this exercise that they prefer Extraversion because they wanted to share their thoughts as they went along—it was hard sitting still and waiting (in some groups, the Extraverted teachers have left their seats or reorganized their book bags while waiting). Others realize they prefer Introversion because they enjoyed the uninterrupted processing time.

Debrief by first asking about reactions to the silence. Then ask for comments and questions about the prompts and in general about Extraversion and Introversion. Usually, responses vary as to which students are more successful in school; emphasize that different environments will honor each preference, making it easier for one or the other to succeed.

Note: Teachers can use a similar exercise with students and report to their PLCs about insights and reactions to the experience. They might ask younger students to sit silently for ninety seconds. They might pose a question to older students and use red card/green card to provide reflection time.

Sensing and Intuition: What Information Catches Your Attention?

According to type theory, people gather information in two different ways:

- *Sensing*—first gathering information through the five senses and through past experiences; reality is the starting place.

- *Intuition*—first gathering information through hunches, connections, and analogies; insight is the starting place.

Tensions arise within PLCs when people don't understand the very different informational needs of people with each of these preferences. Consider the following example:

A school received a large grant to implement an inquiry-based science program. The principal brought in an expert to lead the teachers through several lessons. She then asked each PLC to create a curriculum map and design their first inquiry-based unit. The principal assumed the teachers would love the freedom to devise their own pathways to cover standards. However, almost all of the teachers complained about the lack of guidance. "Haven't other schools done this?" "Can't we borrow from them?" "Why doesn't the expert provide curriculum maps?" "We really shouldn't be doing this . . ." Later, a teambuilding session revealed that the principal preferred Intuition, and all but three of the teachers preferred Sensing.

Sensing types and Intuitive types have profoundly different learning styles because of the difference in how they process information. Here, the principal gave the big-picture directions she likes to receive; she assumed that teachers had absorbed how to make a curriculum map and design units around standards and, therefore, gave them the freedom to pursue the tasks in their own styles. However, the teachers were looking for more details, such as the number of standards to cover in each unit, and specific examples, such as the work of other schools. The teachers were even interested in using the work of others, stating that they lacked enough experience with inquiry to design good units. In this case, the needs of the teachers were so far from being met that before they learned about Sensing and Intuition, they believed the principal lacked leadership skills. The principal admitted that she had believed the teachers were lazy.

Being aware of Sensing/Intuition differences is key to the success of a PLC if it is to be a place of learning for all adults. Areas for conflict between the preferences include the following:

- *Time differences.* Sensing types tend to plan within a six- to twelve-month time frame while Intuitive types tend to look out three to five years.

- *Details.* Sensing types generally prefer to receive more specific instructions before beginning tasks—why would you start before being certain your efforts are in line with expectations? Intuitive types generally prefer general goals and the freedom to pursue them in their own ways.

- *Curriculum.* Sensing types usually try curriculum as it is written, at least the first time around. Intuitive types generally look at curriculum and say, "How can I change it or add to it to make it better?"

- *Learning style.* Sensing types often take a "What can I use tomorrow or this month in my classroom" approach to professional development. Intuitive types often want to explore theories or new philosophies of education or frameworks that may take time to master.

- *Questioning style.* Sensing types can fall into the trap of "right-answer thinking," either asking questions that can easily be judged right or wrong (for example, "What is 2 + 2?") or not probing to ensure understanding ("How do you know the answer is 4? Show me."). Intuitive types can fall into the trap of general discussions (for example, "Let's get a list of at least twenty equations where the answer is 4.") and forget to ensure that basic knowledge is in place or that the standards were actually covered in the midst of a lively what-if discussion.

In each one of these areas, a balance between Sensing and Intuitive needs brings more learning to all if each person understands the needs of the others.

Using handout 2.2, "Sensing or Intuition: Gathering Information" (page 40), place yourself on each of the continuums. Remember that most people have skills on both sides, but you are looking for the preference that comes most naturally. You might even look back on how you processed information in college to gain a true picture of your natural preference.

ACTIVITY 2.2 **Sensing or Intuition?**

Goal: To help participants understand and appreciate the differences in the informational needs of people with each preference

Materials: Handout 2.2, "Sensing or Intuition: Gathering Information," handout 2.3, "Which Test Question?" (page 41)

Directions: Provide each participant with a copy of handout 2.3, or display handout 2.3 to the group. Ask participants to reflect for a minute and then jot down their thoughts on how they would have reacted to each question as a student. Which question would they have preferred to answer? Why?

Facilitate the discussion by asking the following questions:

- Who prefers Question A? Why? (Note whether participants think the question is easier to answer or whether they think it is a better test question.)
- Who dislikes Question A? Why?
- Who prefers Question B? Why?
- Who dislikes Question B? Why?
- Does anyone not have a preference?

After you have finished discussing the test questions, distribute copies of handout 2.2 and ask participants to reflect on whether they prefer Sensing or Intuition, reminding them that while all of us can do both, one is more natural.

Thinking and Feeling: How Do You Make Decisions?

The third preference pair deals with how people make decisions. Thinking types certainly have feelings, and Feeling types think intellectually. However, the two types use psychologically opposite criteria for decision making.

- *Thinking*—making decisions through logical analysis, consideration of precedents, and clear principles

- *Feeling*—making decisions by stepping into the shoes of those involved to determine how each would be affected

Both are *rational* processes. One can be rational without being logical. Further, a logical decision isn't always the best decision. In fact, the overreliance on Thinking for decisions in education often creates situations in which initiatives fail because of lack of buy-in. The best decisions make use of both the Thinking and Feeling functions to include both objective and subjective data. Consider the following example:

Teachers at a high school met to resolve the problem of student tardiness. Several teachers who preferred Thinking wanted to implement a new tardy policy with tougher penalties. One teacher who preferred Feeling said, "I think we should first investigate why students come to class late. Have they given up academically? Are they bored? After all, we already have penalties, and they aren't helping." The group then generated a list of avenues for gathering student input on the topic, discussed specific students whose tardiness rates had increased, and brainstormed transition activities that might motivate students to arrive on time. Most of the teachers grew excited about how they might turn around student attitudes, but one of the Thinking teachers said, "This was a waste of time—we haven't decided what the new penalties should be!"

Thinking types often start with ideas about rewards and punishments, while Feeling types often start with motivations and persuasion. While there is need for both in any classroom, tensions can arise when PLC members favor one approach to the exclusion of the other. The two preferences also often disagree on whose behavior should change first. In this example, some of the Thinking teachers voiced that student behavior should change; they simply needed to get to class on time. Some of the Feeling teachers wanted to redesign how their classes began to motivate students to be on time.

Often, a preference for Thinking or Feeling also drives the kinds of data people are most interested in. Thinking types frequently start from objective data: test scores, behavior statistics, grade books, charts showing time on task, and so on. Feeling types frequently prefer subjective data: student focus groups, journaling assignments about projects, the opinions or experiences of people they trust, or student work samples. *All* kinds of data provide unique information that can lead to more balanced decisions.

Similarly, Thinking types often consider objective criteria for decisions: costs, time frames, statistical information, and so on. Feeling types often place more weight on subjective criteria: the opinions of those most affected, community values, or the level of student engagement. Again, the best decisions often result when the most relevant objective and subjective criteria are both considered. Conflicts frequently arise within PLCs when Thinking types see Feeling types as wishy-washy and downgrade the importance of "soft" data, or when Feeling types see Thinking types as "cold" and downgrade the importance of replicable results or consistency in approaches.

Using handout 2.4, "Thinking and Feeling: Decisions" (page 42), place yourself on each of the continuums, remembering to use the context of decision making. Again, while you no doubt have skills at both ends, be sure to consider which ones are most natural for you.

ACTIVITY 2.3 **Thinking, Feeling, and Policies**

Goal: To understand how a preference for Thinking or Feeling influences the rules people set and the data they consider important

Materials: Flip-chart paper, markers, and copies of handouts 2.4, "Thinking and Feeling: Decisions," and 2.5, "Giving Zeros" (page 43), for each participant. Hand out "Giving Zeros" *after* the group discussions.

Directions: Let participants complete handout 2.4. Ask participants to form groups based on whether they believe they prefer Thinking or Feeling. If participants are unsure, ask them to be observers of a group and take notes on the discussions.

Tell participants that you will read aloud a dilemma a teacher faces with a student, as follows:

All students were to turn in a project today that is worth 100 points. One of your students, who is frequently a discipline problem and chronically turns in assignments late, asks for an extension. What should you do?

Record on flip-chart paper the points made by your group during your discussion, including questions you have, suggested consequences, and opinions or reasoning voiced about each suggestion.

After about eight minutes, ask for everyone's attention one more time and say you would like to add the following details to the scenario:

This particular student struggles with reading grade-level material and has little support for academics at home; neither parent finished high school. You offered after-school help sessions on this particular project, but this student did not attend any of them or seek any other help.

Allow about fifteen minutes in total for discussion. Then, post the group flip-chart papers on a wall, with the reports of each of the two groups clustered together. Ask participants to do a "poster walk," reading the different responses quietly, looking for similarities and differences. After a few minutes, ask them to share their observations with the group.

Typical Thinking responses include the following:

- Discussion of the natural consequences provided by giving a zero on the assignment if it is turned in, or not allowing late work at all

continued on next page →

- Discussion of a sliding scale of points, down to zero, depending on how late the assignment is submitted

- Discussion of the need to teach the student a lesson about responsibility

- Discussion of whether similar students will ever turn in the work, even if given a second chance

- After receiving the extra information, participants may discuss fairness as having consistent rules. They may want to ensure the student understands that the later the assignment is, the more severe the consequences. They may also use if/then reasoning such as, "If you come after school today or tomorrow so that I can make sure you're on track, and you finish it within three days, then I'll take off only 25 percent of the grade you would have had." Or "If the work is late, your maximum score is 60 percent no matter when you turn it in."

Typical Feeling responses include the following:

- Requests for more information about why the assignment is late, such as details about the student's home life or difficulties with schoolwork

- Discussion of whether any penalty should be dependent on the student's circumstances

- Suggestions for providing more help to the student to ensure he or she is on track to finish the assignment in a reasonable period of time

- After receiving the extra information, discussion of fairness as ensuring students have an opportunity to succeed

- Discussion of ways to scaffold this student for success in this assignment—offering special before-school or lunchtime help, with the goal of ensuring that the student completes the work

- Discussion of a way to make an exception, such as "Let's get the student to agree on a plan and then, if he or she follows it, we'll give full credit. Success motivates more than failure."

- Discussion of the theme of "effort creates ability" and how they would communicate to the students, "I know you can do this and I'm here to support you, but you absolutely need to complete the assignment. That's how you get smarter."

After the poster walk, provide copies of handout 2.5 to all participants. Ask them to read through the passage, marking C next to passages that confirm their own thinking, D next to ideas they disagree with, and Q next to anything that raised further questions. Also, ask them to write down any questions they have. Consider using a protocol such as the one in activity 5.2, "Evidence-Based Discussions" (page 92), for debriefing the reading as a large group.

Judging and Perceiving: How Do You Approach Life and Work?

Have you noticed that educators have different approaches to scheduling, planning, and bringing projects to a close? The last preference pair describes two very different approaches to life in general:

- *Judging*—approaching life by focusing on coming to closure (to judgments); they plan their work and work their plan, drive toward conclusion, and control their time.

- *Perceiving*—approaching life by focusing on staying open to more perceptions; they seek to do what is best in the moment, search out more information or alternatives, and experience time.

Judging types who use their preference well bring an instinctive "clock" to PLCs. They estimate accurately how long projects, activities, and tasks will take; understand how to chunk those projects into manageable pieces; and constantly reevaluate the ability to meet the initial timeline.

Perceiving types who use their preference well bring an instinctive curiosity to PLCs. They focus on urgent rather than scheduled matters, press the group to delay decisions until new information becomes available, or experiment with a few ideas before eliminating all but one. Consider the following example:

An instructional coach emailed all teachers in an elementary grade-level team, asking them to conduct a short exercise with students any time during the three days before their next PLC meeting. Two of the teachers, who prefer Judging, responded quickly that they could not fit the exercise into the units they were teaching. However, they came to the meeting with samples of student work from the exercise. The coach asked why they seemed upset, yet completed the exercise. One admitted, "My first reaction was, 'Every minute of those days was already taken. The semester is almost over!' But later I saw how it could fit into our morning schedule." The Perceiving teachers commented that because they had been given three days, they were not worried about whether they could fit it in. All of them, though, used the exercise the afternoon before the meeting.

PLCs that can balance the needs of each preference often experience rich processes while progressing toward stated goals. They explore different alternatives before making decisions and, even while they act on that decision, work to gather information to ensure another alternative would not, in fact, be better.

Using handout 2.6, "Judging and Perceiving: How Do You Approach Life?" (page 45), place yourself on the continuums to determine which preference describes you best. Because education in the United States overwhelmingly favors Judging (for example, curriculum maps, school calendars, testing dates, and distinct units of study), you might need to reflect on how you approached college assignments to determine your true preference.

ACTIVITY 2.4 Judging and Perceiving: Approaching Life and Work

Goal: To help participants understand and appreciate the two preferences for how people approach life

Materials: Copies of curriculum maps, pacing schedules, or other similar documents used by your school or district

Directions: Discuss how each of the preceding documents favors a culture of Judging: there are set goals and timelines. Ask participants to discuss the pros and cons of these devices. Where is there room for flexibility or other evidence of Perceiving? Is there enough balance? How can schools provide guidelines and still recognize and respond to the wisdom of the Perceiving function as they try to give each child the time he or she needs to reach mastery of learning goals?

Verifying Your Personality Type

Take a moment to record your preferences:

_____	_____	_____	_____
E or I	S or N	T or F	J or P

If you are still unsure of your preferences, appendix A (page 155), contains full type descriptions for each of the sixteen personality types. Someone who believes he has preferences for E, S, and T, but cannot decide between J and P, for example, can read the descriptions for ESTJ and ESTP and then choose the one that fits best overall.

Note that we purposely allowed you to self-select your preferences rather than provide you with checklists to score. Many excellent type sorters exist, the most recognized being the MBTI.[1] However, ethical interpretation of the MBTI requires that people first learn about the preferences and self-select the ones they believe describe them best. Participants are then given their MBTI results for comparison, and the majority agree with those results (Myers, McCaulley, Quenk, & Hammer, 1998). When they disagree, a qualified facilitator helps them analyze why they answered differently when they self-selected and when they took the self-reporting MBTI instrument.

---

[1]An online version of the MBTI is available at www.mbticomplete.org. Alternatively, individuals or groups can visit www.aptinternational.org and check the referral network for practitioners in their area if they wish to take the instrument. Alternative type indicators are also available; none of the free online indicators, however, are research based.

The type instruments were designed this way so that people don't feel labeled. Each participant discerns for his or her true preferences, just as you were guided throughout this chapter. In conversations about their results, people often come to conclusions such as the following:

- "I was thinking of work, and I really don't get to be myself at work."

- "I've been working hard on those skills, and my answers reflect that."

- "My parents really valued that preference."

- "I think being in grad school (or a new position or having a baby) has me focused on developing balance in some of these areas."

If you are still struggling to determine which preferences fit you best, take a moment to journal about them. When do you use Introversion and Extraversion, for example? Make lists and then think about which list is more energizing. Which is more natural? If you think back to your teen years, which preference was more natural then?

Why does identifying your own type matter? Because you can tap into the wisdom of thousands of people with the same preferences to learn how they continued to develop and grow, improved their ability to resolve conflict, fostered better collaborative teams, and made better decisions. If you know your own type, then you can recognize when a situation calls for other skills. As you will see in chapter 3, this self-awareness is key to the leadership of sustainable PLCs.

Do Our Type Preferences Change?

Frequently, people comment that their preferences changed as they grew older. Type theory holds that preferences are inborn, but that people develop skills as they mature. Research using brain scans and longitudinal studies of children confirm this theory (Alcock, Murphy, & Ryan, 2000; Murphy, 2007). However, certain careers and life experiences can accelerate skill development, just as skilled coaching can improve a tennis player's backhand. Teaching is one of those careers. Extraverts learn to listen to students. Introverts find ways of being with others all day long without losing all energy. Sensing types learn to push students toward big ideas. Intuitive teachers learn to press students for justification. Thinking types learn to make exceptions and consider the needs of each child separately. Feeling types learn the importance of consistency and objective standards. Judging types learn to let go of plans when dealing with children. Perceiving types learn to plan so that they cover the guaranteed curriculum.

One way to describe this change in preferences is that while preferences are innate, *behavior* changes over time. A child who prefers Judging may be upset by changes in plans. A mature person who prefers Judging understands how to deal with changes in plans. A child who prefers Extraversion blurts out things better left unsaid. A mature person who prefers Extraversion has techniques for leaving things unsaid.

Note that Beth, for example, prefers ENFP, but her years as a school administrator provided excellent practice in developing her Judging side. Jane prefers INFJ, but working as a facilitator and coach provides plenty of opportunities to expand her Extraversion skills. Type, though, helps us pinpoint what we find most exhausting or tedious and then locate strategies to help us do the best we can.

The Case of the Critical Colleagues

Returning to our opening story, Teacher 1 preferred ENFP while Teacher 2 preferred ENFJ. That one-letter difference caused them to pass judgment on each other. Yes, Teacher 2 used more structure and routines, but careful observation showed that her hallway marionettes were actually playing a version of follow-the-leader. Her students looked forward to their turns. As for homework at recess, Teacher 2 used those infrequent moments to get to know each student better. Yes, students missed recess, but they thrived on the one-on-one attention.

And while Teacher 1 hadn't unpacked all of her books, she covered all of the materials, using various technologies and small groups, rather than assigning books to each student. She also found value in following the Finnish model of interspersing fifteen minutes of outdoor time with sixty-minute blocks of learning time. In her experience, the result was less time wasted on classroom-management issues.

Neither teacher had ever asked the other about why they ran their classrooms the way they did. When they learned about their differing personality types, they began to grasp how well each other's classrooms really worked. They could then make constructive use of differences in their PLC.

Reflection

Appendix A (page 155) contains full-page type descriptions for each of the sixteen types. Read through the page for your type, and use the following questions for reflection:

1. What factors are key in motivating you to participate fully in a PLC? What factors discourage you?

2. Reflect on prior frustrations you may have had with group work or collaboration. Consider your personality type to identify ways your needs were not met in those situations.

3. Write a note to your colleagues (although you may never share it) in answer to the prompt, "If you want me to be an effective PLC member, please . . ." If everyone in your PLC agrees, share these statements with one another.

Handout 2.1

Extraversion or Introversion: How Are You Energized?

Place yourself on each of the continuums. How do you prefer to interact? Remember, mature people develop skills with both preferences; try to reflect on which one is most natural for you and provides the most energy.

E |____|____|____|____|____|____| I

I form ideas best through actions and interactions with others.

I form ideas best when I have a chance to reflect before having to share them.

E |____|____|____|____|____|____| I

Silence during meetings is usually painful.

Silence during meetings lets me pull my thoughts together.

E |____|____|____|____|____|____| I

Usually, I'd rather talk with others or attend interactive workshops to get new information.

Usually, I'd rather read or listen at a workshop to get new information.

E |____|____|____|____|____|____| I

I like to try things with my students or PLC and then reflect to decide how it worked.

I like to reflect about how something might work before trying it.

E |____|____|____|____|____|____| I

In groups, I offer ideas quickly.

In groups, I struggle to contribute unless I've had time to reflect or prepare.

E |____|____|____|____|____|____| I

A variety of activities keeps me energized.

I prefer depth—spending significant time with an activity.

E |____|____|____|____|____|____| I

"Live" communication, in person or via telephone, works best for me.

Communicating via emails or memos is more comfortable for me.

E |____|____|____|____|____|____| I

Sometimes I share too readily, when I should be thinking it through.

Sometimes I take too long in reflection; decisions are made without me.

Reflect for a moment on the information. Which preference describes you best? Circle one:

Extraversion   Introversion

Handout 2.2

Sensing or Intuition: Gathering Information

Place yourself on each of the continuums. Remember, most people develop skills with both preferences; try to reflect on which one is most natural for you. You might even look back on how you provided information in college to gain a true picture of your natural preferences. Note that *N* denotes *Intuition*, because *I* was already used for *Introversion*.

S | | N

I prefer receiving clear instructions and getting my questions answered.

I prefer receiving clear goals and charting my own way to meet them.

S | | N

I tend to try something new and then practice to improve it.

I tend to try many new things, often not using them more than once.

S | | N

Past experiences and facts are reliable guides.

Future possibilities and ideas are reliable guides.

S | | N

I prefer receiving relevant facts and examples.

I prefer receiving relevant theories and ideas.

S | | N

Curriculum provides structure for units and lessons.

Curriculum provides ideas that can be modified and improved.

S | | N

I gather facts and then make decisions.

I often know what to do and then use research to support my decision.

S | | N

Professional development should provide immediate classroom tools.

Professional development should stimulate new ways of thinking.

S | | N

I like using proven methods.

I like devising new methods.

Reflect for a moment on the information. Which preference describes you best? Circle one:

Sensing   Intuition

Handout 2.3

Which Test Question?

Which test question would you rather answer? Which is more like the test questions you usually write?

A. During the Constitutional Convention, Ben Franklin made the following statement to urge a compromise between the Virginia Plan and the New Jersey Plan concerning central representation:

> When a bread table is to be made and the edges of planks do not fit, the artist takes a little from both and makes a good joint. In like manner, here both sides must part with some of their demand in order that they may join in some accommodating proposition.

Write an essay that shows how Roger Sherman was able to do just what Franklin suggested when he developed the Great Compromise.

B. Write an essay on the Great Compromise. Be sure to answer each of the following:

- What did the Virginia Plan recommend for the states? Why?
- What did the New Jersey Plan recommend for the states? Why?
- What did Roger Sherman propose in the Great Compromise?
- Explain why the Great Compromise was given this name.

Source: Tallevi (1997, p. 37)

Note: Question A was written by an Intuitive teacher before he learned about type preferences. When he learned about Sensing and Intuition, he wrote Question B and allowed students to choose between the two questions on the test.

Handout 2.4

Thinking and Feeling: Decisions

Place yourself on each of the continuums, remembering to use the context of decision making. While you no doubt have skills at both ends, be sure to consider which ones are most natural for you.

T ——————————————————————————————————————— F

I enjoy working with data and identifying patterns and useful information.

I enjoy working with people and building relationships.

T ——————————————————————————————————————— F

My decisions come from logic, awareness of precedents, and cause-effect reasoning.

My decisions come from values-based analysis and the impact on people involved.

T ——————————————————————————————————————— F

I value being viewed as competent.

I value being viewed as caring.

T ——————————————————————————————————————— F

Critique helps me improve.

Critique is hard to hear unless you also share what I'm doing right.

T ——————————————————————————————————————— F

I emphasize fairness through adherence to rules.

I emphasize fairness through consideration of circumstances.

T ——————————————————————————————————————— F

I tend to first see the flaws in ideas and practices.

I tend to first see the positives in ideas and practices.

T ——————————————————————————————————————— F

I put work first and seek competent colleagues for collaboration.

I thrive through relationships and seek caring colleagues for collaboration.

T ——————————————————————————————————————— F

Using data to inform instruction seems natural to me.

Using data to inform instruction is less interesting than considering student engagement.

Reflect for a moment on the information. Which preference describes you best? Circle one:

Thinking   Feeling

Handout 2.5

Giving Zeros

Read the following text, marking C next to passages that confirm your thinking, D next to ideas you disagree with, and Q next to anything that raises further questions. In your groups, discuss the passages you marked, as well as how each passage ties to the Thinking and Feeling preferences.

In *The Learning Leader* (2006), Douglas Reeves makes a case that giving zeros on work not turned in is unsupportable as a practice. First citing research that shows that using grades as punishment does not motivate students, he points out that a four-point scale (A–F) has only a four-point difference between an A and the 0 resulting from an F. On a hundred-point scale, however, the difference between grades A–D is only ten points, while the difference between grades D–F is sixty points:

> To insist on using zero on a 100-point scale is to assert that work that is not turned in is worthy of a penalty that is six times greater than work that is done wretchedly and worthy of a grade of D . . . [If] the value of D is 61 points, then the mathematically accurate value of F is 51 points. This is not, contrary to popular mythology, "giving" students 50 points but rather awarding punishment that fits the crime. The students failed to turn in an assignment, and they received a failing grade. They are not sent to a Siberian labor camp. There is, of course, an important difference. Sentences at Siberian labor camps ultimately come to a close, while grades of zero on a 100-point scale last forever. Just two or three zeros are sufficient to cause failure for an entire semester, and just a few course failures lead to high school dropouts, with a lifetime of personal and social consequences. (pp. 121–123)

At the opposite end of the spectrum from giving zeros is having low expectations for students, which might be disguised as, "Of course this student had trouble with this assignment. I just won't push him so hard and maybe he will stay motivated." Perhaps teachers accept substandard work with no consequence for lateness. Or, their grading system ensures enough points from busywork so that no student actually fails. In her article "Making America Smarter," Lauren Resnick (1999) argues that low expectations trap students into thinking they just aren't good at school. For students to understand that working hard makes them smarter, they need to do the work. Teachers who believe that effort creates ability would say that the only acceptable consequence for the student who did not turn in the report is to finish and turn in the report—if the assignment was not helping the student learn, why was it assigned in the first place?

We watched a team implement a "No More Ds and Fs" policy that took the failure rate on major projects from 25 percent to less than 1 percent. Poor work? Students needed to do it over. They protested loudly when the first teacher implemented the policy, but by the time students heard it from a third teacher, they began to accept that their teachers had high expectations and that effort would create ability. Then the teachers *taught* students how to break projects into chunks, estimate how long each step would take, determine how late they could start and still finish on time, and other project-management skills that the students simply had not developed. Sometimes, if students fell behind, they lost the privilege of choosing topics and had to switch to more teacher-directed projects. As one boy reluctantly met with the teacher to make such a switch, he said, "You know, I'd done a lot of reading for my first project but then fell behind. If I'd stuck with it, I'd actually have done *less* work, right? 'Cause now I have to do this work too . . ." Now that's a natural consequence that motivates students to persevere the next time around.

Handout 2.6

Judging and Perceiving: How Do You Approach Life?

Place yourself on each of the continuums. Because education in the United States overwhelmingly favors Judging, you might need to reflect on how you approached college assignments to determine your true preference.

J | | | | | | | P

I work best when projects are under control and I know I can make the deadline.

I work best when I can change my work up until the last minute.

J | | | | | | | P

I do my best work when I'm not under pressure.

I do my best work when an upcoming deadline adds pressure.

J | | | | | | | P

I have a built-in clock; I know how long something will take.

It's hard for me to estimate how long something will take.

J | | | | | | | P

I want meetings to stay on task, follow the agenda, and finish on time.

I want meetings to cover pressing issues and often disregard agendas.

J | | | | | | | P

I know when I have too many things to do; then I can say no to new commitments.

I say yes to new commitments and then struggle to keep things under control.

J | | | | | | | P

I like to implement a plan.

I like to respond to a situation.

J | | | | | | | P

I like to choose an option and get working on it.

I tend to resist closing off options and may seek more information.

J | | | | | | | P

Timelines and goals improve my satisfaction with the work of PLCs.

The learning process and collaborative discussions improve my satisfaction with the work of PLCs.

Reflect for a moment on the information. Which preference describes you best? Circle one:

Judging   Perceiving

Creating a Coaching Culture © 2010 Jane A. G. Kise and Beth Russell • solution-tree.com
Visit **go.solution-tree.com/PLCbooks** to download this page.

Coaching Yourself as a Leader

Before you begin reading this chapter, take a moment to reflect on the following questions. (This reflection is private; the more honest you are about writing down what comes to mind, the more accurately you will be able to strategize for increasing your leadership capacity.)

- How would you gauge teacher readiness for effective collaboration?

- What topics would you cover during an initial PLC meeting?

Launching PLCs is a delicate leadership task that requires reflection and planning. According to Hargreaves,

> while leadership of PLCs sometimes needs to convey and develop a sense of urgency about improvements, leaders who rush the work of PLCs will only meet with resistance and resentment later on. And leaders who guide the process too closely, imposing their own visions and having the school share them, will find that their efforts and achievements will not survive their departure and succession, since these efforts have been too dependent on, and closely controlled by, the leader's own decisions and desires. (2007, p. 188)

Establishing effective, sustainable PLCs requires careful leadership. Several bodies of research document at least three distinct stages in the development of effective PLCs (DuFour et al., 2006; Grossman et al., 2001; McLaughlin & Talbert, 2006; Mohr & Dichter, 2001). The research also reveals that most schools do not make it to the second or third stage. McLaughlin and Talbert (2006) summarize:

> Significantly, many schools involved in initiatives that aim to develop teacher learning communities do not move from the novice to the intermediate stage, and most do not transition to an advanced stage after several years. They become stuck in a stage of collaborative work that falls short of teacher learning community practice. This reality highlights the need for clearer understanding of the problem of change. The stagnated development of teacher community stems from weak leadership for change among school administrators, reflecting their limited opportunities to be effective in these roles. It also testifies to the complex challenges entailed in developing teacher learning communities widely in U.S. schools. (p. 59)

Reviewing the demands each stage places on leaders through the lens of type indicates that each stage requires an entirely different leadership style and skill set. This chapter is designed to help you coach yourself as a leader. As you read through the crucial leadership roles for each stage of PLC development and the preferences for which each role is most natural, you can identify the roles in which you are most effective. The goal is to help make the most of your strengths over the three- to five-year effort required to establish PLCs. And since few leaders have all of the strengths needed, and most PLCs fail to reach sustainability without shared leadership, this chapter looks at processes for effectively sharing leadership as a PLC moves through each stage.

Type and Leadership

Type research from around the world shows that the vast majority of leaders and managers in all fields prefer Thinking and Judging. The same is true of school principals and district leaders—70 percent prefer Thinking and Judging, compared with 27 percent of teachers (Macdaid, McCaulley, & Kainz, 1991). The language of grade levels, objective standards, adequate yearly progress, testing windows, curriculum maps, data-driven instruction, and so on all reflect those preferences. The preceding Hargreaves quote on the tendency to "rush the work of PLCs" describes an unintended consequence of the Thinking/Judging style of leadership.

To grasp how prevalent the Thinking/Judging mindset is, consider what a Feeling/Perceiving system might look like: individual learning plans for each child with time to pursue every concept to mastery; continuous progress rather than grade levels; curriculum guidelines that flex with current events, student interests, and teacher experiences; and cooperative rather than competitive processes throughout educational systems. If this sounds like impossible chaos, consider whether decades of Thinking/Judging influence have blocked our ability to imagine other systems.

As we reviewed the literature on effective PLC implementation, two things became clear:

- *Leadership is key.* DuFour et al. (2006) summarize:

  > The current emphasis on shared decision-making, dispersed leadership, staff empowerment, collaboration, and collegiality has tended to obscure another harsh reality about substantive change: It demands the sustained attention, energy, and effort of school and district leaders. The idea of bottom-up reform is great, but it is unrealistic to assume that one day a group of educators gathered together in the faculty lounge will suddenly begin to re-examine the basic assumptions, beliefs, and practices that constitute the culture of their school. (p. 191)

- *There are very few schools in which a purely Thinking/Judging style of leadership will produce effective, sustainable PLCs.* Leaders need to be visionary yet collaborative, transformative yet systematic, directive yet empowering for teachers, results oriented yet long term in focus, and fostering adult learning while focusing intensely on student achievement—the role calls on every type preference.

Fortunately, none of us is limited by our preferences. All types can be effective educational leaders. Pearman (2001) writes:

> Three qualities seem essential for leaders at all levels if they are to continue to grow in their effectiveness: openness to experience, confidence in meeting challenges, and eagerness to gain feedback to feed forward to performance. All types can display these qualities. Further, all types can be equally effective in their leadership roles or derail in those roles. . . . My hope is that we can gain clarity about the leadership strengths of our type and learn how to avoid our potential blind spots that derail our best intentions and efforts. In this way, we can boost our confidence and step forward toward greater performance and satisfaction. (p. 1)

In leading PLCs, considering type can help leaders pinpoint potential blind spots and move forward more quickly.

PLC Development Stages and Leadership Priorities

Because the move from independent classroom teaching to professional learning community goes against the traditional culture of many schools, each stage of PLC development has unique characteristics and leadership requirements. Researchers tend to agree on three similar stages (Grossman et al., 2001; McLaughlin & Talbert, 2006; Mohr & Dichter, 2001); the following category names are from DuFour et al. (2006).

- *Stage 1: Pre-Initiation/Initiation Stage*—For this stage, leaders are ***catalysts** for launching PLCs*. Essential roles include building shared vision, building relationships, establishing trust, and identifying issues or foci that motivate change. While people of all types can fill these roles, they are the more natural realm of Intuition and Feeling (NF).

- *Stage 2: Developing Stage*—In this stage, leaders are ***strategists** for building PLC capacity*. Essential roles include setting clear expectations and public accountability, evaluating PLC effectiveness for adults and students, and promoting risk taking. All of these are more the natural realm of Thinking. Another key role at this stage, though, is ensuring shared leadership, which is often more natural for Feeling types.

- *Stage 3: Sustaining Stage*—For this stage, leaders are ***managers** for PLC sustainability*. Essential roles include instituting proven tools and processes (Sensing and Thinking) and sustaining the community (Sensing and Feeling), even as leaders ensure that PLCs continue to seek improvement and share leadership.

Our own experiences in various schools in which we knew the personality types of the leadership teams point to the importance of understanding your own capacity to lead at each stage.

We've seen Intuitive/Thinking leadership teams assume that PLCs could immediately implement shared practice, risk taking, and accountability. In most cases, lack of sufficient trust or group processing skills hampered PLC effectiveness.

We've seen Intuitive/Feeling leaders concentrate on building community, trust, and shared vision. In many cases, they underestimated the amount of structure or clear expectations required for groups to focus on shared initiatives.

We've seen Sensing/Thinking teams develop detailed data systems that cost teachers significant time to disaggregate test results, and yet the ensuing classroom changes focused on a narrow band of test score improvement strategies rather than authentic, rigorous learning.

We've seen Sensing/Feeling teams develop groups that provided collegial support, but discussions stayed shallow because teachers were uncomfortable sharing feedback with each other.

At this point, some readers might be saying, "But this is stereotyping! Any good leader can move schools through each stage." This is true, but each of us is wired to direct our energy toward some of these roles more than others—and our review of the literature revealed at least nineteen roles, detailed in the next section. To illustrate how difficult it is to effectively carry out every role, we want to share our personal experience with moving PLCs through these stages.

- *Stage 1: Leader as PLC Catalyst*—We both prefer Intuition and Feeling. Our natural forte is creating shared experiences that build trust, articulating a common vision, and focusing the work in ways that motivate teachers to engage in PLC work.

- *Stage 2: Leader as PLC Strategist*—We easily planned professional development to introduce classroom practices that promote academic rigor. However, in our initial experience with this work, we realized the need for accountability measures only after classroom walkthroughs revealed that professional development wasn't changing classroom practices. Thereafter, we devised reflection questions, asked teachers to bring samples of student work, asked groups to record main discussion points, and otherwise structured ways to ensure public accountability. See handout 3.2 (page 62) for a sample PLC assignment.

- *Stage 3: Leader as PLC Manager*—This stage is the least exciting for us; once we see results, we are ready to move on to the next initiative. Fortunately, other members of Beth's leadership team had different strengths. They kept the focus on a narrow band of comprehensive strategies. Beth's team also naturally focused on key administrative tasks, such as orienting new teachers to the PLC framework and other roles that promoted PLC sustainability.

Yes, we realized what was necessary to move from stage to stage, but the people around us were better suited to some of the roles than we were. When PLCs were not progressing as we thought they should, we learned to ask, "What aren't we doing? What leadership role is critical?" If you are in the midst of PLC development, as you read through the roles for each stage, consider how the necessary leadership roles might explain what is or is not happening.

Stage 1: *Leader as Catalyst* Roles for Launching PLCs

Community cannot happen without trust and effective collaboration. Consider the different needs of different schools we worked with as they began the work of PLCs:

- At one school, we learned that staff had broken into two sides. Each side thought that the other side didn't care about the students.

- In another school, the principal had moved several teachers to different grade levels. The "old" first-grade teachers thought the "new" teachers needed their advice, leading to power struggles.

- In a new magnet school, the teachers had never worked together.

- In one school, teachers had always been free to use (or not use) district curriculum, resulting in significant differences in classroom instruction.

- In another school in which more than 90 percent of the students met state proficiency standards, the teachers admitted that they feared that their classrooms might have the most underperforming students. "What if I'm the worst teacher? Why would I want to share results?"

These teachers were not ready to share student work or discuss teaching methods. Furthermore, laying the groundwork for effective collaboration in each school required distinctly different tools, timelines, and strategies.

Thus, the roles of PLC leaders at this stage involve designing the groundwork for trust, group processes, and buy-in for the vision and goals while the school shifts its attention from teaching to student learning. As you read through the roles, note which ones are energizing or naturally appealing, and which you hadn't consciously considered.

Role 1: Assessing Current School Culture and Its Readiness for PLC Work

Research base: Hord, 2004; Marzano, Waters, & McNulty, 2005

This role, also called *situational awareness*, is often more natural for Extraverted types since it involves interacting and engaging in conversations. Feeling types naturally gauge relationships, so they may be adept at unearthing trust issues or conflict. Intuitive/Feeling types might adeptly ascertain the climate of a building, but Sensing/Feeling types might pick up on nuances within each team or between teams more easily. Thinking types might note power struggles and informal leaders. In Hord's research, this role was often filled by an outside facilitator who could objectively assess interactions and issues. Perhaps this is because less than 15 percent of school principals prefer Sensing and Feeling—it is seldom a natural role for administrators.

Role 2: Building Relationships by Understanding Each Teacher as an Individual

Research base: Kise, 2006

Sensing/Feeling types usually thrive on working with people one on one. This role facilitates understanding each person's hesitations, needs, and potential contributions. Leaders identify individual difficulties with data analysis or how, because of past conflicts, one grade-level team might need more time to develop norms and protocols. Leaders may also seek out seemingly resistant teachers to better meet their needs.

Role 3: Building Social Trust

Research base: Bryk & Schneider, 2002; DuFour et al., 2006; Hord, 2004

Intuitive/Feeling types often think in terms of community—how to get groups of people collaborating toward the same goals. This includes helping people understand that conflict can be negotiated and is helpful in evaluating different viewpoints and making wise decisions.

Role 4: Identifying Issues That Focus Work and Influence Teacher Beliefs

Research base: McLaughlin & Talbert, 2006; Resnick & Hall, 1998; Sparks, 2006

In this role, leaders acknowledge that change is hard work and generally requires the intrinsic motivation that personal vision brings. They discover teacher concerns, interests, and beliefs that are blocking change. They then create implementation plans that focus on teacher-developed goals, while at the same time advancing school initiatives. This big-picture focus—with constant connections among teacher needs, initiatives, and overall frameworks—is generally the realm of the Intuitive type.

Role 5: Building Norms for Shared Decision Making and Conflict/Problem Solving

Research base: DuFour et al., 2006; Hord, 2004; Kise & Russell, 2008; McLaughlin & Talbert, 2006

Research indicates that without careful attention to protocols that unearth biases or blind spots, PLCs can reinforce ineffective teacher practices. Further, bringing teachers together can foment conflict that isolation had kept quiet. These factors make developing protocols and skills for decision making and handling conflict an important part of the work of PLCs. Sensing/Feeling leaders often naturally seek effective processes for working with others.

Role 6: Designing and Building the Practice of Collaboration

Research base: DuFour et al., 2006; McLaughlin & Talbert, 2006

Few people possess natural collaborative skills; this is especially true for professionals, such as teachers, who are used to working in isolation. Decades of practitioner experience and research indicate that Thinking types are more task-oriented than relationship-oriented and spend less time than Feeling types on collaboration skills (Fitzgerald, 1997; Myers et al., 1998). Team building for effective, ongoing collaboration falls within the realm of Intuition and Feeling.

Role 7: Coordinating Professional Development for Evidence-Based Decision Making

Research base: DuFour et al., 2006

This role involves quickly identifying and streamlining the collection of data that provides information on student academic progress, the "How will we know if students learned it?" goal of PLCs. Leaders ensure that professional development and data collection and analysis are efficient and encouraging. While all types are capable of this kind of strategic thinking, this role is the natural playground for Intuitive/Thinking types, who also, incidentally, tend to enjoy evaluating and synthesizing data.

Stage 2: *Leader as Strategist* Roles for Building PLC Capacity

After the foundation for collaboration is well underway, the leadership focus turns from culture to learning—that of adults and students. Yes, leaders still need to be cognizant of Feeling function skills such as maintaining social trust and influencing beliefs, but it is time to get tough about the tough work of PLCs: adults learning together and making decisions to improve classroom instruction so that all students achieve.

Role 8: Setting Clear Expectations and Providing Related Feedback

Research base: DuFour et al., 2006; Kise & Russell, 2008

If PLCs are to advance the strategic goals of the school, then the leadership needs to clarify expectations and provide feedback to PLCs in several areas: goals, activities, communication to leadership and to other teams, and classroom implementation. Sensing/Thinking types often naturally excel at developing procedures, timelines, check-in tools, and progress charts or other mechanisms.

Role 9: Aligning School Culture and Structures to Promote Adult and Student Learning

Research base: Stoll & Lewis, 2007

PLCs can easily lose the balance between adult learning and student learning; this role involves ensuring that teachers look beyond quick-fix strategies and instead have the time and tools to examine practices, investigate alternatives, and change their classrooms. Ideally, students see adults who are excited about learning. The Intuitive/Thinking types often seek the big ideas behind strategies and strive for holistic implementation, as required in this role. In addition, rigorous classroom strategies that involve analysis, synthesis, evaluation, and other higher-order thinking skills are usually far more attractive to them than teaching procedures or factual information.

Role 10: Prioritizing Teacher Learning of Both Content Knowledge and Teaching Strategies

Research base: DuFour et al., 2006; McLaughlin & Talbert, 2006

With a nearly infinite number of possible initiatives, leaders need a clear strategic focus that balances teacher mastery of content knowledge and instructional strategies. Picture a mathematics major who mastered differential calculus, yet struggles to facilitate inquiry-based tasks—this teacher needs instructional strategies. In contrast, picture the teacher who knows how to run small groups and encourage student-directed discussions, yet cannot identify the incremental building blocks in student knowledge of addition—this teacher needs to build content knowledge. The Sensing/Thinking leader might emphasize sequential knowledge teachers need, while the Intuitive/Thinking leader might emphasize strategies that are useful in multiple settings.

Role 11: Nurturing Public Practice to Establish Collective Responsibility for Student Learning

Research base: DuFour et al., 2006; McLaughlin & Talbert, 2006

This role is a continuation of building social trust by building awareness of all-community responsibility for student learning. Establishing this as a norm is essential for moving to Stage 3; failure to do so is a major reason so many PLCs never become sustainable. Intuitive/Feeling leaders often naturally uphold community values and facilitate conversations that allow teachers to share their struggles and successes.

Role 12: Promoting Risk Taking

Research base: Hord, 2004; McLaughlin & Talbert, 2006

Change is inherently risky. The students, teachers, and cultural environments in which schools operate are different in every situation, and results can be unpredictable—no matter how proven the practices. Role 12 involves nurturing the courage to try practices that have a reasonable chance of improving student learning. Rather than expecting instant results, leaders support teachers in sustained efforts to master content or implement strategies, acknowledging that five to seven classroom attempts may be necessary before results are seen. Intuitive/Thinking leaders often need less evidence than Sensing/Thinking leaders to try a practice—a key component of risk.

Role 13: Building Shared Leadership Capacity

Research base: Brown & Isaacs, 1994; DuFour et al., 2008; Hord, 2004; Huffman & Jacobson, 2003; Snyder, Acker-Hocevar, & Snyder, 1996

Nearly every resource on PLCs lists this role, which includes developing leadership in each teacher, as an essential component of leadership, especially if PLCs are to continue through multiple changes in school leadership. The natural leadership style for many Intuitive/Feeling types emphasizes shared leadership.

Role 14: Evaluating Effectiveness of Professional Learning by Improvement in Student Learning

Research base: DuFour et al., 2006

In this role, leaders focus on whether students are learning. Is the school becoming more successful at its core mission of academic achievement for all students? The Sensing/Thinking leader may most naturally seek measurable results, while the Intuitive/Thinking leader usually uses different measures to identify progress toward long-term results.

Stage 3: *Leader as Manager* Roles for PLC Sustainability

At this stage, PLCs are as much a part of school culture as whiteboards, buses, and libraries. Adults know their collaborative work improves outcomes for students. For PLCs that make it to Stage 3, leadership efforts revolve around ensuring stability. Elias (2008) found that programs erode quickly without plans for incorporating new staff, review, and ongoing training for existing staff, and continued funding—especially if leaders leave. Overall, developing consistent processes and monitoring mechanisms involves the administrative skills natural to Sensing and Thinking leaders.

Role 15: Institutionalizing Proven Routines, Tools, and Support for PLCs

Research base: Elias, 2008; McLaughlin & Talbert, 2006

This role involves monitoring and evaluating PLC protocols, activities, decisions, and classroom impact, as well as determining both internal and external support needs. Keeping what works and developing sustainable routines are hallmarks of Sensing and Thinking types.

Role 16: Sustaining Community via Norms and Habits

Research base: McLaughlin & Talbert, 2006

This role involves sustaining community focus on the values and purpose of PLCs—including assessing and improving teaching and learning—even as members of the community come and go. Sensing/Feeling types may more naturally develop ongoing rituals or routines that keep vision and values at the forefront of activities.

Role 17: Sustaining the Vision of Continuous Improvement

Research base: McLaughlin & Talbert, 2006

Schools in which students have always performed well on measures of academic achievement or that make significant progress toward closing the achievement gap can grow complacent over instructional improvement. This leadership role involves the ongoing search for better content knowledge and instructional strategies, as well as for professional development opportunities that inspire teachers. Intuitive/Thinking types may most naturally press others to join them in working toward ever-higher levels of excellence.

Role 18: Continuing Shared Leadership

Research base: Hord, 2004; Gunn & King, 2003

True sustainability incorporates teacher input for decisions that affect their PLC, their classrooms, and the overall school community. Through this role, leaders ensure that shared leadership becomes a part of the culture. Intuitive/Feeling types often naturally seek to develop leadership qualities in others.

Role 19: Developing Social Networking That Facilitates Community

Research base: Bolam, McMahon, Stoll, Thomas, & Wallace, 2005

Sensing/Thinking types often enjoy exploring efficient ways to use technology and may be most interested in determining how to use Web 2.0 tools to capture PLC data; provide easy ways for members to be resources to each other and to network outside their buildings; or to warehouse pertinent information, articles, or tools for data or instruction.

Again, the point in identifying which types might most naturally excel at these roles is not to limit leaders but to help us evaluate what we might overlook during the difficult journey required for sustainable PLC development. Furthermore, if you are a school administrator, these nineteen roles are in addition to the twenty-six leadership roles (with slight overlap) that research shows are essential for student achievement (Kise & Russell, 2008). Examples of these additional roles include:

- Advocating for the school

- Acting as school change agent and optimizer

- Gaining extensive knowledge of curriculum and assessment

- Setting clear expectations and providing related feedback

- Showing appreciation and recognizing accomplishments

While a few "superleaders" might be able to do them all, few buildings sustain the programs started by these overachievers once they leave.

The reflections and exercises at the end of this chapter are designed to help leaders and leadership teams determine how to cover the roles. However, let's look at one other dilemma of leadership first: granting autonomy in processes while maintaining control of the end goals. This is called *loose/ tight leadership* (DuFour et al., 2008; Sagie, 1997).

Balancing Loose/Tight Leadership

The complex task of leading PLC implementation requires planning, yet initiatives seldom proceed as planned. Personality type can be useful in analyzing the tendency to over- or understructure initiatives, protocols, or activities, thus helping schools balance the need to plan with the need to flex as events unfold.

Picture leadership as falling on a continuum between the extremes of a purely Sensing/Judging style (PLC implementation happens uniformly and in adherence to a schedule) and a purely Intuitive/ Perceiving style (PLC implementation emerges according to the ideas and desires of its members). Both ends create problems. On the SJ extreme, PLCs usually disintegrate once the leader is gone, and on the NP extreme, PLCs often never get off the ground. Fortunately, few leaders tend to be either extreme.

So how do you find balance on this continuum? By planning for flexibility, allowing choices while setting clear expectations, and encouraging creativity in conforming to PLC norms. Activity 3.1, "Checking Loose/Tight Balance," contains a checklist of common responsibilities for PLCs and their leaders. Use it alone or with your team to consider whether your approach is too loose, too tight, or just right. Then, activity 3.2 provides a loose/tight PLC activity that you can compare to your own protocols.

ACTIVITY 3.1 Checking Loose/Tight Balance

Goal: To evaluate the degree of control that leadership has over PLC implementation and whether that amount is effective

Materials: Copy of handout 3.1, "A Checklist for Loose/Tight PLC Leadership" (page 61), for each participant

Directions: Have team members individually reflect on each of the questions in handout 3.1 before the group discussion. Encourage them to think of specific examples of a time when the answer would be *yes* and also when it would be *no*.

Then, for each item, ask for a show of hands to indicate *yes* or *no*. Ask participants to provide evidence that supports their answers. Work toward consensus on whether the team is loose, tight, or balanced on each question.

ACTIVITY 3.2 Loose/Tight PLC Assignment

Goal: To help PLC leaders understand their natural tendency to differentiate implementation activities to meet the various needs of each group

Materials: Copy of handout 3.2, "Sample PLC Assignment: Student-Focused Discussions Task" (page 62) for each participant

Directions: Examine handout 3.2. How is it similar to or different from activities you might design? How might groups use it differently? (Loose) Does it provide clear expectations? (Tight) Explain.

Which Roles Will You Fill?

At each stage of PLC implementation, which roles make the best use of your strengths? Use handout 3.3, "Leading Effective Professional Learning Communities" (page 63), to reflect on how you would like to lead. Then, activity 3.3, "PLC Shared Leadership Analysis," is designed to help teams share the roles. Type, of course, is not destiny; you may have taken specific training or been motivated by certain experiences to develop skills with roles that are less natural for you. However, for most people, the lens of type assists in deciding where to concentrate their efforts and when to partner with others.

ACTIVITY 3.3: PLC Shared Leadership Analysis

Goal: To analyze the strengths of a team and which leadership roles are being overlooked

Materials: Copies of handout 3.3, "Leading Effective Professional Learning Communities," (page 63) for each participant, a poster of handout 3.3, increased to at least 200 percent, and five green and five red garage sale stickers (three-quarters of an inch circles) for each participant

Directions: Have each participant work alone to complete handout 3.3. Then have them select the five "green" roles for which they have the most energy and interest and the five "red" roles for which they have the least energy and interest. When they finish, have them place the appropriate-colored stickers next to the roles they chose on the handout 3.3 poster.

When everyone has placed their stickers, remind the group that while each of them may fill more than five roles, most leadership teams find that the patterns of red and green explain what is and is not happening. Use the following questions to facilitate discussion:

- For the roles that have multiple green stickers, in what ways is this area emphasized in how we lead PLCs? Is there too much emphasis?

- For the roles that have multiple red stickers, what evidence suggests that this role is not being covered? What do we need to do?

- What action steps should we take, based on our analysis of the roles we like and dislike? Do some of us need to develop skills? Should we tap others for leadership? What specific actions have we overlooked that require immediate attention if we are to further the work of our PLCs?

Reflection

1. Use handout 3.3 (page 63) as a tool to gauge how your PLC is progressing toward sustainability. If you are just beginning, flag any areas in stage 1 that are at risk of being ignored or rushed. If you are in the midst of an initiative, consider which roles need more attention. What actions will improve effectiveness and sustainability?

2. Peck (1987) wrote, "Communities have sometimes been referred to as leaderless groups. It is more accurate, however, to say that a community is a group of all leaders" (p. 72). Is the leadership of PLCs shared in your building? Why or why not? Given that research indicates that sharing leadership is essential to PLC sustainability, what steps are needed to make this a reality?

3. If you are a schoolwide leader, identify the roles in handout 3.3 that you consistently take and those that are hard to fill. Develop some action steps: how will you develop skills or share leadership for those out-of-strength leadership requirements?

Handout 3.1

A Checklist for Loose/Tight PLC Leadership

Individually, or as a leadership team, reflect on each of the following questions regarding the work of PLCs. For each question:

- Cite specific examples to illustrate how loosely (the Perceiving strength) or tightly (the Judging strength) this item is controlled.

- Consider whether moving either way on the loose/tight continuum would improve PLC effectiveness.

- Write down action steps to take to achieve balance.

1. Do you have a professional development plan for covering topics your PLC needs? Does it cover an adequate time frame? (Judging)

2. Do you have procedures for evaluating whether the professional development is resulting in classroom changes or improvements in student achievement? (Judging)

3. Do you regularly revise the professional development schedule based on classroom evidence or changes in teacher or student needs? (Perceiving)

4. Are expectations clear when PLCs decide to implement new strategies? Do teachers agree on what those expectations mean? (Judging)

5. Is there room for innovation or differences in style as to how teachers meet those expectations? (Perceiving)

6. Have you established procedures for assessing whether students are learning what is taught? (Judging)

7. Are teachers encouraged to seek new ways to assess student progress? (Perceiving)

8. Does your school or PLC have clear procedures for helping students who are struggling? (Judging)

9. Do you have regularly scheduled meetings? (Judging)

10. Is the meeting routine set (Judging), or does it vary according to needs (Perceiving)?

Handout 3.2

Sample PLC Assignment: Student-Focused Discussions Task

When we last met, the consensus of the group seemed to be that we needed a more concrete plan to facilitate productive, student-focused discussions in our classrooms, as opposed to teacher-directed discussions. In response, we are asking each PLC to create an implementation plan for trying out a student-focused discussion in each classroom. You will work together to plan a similar lesson and then share data about your experiences. Please use the following guidelines to create your plan. Each PLC will turn in one plan at the end of the session.

Step 1. Decide on the lesson content. Brainstorm similar lesson content (a topic, activity, or strand, for instance) that each PLC member will implement sometime during the next two weeks. For example, social studies teachers could focus on current events, language arts or math teachers could look at sample constructed responses from accountability tests, and science teachers could develop a lesson for experiments. Then make a final choice.

Our PLC will facilitate student-focused discussions on the following:

Step 2. Decide how student-focused discussions best fit into the lesson. Would the lesson work best with an all-class discussion? Small groups? A fishbowl? Any of the other techniques we have talked about or you have learned about elsewhere? Reach a conclusion about how all of you will facilitate the discussion.

Our PLC will use the following discussion strategy:

Step 3. Decide on the data you might record for the lesson. Consider what data will be useful for your PLC discussion about this common experience: student engagement rate, work completion rate, or types of specific comments from students (levels of questions, elaboration, accuracy)? Think about how students could reflect on the situation and give you feedback as well.

Each member of our PLC will gather the following data for our discussion:

Note: Each PLC member will bring the data from his or her experience to our meeting scheduled for two weeks from now, along with a written reflection on what went well, what was challenging, and what your next step might be.

Handout 3.3

Leading Effective Professional Learning Communities

Researchers are beginning to form a consensus that it takes three to five years to form effective PLCs and that strong leadership is key to moving through various stages of development. The following chart lists the three PLC stages, the leadership roles emphasized at each stage, and the most natural type preferences for each role. Review the roles required of leadership to successfully move through each stage, and rate your affinity for that role using the following rating key:

1. I don't think I am best suited to this responsibility.
2. I understand this responsibility and could cover some of it.
3. I have strategies and ideas that work for me in this area, although I prefer other roles.
4. I can do this easily.
5. I do this easily and can share with others what I've learned.

Note: Bracketed letters refer to best-fit preferences for the role.

Stage 1: *Leader as Catalyst* Roles for Launching PLCs	1	2	3	4	5
1. Assessing current school culture and its readiness for PLC work [SF]	O	O	O	O	O
2. Building relationships by understanding each teacher as an individual [SF]	O	O	O	O	O
3. Building social trust [NF]	O	O	O	O	O
4. Identifying issues that focus work and influence teacher beliefs [N]	O	O	O	O	O
5. Building norms for shared decision making and conflict/problem solving [NF]	O	O	O	O	O
6. Designing and building the practice of collaboration [NF]	O	O	O	O	O
7. Coordinating professional development for evidence-based decision making [NT]	O	O	O	O	O
Stage 2: *Leader as Strategist* Roles for Building PLC Capacity	**1**	**2**	**3**	**4**	**5**
8. Setting clear expectations and providing related feedback [ST]	O	O	O	O	O
9. Aligning school culture and structures to promote adult and student learning [NT]	O	O	O	O	O
10. Prioritizing teacher learning of both content knowledge and teaching strategies [ST, NT]	O	O	O	O	O
11. Nurturing public practice to establish collective responsibility for student learning [NF]	O	O	O	O	O
12. Promoting risk taking [NT]	O	O	O	O	O
13. Building shared leadership capacity [NF]	O	O	O	O	O
14. Evaluating effectiveness of professional learning by improvement in student learning [ST, NT]	O	O	O	O	O
Stage 3: *Leader as Manager* Roles for PLC Sustainability	**1**	**2**	**3**	**4**	**5**
15. Institutionalizing proven routines, tools, and support for PLCs [ST]	O	O	O	O	O
16. Sustaining community via norms and habits [SF]	O	O	O	O	O
17. Sustaining the vision of continuous improvement [NT]	O	O	O	O	O
18. Continuing shared leadership [NF]	O	O	O	O	O
19. Developing social networking that facilitates community [SF]	O	O	O	O	O

Differentiating the PLC Structure

Before you begin reading this chapter, take a moment to reflect on the following questions:

- What are the three main reasons teachers resist change? Why do you think so?

- What activities do you believe PLC meetings should emphasize? How would you prioritize the work?

In an article on leadership for sustainability, Hargreaves and Fink (2004) discuss how standardizing a curriculum to match accountability tests demotivated an entire teaching team that had previously used curricula differentiated for the diverse backgrounds of their students. Enthusiastic teachers turned into resisters. While recognizing the complexity of the issues, they report that

> standardization is the enemy of sustainability. Sustainable leadership recognizes and cultivates many kinds of excellence in learning, teaching and leading and provides the networks for these different kinds of excellence to be shared in cross-fertilizing processes of improvement. (p. 1)

Have you encountered any resistance to forming PLCs or to the activities you are using? As you start this chapter, we ask you to entertain the premise that *there are no* resistant *teachers, but instead only teachers whose needs have not been met.* Why else would a professional resist reform efforts clearly linked to improved student achievement?

Here is the dilemma: teachers do not want, need, or expect the same things from collaboration; nor, as personality type explains, do they absorb the same kinds of information or base decisions on the same evidence. If you still harbor any doubts that one-size-fits-all PLCs are ineffective, turn to appendix A, "Descriptions of the Sixteen Types," on page 155. Read your own type description, especially the sections titled "Value to the PLC" and "Approach to Data." Then turn to the page for your opposite type. For example, if you prefer ISTJ, you would also read the ENFP descriptions. The two descriptions have nothing in common other than the mutual hope that making time for PLC activities will improve student achievement.

When PLCs differentiate protocols, activities, information resources, and meeting formats, they ensure that each teacher is treated as a valuable resource and is given every opportunity to improve his or her teaching and learning ability. In this chapter, we focus on using the differentiated coaching framework, as discussed in chapter 1, for adult learning within PLCs.

Step 1: Using the Common Framework

The first step in ensuring that all educators feel welcome in their learning community is to honor their needs for energy, information, and decision making, as well as their approach to the tasks at hand—essentially keeping all personality preferences in mind. Chapter 2 contains resources for teams to use for self-identification of preferences. Chapter 6, "Coaching a Group Into a Collaborative Team," helps PLCs learn to use these differences constructively. Here, we concentrate on ensuring that the leaders' preferences, or those of the majority of PLC members, do not result in practices or premises that put others at a constant disadvantage. Activity 4.1, "Evaluating Your PLC Atmosphere," provides a process for groups to discuss the considerations and atmospheres that help people with each personality preference learn best.

ACTIVITY 4.1 Evaluating Your PLC Atmosphere

Goal: To help PLC leaders and members understand the needs of each preference and adjust how the PLC operates to better meet everyone's needs

Materials: Flip-chart paper, pink and yellow highlight markers for each participant, and copies of handout 4.1, "Type Preferences and Learning Needs" (page 77). If you are using this as a group activity, consider creating a poster of handout 4.1 to facilitate the discussion.

Directions: Ask participants to read through the sections on their own preferences, marking in yellow the items they believe their PLC honors and in pink the items they believe need more consideration. Participants can also read through the other preferences, but may wish to leave them unmarked so that they can eventually annotate them based on what people who hold those preferences say.

Debrief by going through the preferences one by one. Ask for comments from people who hold those preferences. On the poster of handout 4.1, mark items that the group agrees need more consideration.

At the end of each preference discussion, ask participants to do a quickwrite on processes they would suggest to meet the needs of their preferences. Ask each person to share one of his or her favorite suggestions. Record these suggestions on flip-chart paper, and discuss which ones should be reflected in group norms.

Step 2: Understanding Teacher Strengths and Beliefs

While every individual is unique, type suggests general patterns in teacher strengths and beliefs, as shown in appendix A (page 155), especially regarding strengths. However, teachers also form beliefs based on their experiences, culture, training, family background, and glimpses they have of their colleagues' classrooms. Working to understand their beliefs about teaching and learning is often key to motivating them to change.

After you establish trust with teachers, the following prompts, posed to individuals or the group, may provide information about their beliefs:

- Why do students struggle in this school? (Note the general question rather than asking about a specific teacher's classroom.)

- Describe a time when you were at your best helping a student.

- What are the characteristics of students you feel least able to help?

- If you could get teachers to be consistent about one thing, what would it be?

- What priorities do you have for your classroom this year?

- If you could wave a magic wand, what two things would you change in your school or district to help the most students achieve proficiency?

You might also engage your PLC in a text-based discussion on the belief that student effort creates ability, as opposed to student aptitude. The following texts might be helpful:

- "Making America Smarter" (Resnick, 1999)

- Appendix C, "Reading on Student Motivation" (page 181), which can be used with activity 5.2, "Evidence-Based Discussions" (page 92)

- Resources posted at the Efficacy Institute: www.efficacy.org

Remember that your purpose is to look for any beliefs that might block the essential work of PLCs: identifying what students should learn, determining how to assess whether they achieved mastery, and planning for what to do if they have or have not mastered the material. If such beliefs exist, Step 3 can help you overcome them.

Step 3: Coaching to Meet Each Teacher's Learning Style and Needs

Appendix A lists the kinds of PLC activities and information that best meet the needs of each personality type. However, planning for sixteen types can overwhelm the time available to plan professional development. We simplify the task by differentiating to address the needs of four main styles: the combinations of Sensing and Intuition (information needs) and Thinking and Feeling (decision-making needs).

ACTIVITY 4.2 Understanding the PLC Styles

Goal: To foster understanding of how teachers with different learning styles would ideally structure PLC activities; to promote constructive use of differences within PLCs

Materials: Copies of handouts 4.2–4.5 (pages 78–81) for each participant

Directions: Ask participants to individually read through the handout for their PLC style—Sensing/Thinking (ST), Sensing/Feeling (SF), Intuition/Feeling (NF), or Intuition/Thinking (NT)—and then reflect individually on the following questions:

- What elements of the description fit your image of the ideal PLC? Note any positive experiences that come to mind.

- How does the description match your beliefs about the purposes of PLCs?

Next, ask participants to individually read over the page for the opposite PLC style and answer the questions that follow for:

The Pragmatic PLC (ST) versus The Collegial PLC (NF) *or*

The Supportive PLC (SF) versus The Intellectual PLC (NT)

- Consider the PLC style your opposite prefers. What elements would be difficult for you to engage in? Why?

- Have you been on teams with colleagues who are your opposite? What worked? What didn't work?

Then, form groups of participants who prefer each style and ask them to discuss the following questions:

- How might we misjudge a teacher whose style is opposite ours?

- What are the most important adjustments we could make to meet the needs of the style opposite ours?

Finally, ask for "aha" moments, stories, or ideas from each group.

While meeting the informational needs of each style can balance PLC activities, the four coaching cultures can also be key in anticipating which teachers might struggle the most with certain initiatives. For example, a school staff might decide that consistency with certain classroom management techniques or discussion protocols would clarify expectations for students as they move from classroom to classroom. This policy might be hardest for Intuitive/Feeling teachers to implement since they may already have developed creative methods that reflect their own interests or personalities.

Often, PLCs work to develop vertical curriculum maps that ensure all students master key content and concepts. Sensing/Thinking teachers may already have their own maps and carefully honed lessons that work well in the order they established. They may need more support or may need a bigger voice that recognizes their expertise in constructing the new maps. Intuitive/Feeling teachers might be challenged if maps leave out their favorite units; leaders may need to reflect on whether loose/tight implementation guidelines might create deeper buy-in for curriculum maps.

Group work is another example. Young Introverted/Sensing/Feeling teachers often report that launching literature circles or small groups for math investigations is stressful—the room is noisier, it is difficult to assess student progress, and they worry about whether they are allowing too much or too little time for activities.

Sensing/Thinking types report hesitations at giving students choices in assignments—a key strategy for motivation—because they worry about consistency in grading.

One way, then, to differentiate staff development is for PLCs to first consider which preferences might struggle with an initiative, curriculum, or teaching strategy; then the group can design professional development that matches the learning style of teachers with those preferences so they receive the highest level of support from the start. *Every* teacher might struggle to some degree, but in very different ways.

Figure 4.1, page 70, illustrates how two different types might struggle with implementing student-focused discussions. Characteristics of these discussions include the following:

- Students, not teachers, do most of the talking.

- Students build on each other's ideas with several taking turns addressing a topic or thought before the teacher asks another question.

- Students use evidence from text, experiences, or other sources to support their reasoning—they do not rely solely on opinions.

- Students prompt each other to explain, clarify, or justify their ideas.

- An atmosphere of respect encourages students to share answers they aren't sure are correct or that they may still be formulating.

- Students work toward group understanding. If one student provides an answer that is clearly wrong (for example, on a mathematics problem), classmates gently probe for his or her reasoning or work together to determine the source of the misunderstanding.

- Student participation and engagement are at a high level.

Leaders can use figure 4.1 to tailor professional development, choosing the activities that best fit the teachers they are working with. Or, they might provide alternative activities and support for teachers with different styles.

Sensing/Thinking teachers might struggle with: Focusing on justification and student thinking, rather than on correct answers Asking open-ended questions that allow for in-depth discussion, rather than ones that explicitly cover content **Professional development plan for STs:** Show a film clip of a student-focused discussion, preferably with students from their own school or a similar school. Ask teachers to take notes and then discuss the following: <ul><li>What the teacher does</li><li>What the students do</li><li>What impresses them about the discussion</li></ul> Hand out the elements of student-focused discussions. Clarify that this is a skill that must be taught and that students in the film clip worked for about six weeks on the technique before the film was made. Engage teachers in an exercise in which they are the students. You might try two different topics to better match the needs of all teachers: <ul><li>A mathematics problem that is not too hard but that can be solved in multiple ways</li><li>An article on text-based discussions, effective group work, or other relevant topics</li></ul> Provide teachers with *prompt cards*—phrases they can use during the discussion and that they can later have students use. Facilitate a whole-group discussion for the first topic and then ask teachers to work in small groups on the second topic, continuing to follow the principles.	**Intuitive/Feeling teachers might struggle with:** Teaching clear protocols and phrases for students to use Clarifying in advance their goals for a discussion so that they can gauge achievement **Professional development plan for NFs:** Show a film clip of a student-focused discussion. Ask teachers to work in groups to compare how the discussion is similar to and different from discussions in their own classrooms. Hand out the elements of student-focused discussions. Emphasize the teacher role in the following: <ul><li>Planning learning goals and questions in advance</li><li>Teaching this skill in steps during a six-week period</li></ul> Ask teachers to work in pairs on a math problem such as the following example. Ask for volunteers to share their work via a document camera. Provide prompt cards to all participants to use in discussing the sample solution. Ask whether other groups have a different solution or approach. Be sure that the group probes for thinking before passing judgment on correctness. *Problem: A palindrome is a word or number that reads the same forward or backward. The year 1991 and the word level are good examples. Your challenge is to determine how many whole numbers between 100 and 1,000 are palindromes.*

Hand out an exercise that each teacher can use to begin instruction on student-focused discussion. Make sure that the content is familiar enough so that teachers and students need only focus on the process. Ask teachers to complete a reflection sheet when they finish the activity with their class and to bring that sheet to their next PLC meeting. Continue to provide exercises for teachers to use in their classrooms and to structure the exercises to address the concerns and needs teachers voice through their PLC meetings.	Hand out a learning progression—skills students need to master to engage in student-focused discussion. Ask teachers to work together to develop an activity to teach the first skill, using the prompts to build on one another's comments. Ask teachers to complete a sheet outlining what they will do in their classrooms and how they will record their observations and report to the next PLC meeting. Continue to have PLCs develop activities to teach each skill, as well as tools to monitor student improvement.

Figure 4.1: Professional development for student-focused discussions.

Another common initiative is helping teachers move students toward higher-level thinking through the model of questioning developed by Costa (2001). *All* types tend to underestimate the amount of effort needed to help students be successful with the highest level of questioning. Figure 4.2 provides examples of the different struggles SF and NT teachers might have and the different PLC activities that would best meet their needs. To meet such diverse needs, professional development might include giving choices or otherwise differentiating for teacher needs, thus modeling what we expect these teachers to do for students.

Sensing/Feeling teachers might struggle with: Moving from questions with a correct answer to open-ended questions Developing a wide variety of questions rather than working from a list **Professional development plan for SFs:** Provide a chart of the three levels of questions and explain how the levels relate to rigor. Hand out a copy of a poem such as Robert Hayden's "The Whipping" or a reading that teachers will be using with students. Let teachers work in pairs to write Level I, II, and III questions based on the text.	**Intuitive/Thinking teachers might struggle with:** Breaking down the levels of questions into steps for students Keeping discussions focused **Professional development plan for NTs:** Explain Costa's (2001) model of Intellectual Functioning in Three Levels. Provide copies of *Developing Minds* for background reading. Distribute a one-page reading, or ask participants to turn to a passage in Costa's book. Ask them to create at least three Level III questions for the passage.

continued on next page →

When the teachers have finished, provide examples of questions in which the words used *do not* make the question or task more rigorous. For example:

> Create a timeline of significant events. In this case, *create* does not make the task more rigorous because students will continue to list facts sequentially. Adding "Explain why each event you chose is significant to the author's message" would make the task more rigorous.

Have teachers review their questions for similar flaws.

Provide a lesson plan for teaching students the levels of questioning. Demonstrate any activities teachers are unfamiliar with.

Offer to model the lesson for any teacher who wants to see how it works with his or her students. Provide the alternative of observing a classroom and giving feedback.

As a group, ask them to brainstorm the problems they anticipate students might have with a discussion or assignment based solely on Level III questions.

- Demonstrate how to plan backward for such a discussion.
- Identify major points the discussion needs to cover.
- Construct Level I and II questions that guide discussion toward those points. Anticipate student responses and possible additional questions that might refocus the discussion.
- Think through the essential prior knowledge students need in order to engage in the Level III discussion.
- Determine an activity aimed to help students process Level I questions about the content of the discussion, such as the following:
  + Constructing a timeline
  + Journaling about the text
  + Reading and commenting on the text with a partner
  + Completing a science experiment
  + Recording a film clip or video
- Discuss the advantages of teaching students about the different levels of questioning. Provide a handout teachers could use with students. Have teachers identify content they might use to teach the model to students.
- Plan for peer observations and feedback on using the three levels of questioning.

Figure 4.2: Professional development used to increase rigor of questioning.

Step 4: Differentiating Concrete Evidence

A quick reading of the four coaching cultures highlights the very different forms of data that influence how people make decisions. You can use activities 4.3, "Using Data in PLCs," and 4.4, "PLC Inventory," to help PLCs provide needed information to all members and to balance the forms of data they use to inform instruction.

ACTIVITY 4.3 Using Data in PLCs

Goal: To understand how each type approaches data analysis and what that means for PLC efforts using data to improve instruction

Materials: Access to the type descriptions in appendix A, "Descriptions of the Sixteen Types" (page 155)

Directions: Do a quickwrite on how your district, school, or PLC currently gathers, analyzes, and uses data, including the kinds and sources of data that are given the most weight in decisions. If you are using this exercise with a group, create a posterboard chart that lists the data, how they are gathered, who analyzes them, and what decisions are based on them.

Each type description has an "Approach to Data" section. Read the one for your own type. Does it match with your overall approach to using data? If not, what factors might have influenced your use of data? Your position? Training? Your colleagues?

Then read through the paragraphs for the other types. You might construct a table, categorizing types by whether their style matches or does not match yours.

Finally, reflect on the information. Are you overlooking key sources of data? Might there be more efficient processes, especially given the natural inclinations of different types? Could your site benefit from a *data inventory*—a hard look at what to use, when to use it, and how to organize it for end users, the teachers?

ACTIVITY 4.4 PLC Inventory

Goal: To take inventory of the activities and information sources a PLC is using by asking: What has happened? What is planned? Who is being left out?

Materials: Copies of handout 4.6, "PLC Activities" (page 82), for each participant. Alternatively, this activity can be done individually by a PLC leader.

continued on next page →

Directions: On handout 4.6, highlight the activities in which your PLC frequently engages as well as the information most frequently provided. Then, answer the following questions:

- Are there any patterns? Does your PLC have an overall "style"? Does the style match the preferences of most teachers? If so, are any teachers constantly put at a disadvantage? How does this affect the role they have in the PLC? What action steps might the group take to be more inclusive?

- If the highlighting is more random, are the needs of some teachers met more than others? What activities might you include to add balance?

- What, if any, missing data might provide key information to improve student learning?

Step 5: Focusing on Problems That Concern PLC Members

The differentiated coaching model contends that meeting teachers' learning needs may not be enough. If their view of the obstacles is different from the overall vision for school change, teachers still may resist collaborating on school or PLC goals. If a teacher cannot get his or her classroom under control, PLC activities might assist by providing routines that also improve instruction. If teachers perceive a lack of trust among students, professional development might focus on building relationships through creating conditions for student-focused discussions. If a teacher is frustrated by too much paperwork, leaders may need to find a PLC focus that incorporates paperless formative assessments. If teachers want students to get to class on time, PLCs may need to concentrate on rigor via improving launch activities so that students want to be on time.

In almost every case, classroom problems are complex enough that addressing them can be incorporated into most PLC initiatives. Teachers see the connection, see the results, and are ready to engage more fully in the overall goals of the PLC or the building. When teachers show a lack of enthusiasm over the chosen topics or goals for the year, leaders may want to probe to discover what needs are not being addressed. Sometimes, schools can give choices; for example, the administration might provide parameters for using school data and supporting school goals, but then allow PLCs to submit their own plans for approval. Or, to understand and plan for teacher needs, they might talk with teachers one-on-one or use an anonymous web survey site such as www.zoomerang.com to gather responses to questions such as those in step 2 on page 67.

Linking problems cited by the teachers with the school initiatives may sometimes be difficult. For example, one school that Jane worked with chose creating consistent lesson plans as its goal for the year. However, when Jane interviewed teachers, the topic of school uniforms came up again and again. The school had a uniform policy, but students were frequently in violation. Some teachers enforced the policy; others did not. The "enforcers" complained that administrators were inconsistent in how they treated the "noncompliers," both teachers and students. Teachers admitted that they were only half-heartedly engaged in the lesson plan project because they expected the same implementation inconsistency on lesson plans that they experienced on uniforms. They assumed that some teachers would work hard on the lesson plans and others would fail to take it seriously, doing little planning. Once the teacher leaders understood the reason teachers were resisting the lesson planning effort, they tackled the uniform dilemma. The teacher leaders then revised the templates for lesson planning to make them directly useful to teachers.

Step 6: Deepening Collaboration

This final element of differentiated coaching is deep collaboration, in which teachers are able to share work from their classrooms, plan together, and give and receive feedback, all while focusing on student achievement. This subject comprises the next chapter.

Reflection

1. Review handout 4.1 (page 77). Where do you struggle most to meet the needs of others? What action steps might you take? Handouts 4.2–4.5 (pages 78–81) might give you some concrete ideas.

2. What evidence might teachers need that the three-to-five year process of creating sustainable PLCs is worth the effort? Consider each of the four PLC styles and the information people with those styles might want to see.

3. Develop a three-year plan for your PLC. Focus on topics, data, and an act-reflect-act model to ensure that PLC activities have an impact on instruction. Reflect on the following:

   + What are we emphasizing in this plan?

   + How can we incorporate the Problem-Solving Model (appendix B, page 173) to move forward in collaboration?

4. Review the strengths of the people in your PLC and your needs by considering the following:

   + Do we receive the support necessary to create the environment for honest, reflective work together?

+ Do we have the designated time necessary to work together? Is it sacred to the school?

+ Do we have the right people working together, given the targets and goals of the school?

Handout 4.1

Type Preferences and Learning Needs

Extraverted types *may:* Need to talk and ask questions to understand—they say what they are thinking Want to explore a breadth of topics Prefer act-reflect-act patterns of learning—the doing gives them something to think about Enjoy productive brainstorming and working with others on plans for action	**Introverted types** *may:* Need to think and reflect to understand—they may share thoughts only when asked Want to explore a few topics in depth Prefer a reflect-act-reflect pattern of learning—background reading sets up an experience Need to know topics or agendas in advance—they get a "deer in headlights" feeling without a chance to reflect
Sensing types *may:* Thrive on direct application and relevant examples Prefer step-by-step instructions and details that take them from what they know to what is new View theory as beside the point—they want to know what will work in their classroom Be stressed by removal of what is working with no proof that the change will be better	**Intuitive types** *may:* Thrive on vision, metaphors, and new theories View curriculum or instructional practices as a starting place for innovation unless given clear reasons not to deviate from them Be less interested in isolated skills than in how they fit into overall theories and strategies Be stressed by details and structure with no room for creativity
Thinking types *may:* Seek competent, knowledgeable team members Challenge the ideas first, then look for points of agreement Use objective criteria for decisions—data, precedents that might be set, unintended consequences Need logic and the rationale for changes	**Feeling types** *may:* Seek caring, collegial team members Look for points of agreement first, then challenge the ideas Use subjective criteria for decisions—the impact on each person and on community values Need to consider the impact of changes on the *whole* person—teachers and students—not just academic achievement
Judging types *may:* Find good practices and stick with them Drive for closure and action—they want to start planning Thrive on schedules, agendas, and goals Be aware of what is doable—available time and resources	**Perceiving types** *may:* Avoid planning very far ahead—things could change Prefer delaying decisions to search for options Thrive on allowing for processing of emerging concerns and ideas Be more likely to over- or underestimate how long activities will take

Handout 4.2

The Pragmatic PLC

Sensing and Thinking (ST)

Teacher strengths include administrative tasks, setting up systems, using data, and working with established curriculum. They take a pragmatic approach to teaching and learning.

- STs thrive in a hands-on, relevant setting in which they can easily connect adult learning activities with how those activities improve student learning.

- They want strategies and lessons that are easily customized to their content areas and student grade level. They may dismiss examples that do not deal with their specific responsibilities.

- They naturally prefer to see results rather than read about theories. Background information is almost irrelevant. Their concern? "Show me it works." ST teachers have often modified their practices over time and believe they work quite well.

Preferred PLC Activities

- *Learning through demonstrations, modeling, or film clips of real classrooms.* STs often thrive when using the Gradual Release of Responsibility Model (Pearson & Gallagher, 1983). They want to hear about a strategy, see it used with their students (or students like theirs), talk through questions and anticipated problems before they try it themselves, and finally try it and receive suggestions afterward.

- *Lesson study.* At first, ST teachers prefer studying existing lessons with clear directions. Once they see how a lesson works with students, they enjoy collaborating to improve it. Eventually, they become comfortable creating lessons from scratch.

- *Focused action research.* With their drive for "Does it work?" ST teachers find motivation in short investigations. They want to choose a goal and a strategy, try it with their students, and evaluate the results efficiently. If it works, they embed the strategy in other creative ways.

- *Examining student work.* ST teachers want this activity to concentrate on improving assignment construction and grading consistency. They thrive when PLCs develop rubrics that facilitate uniformity in evaluating student work. They also appreciate tips for streamlining tasks to better assess student learning. They may have a tendency to concentrate on right answers rather than student thinking.

Preferred Information

- *Data that tie tightly to their teaching.* STs want to know what to teach to which students. They want quick formative assessments, not test data from last year's students.

- *Implementation details.* ST teachers want clear information about their responsibilities, timelines, training, and troubleshooting contacts. They want their questions answered immediately. If this does not happen, they may hesitate and appear resistant to the initiative.

- *Summaries.* While STs can be as intellectual as anyone else, they also value efficiency. They may prefer to receive condensed articles for text-based discussions, summaries of research, charts and graphs that highlight relevant data, and so on.

Handout 4.3
The Supportive PLC

Sensing and Feeling (SF)

Teacher strengths include handling details, working one-on-one with students, creating a respectful classroom atmosphere, and implementing curriculum and day-to-day classroom routines.

- SFs want leaders who meet their needs for encouragement, clear goals, and concrete tasks. They take student progress personally and assume that deviations from perfect results are their own fault.

- They want on-the-job help. They want leaders who show them what is going right and make concrete suggestions to fix molehills that seem like mountains because of their conscientiousness.

- Too many new strategies or initiatives can overwhelm SFs. They thrive when PLCs concentrate on one change at a time and provide methods to document progress. Leaders should keep the focus on the overall objective; otherwise, the teacher may get sidetracked by perfectionism over details.

Preferred PLC Activities

- *Learn-by-doing activities.* SF teachers would rather, for example, experience a text-based discussion than read or hear about how to do it. They learn to facilitate group work by participating in protocols. They get frustrated, though, if examples are too far removed from what they can envision using in their own classrooms.

- *Action research that reveals student engagement.* SF teachers see each child as an individual. Their interest in action research increases when assessments include student voices regarding learning or what makes school engaging.

- *Modeling or co-teaching.* SF teachers enjoy learning through collaboration. A second set of eyes can point out what is working well. Because things seldom go smoothly when introducing something to students for the first time, SF teachers may need an objective voice before they are willing to try it again.

- *Lesson planning.* SF teachers often enjoy brainstorming ideas with others. They may not see themselves as inherently creative, but a suggestion, or an example of what worked for another teacher, often jump-starts their ability to innovate.

Preferred Information

- *Data that tie to students they know.* Many SFs thrive on the detailed work of statistics. However, because numbers have little to do with people, a high percentage of those who prefer SF experience math anxiety. Leaders should summarize data or provide charts. Often, SFs find analyzing their own grade books or assessments compelling.

- *Stories and examples from peers who have used the strategy or technique.* SF teachers also respond to stories of specific students who experienced growth.

- *Specific, step-by-step instructions.* SF teachers appreciate opportunities to get all their questions answered.

Handout 4.4

The Collegial PLC

Intuition and Feeling (NF)

Teacher strengths include starting new programs, motivating others, developing creative projects, and engaging students in large-scale creative writing/dramatization/simulation units.

- NF teachers march to their own beat. When PLCs provide space for creativity, NFs can become staunch supporters of any strategy. Leaders should let them generate their own ideas for adjusting curriculum or mandates, while making space within PLC meetings for critique from colleagues.

- They may resist initiatives or strategies that seem too structured because they thrive on allowing students to express their individuality and creativity. Examples of rubrics or objectives that give clear direction yet avoid overstructuring may persuade them.

- NFs need to explore ideas and entertain multiple possibilities before they can buy into group decisions.

Preferred PLC Activities

- *In-depth study.* NF teachers often like to read about and discuss new ideas. If they prefer Introversion, their best route to change is independent study; if they prefer Extraversion, they enjoy text-based discussions.

- *Peer observations.* They thrive on the cognitive coaching model and usually have ideas about the areas in which they would like to receive feedback.

- *Professional development leadership.* NFs enjoy helping others grow and often volunteer to identify materials or activities that meet adult learning needs as well as to facilitate PLC meetings.

- *Lesson study.* NF teachers often prefer to go as far as they can on their own with a new idea. Rather than collaborating in the early stages of lesson planning or strategy implementation, they may volunteer to outline their ideas and then seek group input. They often enjoy developing rigorous, integrated activities.

Preferred Information

- *The big picture.* These teachers are motivated by vision and values.

- *Data that incorporate student voices.* NFs want to improve students' motivation, self-esteem, and altruism, as well as their academic performance. Objective data leave them cold unless they are accompanied by qualitative evidence of student growth.

- *Stories of systemic change.* NF teachers often pursue in-depth knowledge of a model or theory if it is presented with case studies of how a school changed or how a targeted group of students embraced academics.

Handout 4.5

The Intellectual PLC

Intuition and Thinking (NT)

Teacher strengths include theorizing ways to improve student learning and then logically testing them, providing rigorous assignments, getting students to think, and using data.

- NT teachers tend to challenge their colleagues—not intentionally, but because NT teachers learn by comparing any new instructional strategy or change to the models and schemas they developed about how students learn.

- Leaders should allow for debate on new strategies or theories. A response of "That's plausible" to a most brilliant idea is high praise from an NT. Often, people with this learning style are viewed as contrary, resistant, or abrasive rather than the deep thinkers they are.

- Leaders should meet their needs for evidence and data. If NT teachers embrace a change as valid and important, they often become enthusiastic champions.

Preferred PLC Activities

- *Co-leadership.* NT teachers thrive when they have a say in implementation planning. Carefully considering their critiques often increases buy-in. Ask about areas where they feel competent to lead the group.

- *Peer observation.* NT teachers are generally interested in making improvements and appreciate the preconference-observation-postconference model. The model can also help them give feedback to others without seeming overly critical.

- *In-depth study.* NTs seek competence and may prefer studying research or theory-based books or having more than one meeting on the same topic in their quest to be knowledgeable about the practices they implement.

- *Writing common assessments.* NTs enjoy creating the systems and structures that common assessments make possible. Their strengths in logical thinking and analysis often facilitate this work.

Preferred Information

- *Expert knowledge.* NT teachers often prefer to learn from an outside expert through workshops, websites, books, articles, and other resources, as opposed to text-based discussions with peers.

- *Data and statistical studies.* This is the one group of teachers that is very interested in objective research studies and data, and may be instrumental in streamlining access to and analysis of student data to inform instruction.

- *Logical theories and models.* NTs need to know how and why things work.

Handout 4.6

PLC Activities

The Pragmatic PLC Sensing/Thinking	The Supportive PLC Sensing/Feeling	The Collegial PLC Intuition/Feeling	The Intellectual PLC Intuition/Thinking
Preferred learning activities: Demonstrations, modeling, and film clips Focused action research Examination of student work Lesson study, existing lessons	**Preferred learning activities:** Learn-by-doing activities Action research, including student engagement Modeling or co-teaching Lesson planning	**Preferred learning activities:** Professional development leadership Reading about ideas, strategies, or programs that foster student growth Peer observations Lesson study, including initial development	**Preferred learning activities:** Professional development leadership Book study or reading the research on a topic, with some individual choice Peer observations Writing of common assessments
Preferred information: Data from their classrooms Implementation details Summarized information	**Preferred information:** Data on students they know Stories, examples, and testimonials Specific, step-by-step instructions	**Preferred information:** Data that incorporate student voices Big-picture overviews and vision Stories of systemic change	**Preferred information:** Data and statistical studies Expert knowledge Logical theories and models

5

Coaching for Genuine Community

Before you begin reading this chapter, take a moment to reflect on the following questions:

- What are your reactions to the following statements? Do you agree or disagree? Why?

    + Conflict allows for community renewal, not destruction.

    + Adult learning is as essential as student learning.

    + Correctly defining a problem may take longer than solving it, but you cannot solve a problem until you define it.

    + Your greatest resource may be the colleague with whom you have the most trouble connecting.

- What examples or experiences come to mind?

The last word in the phrase "professional learning community" is as important as the first two. Communities are a far cry from a group of individuals who gather at a designated time; they're defined by having things in common such as values, beliefs, resources, intentions, and a desire for continuity. However, trying to impose the leadership's values and beliefs may not lead to optimal outcomes. The hard work of coming to consensus is what builds community.

> Community does not solve the problem of pluralism by obliterating diversity. Instead it seeks out diversity, welcomes other points of view, embraces opposites, desires to see the other side of every issue. It is "wholistic." It integrates us human beings into a functioning mystical body. (Peck, 1987, p. 234)

Transforming a group into a team takes more than norms, protocols, or even a common vision; it takes more than trust and respect. Members of authentic teams know that they truly need each other. If they cannot arrange for interactions, they find themselves asking, "What would the others think? What have they told me before?" While educators may have a few close colleagues they could describe in this way, groups—historically—seldom become teams. Even when gathered for the purpose of improving teaching and learning, teachers often keep interactions superficial, offering little substantive analysis or critique (Hargreaves, 1994; Little, 2003; Stein et al., 2009).

DuFour et al. (2008) describe professional learning communities as "collaborative teams whose members work *interdependently* to achieve *common goals*—goals linked to the purpose of learning for all—for which members are held *mutually accountable*" (p. 15). This chapter guides you through four important processes to use before delving into teamwork:

- Assessing the quality of relationships
- Building collaboration skills and group norms
- Setting a vision
- Establishing collaboration time

Process 1: Assessing the Quality of Relationships

Toole and Louis (2002) suggest that PLC members should be interested "not only in discrete acts of teacher sharing, but in the establishment of a school-wide culture that makes collaboration expected, inclusive, genuine, ongoing, and focused on critically examining practice to improve student outcomes" (p. 247). That is a tall order. Knowing how close or far away a school is from establishing that kind of culture is crucial to creating the culture.

Honest evaluation of the quality of relationships is essential. At one school, Jane was asked to help each grade-level team set goals for the year. The principal assured her that all the teams were functioning well, adding that the fourth-grade team had been working hard on communication. The fourth-grade team told Jane, "We want to work on collaboration skills. With a little jump start from you, we'll be fine. We already collaborated for parent night!" However, when Jane started a tried-and-true team-building exercise with them, one of the teachers calmly told another, "I will never have anything nice to say about you." Finally, the teachers disclosed that they had been at each other's throats the entire previous year. The principal burst into tears when Jane shared the depth of the problem, saying, "I guess I hoped it had all gone away." While the school made some progress toward collaborative teaming that year, the troubles of the fourth-grade teachers affected everyone's ability to focus on student learning.

Compare that with another school in which the principal was well aware of and up front about existing conflicts. Jane met separately with two teachers who were finding it hard to respect each other, listened to their concerns, and helped them develop new methods of interaction. With that groundwork laid, Jane was able to facilitate their team in successfully using a lesson-planning protocol. The two teachers listened to each other, took each other's suggestions, and agreed that they could work together if they used the protocols to navigate their very real differences.

Again, sometimes bringing teachers together surfaces conflicts that simmered under the surface as long as teachers stayed isolated in their classrooms. Sometimes teachers are insecure about their abilities and cannot imagine making their practices public. They assume their colleagues will judge them as failures. Or perhaps an unwritten chart categorizes teachers as good or bad. Sometimes the principal doesn't expect all teachers to work hard, ignores a group, doesn't set clear expectations that collaboration is expected, or gives no focal point to set a vision for PLCs. Sometimes everyone acquiesces to informal leaders.

Any of these relationship issues, and many others, can prevent a PLC from becoming a team, which is why the leadership roles of building relationships and understanding the current culture of the school and its readiness for PLC work are so essential in Stage 1 of PLC development (see page 51). In many cases, schools found they needed an outside facilitator to do this well *and* to begin the work of building a collaborative community of shared practice (Hord, 2004; McLaughlin & Talbert, 2006).

Sometimes school or district leadership believes that there is no time for issues; they believe adults need to set their differences aside and focus on student learning, especially in schools in which the achievement gap looms large. Their implementation plans jump right to action planning, with instructions for the first PLC meeting focused on using data to identify a goal for instruction. In many such cases, however, the results are shallow because of lack of trust. In *Trust in Schools: A Core Resource for Improvement*, Bryk and Schneider (2002) highlight four ways that relational trust is a *resource* for school improvement—a resource well worth the investment of time and, if necessary, outside assistance:

1. Organizational change involves high risk. When teachers are asked to make private practice public and change their classrooms, trust moderates the uncertainty and vulnerability they feel.

2. Trust facilitates problem solving and decision making. Teachers are able to share concerns and feel heard, as opposed to acquiescing and then not buying into the decisions.

3. Roles are easier. Trust allows for clear expectations and makes implementation of new improvement efforts much easier.

4. Trust means that people can concentrate on the ethical imperative to advance the best interests of children rather than their own interests.

So how do you go about ensuring that the existing climate is healthy enough to build trust? The following suggestions can help you answer that question.

Leadership Team Consensus

Start by assuming that your team has the skills to assess building climate, and meet as a group to discuss the following questions. Again, your goal is to identify issues that might block groups from becoming collaborative teams.

- Do we have enough information on every team (grade level, content area, or other suggested PLCs)? Do we need to talk with anyone, observe interactions, or otherwise ensure we are not overlooking trust issues or serious conflicts?

- Will the issues we know about get in the way of collaboration, or will general collaboration training most likely improve relationships or trust?

- For any relationship issue that needs resolution, can one of us handle the situation? Is there a district mediator who might help? Is the lack of trust deep enough that we need outside help (just for this issue)?

- Could informal leaders or power structures interfere with making private practice public? Would changing staff assignments be wise in any of these cases, or might the individuals involved become resentful? What launch efforts might make these teams more collaborative?

- What else might we have overlooked before we begin the work of collaboration?

Then, step back from your answers. In which areas, if any, are you uncertain about the trust levels or relationship quality? Remind yourselves that many PLCs never become sustainable or fully effective, and then list any areas where you may need to gather more information. You can use team inventories, online surveys, and other tools described later in this section.

Team Inventories

Several resources contain excellent surveys you can use with your staff to gain their perspectives on school climate and readiness for collaboration.

The Southwest Educational Development Laboratory makes available a free, seventeen-question survey developed by Shirley Hord, Merrill Meehan, Sandra Orletsky, and Beth Sattes (1999) that has teachers rate their school on a scale of 1 to 5 regarding such factors as "School administrators participate democratically with teachers sharing power, authority and decision making."[1]

Kise and Russell (2008) also include a simple chart for teams to use in assessing their current collaboration level. Leaders can use this chart to differentiate the needs of each PLC.

---

[1] An article regarding this survey and information on how to receive permission to use it can be found at www.sedl .org/change/issues/issues71/

Handout 5.1, "Collaboration Survey" (page 97), contains a different kind of survey that teams can use to evaluate their overall collaboration ability and may be appropriate if you are fairly certain that relationships are solid.

Online Surveys

Websites like www.zoomerang.com and www.surveymonkey.com make it easy to develop free surveys that your staff can answer anonymously via an email link. You should add at least one open-ended question so that staff can make specific comments or share concerns. The following list includes some sample statements you might consider:

- I'm comfortable having other teachers observe my classroom.

- If I share lesson plans or samples of student work, I trust that my colleagues would provide helpful, nonjudgmental feedback.

- Existing conflicts among staff may interfere with PLC work.

- On our team, one person seems to hold authority—I'm not sure the rest of us are heard.

You can also use surveys to mark progress. At one school, we asked the questions in figure 5.1 (pages 87–88) after completing several team-building modules. The questions we asked were specifically tied to the conflict and relationship problems the school had identified before the team building and the goals of the process. Delivering it as an online survey was efficient and, according to feedback from the teachers, continued to build the trust the team needed.

1. The team discussed the need to drop past hurts and that new protocols will not help unless the staff begins the year with a fresh start. Which best describes your current view?
   - I believe I can drop past hurts and am ready to start fresh with my colleagues.
   - I need to discuss a past hurt with a colleague but am confident that I can do this productively.
   - I need help to deal with past hurts before I can move forward.

2. Please mark the answer that best fits how you would describe the current status of the staff.
   - We haven't made any progress. We are still divided.
   - Many of us are ready to move forward, but some are not and are holding us back.
   - We understand why past conflicts happened, but still need to heal them.
   - We are ready to use what we've learned about our differences to move forward, but need more tools.
   - We are already moving forward.

continued on next page →

3. How would you rank the following concerns raised about moving forward? Rank your biggest concern as 1, your second biggest concern as 2, and so on.

    •   Since most of the staff is nonconfrontational, how do we best go to the source?

    •   How do we confront without it being seen as an attack?

    •   How do we learn to reserve judgment and not take things personally?

4. How comfortable are you with your ability to calmly speak with colleagues about possible misunderstandings, using a protocol such as, "I sense you're_____ (frustrated/angry/upset/ overwhelmed). Can you explain? Am I misinterpreting? How can we resolve this?"

    •   Not comfortable

    •   Somewhat comfortable

    •   Comfortable

    •   Very comfortable

Figure 5.1: Post-team-building survey.

Outside Facilitation

We regret that we are often called to consult in schools in which the relationships have deteriorated to the point where the principal says, "You probably can't help us, either"—and that is a direct quote. In the press for time and with scarcity of resources, schools often bury conflict until it erupts in damaging ways. Please don't wait that long! We have many success stories, but far less time would have been spent on conflict resolution if issues had been addressed earlier.

If your team has not completed activity 3.3, "PLC Shared Leadership Analysis" (page 59), use it to help you identify whether those in leadership have energy around the roles required for building relationships and trust. If you determine that you do need outside assistance, be wary of anyone who suggests a simple process. Usually, a facilitator needs to observe a few classrooms and perhaps a staff meeting to get a sense of the overall atmosphere; interview several or all staff members, with a guarantee of confidentiality, to grasp all perspectives of school climate and relationships; summarize findings, maintaining confidentiality, for use with the leadership team in planning team building; conduct interventions such as Jane did with the two teachers who did not respect each other; and finally, spend a significant block of professional development time on helping team members understand their diversity, improve communication, and take first steps in collaboration. Generally, schools also benefit from the outside facilitator doing another survey to gauge whether the climate is improving, as well as some follow-up sessions until the new ways of relating to each other become habits for the staff.

If the relationship problems are between administration and staff, often in our experience the problems result from misunderstandings about the motivations, needs, and communication styles of people with very different personality types. If this is the case, creating a common framework, as discussed in chapter 2, goes a long way toward establishing trust. Skilled facilitators can choose team-building exercises whose purposes are twofold: building trust and collaboration skills but using exercises or protocols that jump-start the real work of PLCs in setting goals, looking at student work, and holding respectful conversations about teaching and learning. Time spent on trust furthers the work of focusing on learning while simultaneously ensuring that PLCs become effective and sustainable.

Next: Collaboration Skills

Remember that within a coaching culture, one pays constant attention to communicating and providing assistance in ways that meet each person's learning style. Everyone—adults and students—needs to be able to learn in every style. Reading, for example, requires Introversion and Intuition, while conducting science experiments requires Extraversion and Sensing. The content being learned often dictates the style required. However, a coaching culture works to ensure that no one is so "out of style" that they feel exhausted by the sequence of activities.

Through the lens of type, two factors are the starting place for learning styles (since sixteen types would be overwhelming for a differentiation structure). Adults and students alike need energy to learn, through Extraversion and Introversion, and information that meets their perceiving style, whether it is Sensing or Intuition. This results in four basic learning styles, as described in handout 5.2, "Learning Styles Summary" (page 99), and in more depth in handout 7.1, "Learning Styles, Favorite Activities, and Motivating Words" (page 151). Handout 5.3, "Differentiating PLC Meetings for Learning Styles" (page 100), provides an example of how to plan a PLC meeting that meets the needs of all four styles.

A basic understanding of learning styles often helps groups recognize and accept one another's needs. For instance, Beth often jokes that her own learning style, Extraversion and Intuition, is the "Let's lead" group. They would rather brainstorm how to use an activity than read about it, or lead everyone else in trying a new strategy rather than hear a word about the theory. However, in group settings Beth knows that others want to see specific examples, and that she will gain different insights by reading some of the more theoretical information.

Still, exercises and protocols need to be carefully tailored so as not to make one group inordinately uncomfortable. Many protocols are clearly biased toward Extraversion *or* Introversion, are so overstructured that they frustrate Intuitive types, or are so objective and task-oriented that Feeling types feel like robots during the process. In fact, one of our favorite tricks is to take a biased protocol and tweak it just a bit so that *no one's* needs are met. Why? Because everyone experiences frustration at the same moment, creating buy-in for the idea that meeting learning style needs makes a difference in whether or not adults engage; participants then realize their students may have even deeper needs for learning in their own style. One such experience is worth a thousand lectures.

For example, in differentiation workshops, we often include a poster walk of three or four different lesson plans. Each lesson is set up at a different station in the room. Every station also has flip-chart paper and markers. Participants are to view the stations silently and write any comments they have on the flip-chart paper regarding their reactions to teaching or learning from the activity. People report the following frustrations:

- IS types are frustrated if there is no opportunity to raise questions about formats or activities. They also hesitate to write down comments and wish that they could ask opinions of others about whether they are focusing on the right aspects of the lessons.

- ES types are usually pretty blunt that if they cannot talk about it, they soon lose interest. They are usually the first ones finished.

- IN types would rather sit still, receive a packet containing the lesson plans, and be able to write notes directly on them as they compare and contrast the formats.

- EN types want to engage in discussions of how to improve the lessons or what is right or wrong with each one. They find the writing process frustrating and limiting.

When we explain the structure, the group has a good laugh and quickly grasps how everyone's needs *could* have been met by giving choices, providing a discussion protocol, or making other simple adjustments.

Building Understanding of Collaboration Needs and Group Norms

The more thought that goes into norms and the more they are tailored to the needs of a specific group, the more likely they will lead to the deep collaboration needed within PLCs. Activity 5.1, "Group Norms and Collaboration Cues," is designed to help teams recognize one another's collaboration needs and thereby target ways to improve their own ability to participate productively in team tasks. Note that teams that consider all of the preferences will automatically build in some of the loose/tight structures needed to move forward strategically while ensuring that the chosen plan is still optimal.

ACTIVITY 5.1 **Group Norms and Collaboration Cues**

Goal: To generate group norms by helping each person develop a cue card that reminds him or her of ways to adjust his or her natural style for more effective group dynamics and processes

Materials: Copies of handout 5.4 (page 101), "Tips for Working With Opposites," two different colors of highlight markers, and a blank index card for each participant

Directions: Ask each person to read through handout 5.4, highlighting items they think the team might benefit from considering with one color and items they need to remember themselves with the other color.

Hold a group discussion about the team items. Reach consensus about which items should be group norms. The norms may look similar to those generated through other processes, but the framework of type often increases buy-in since people understand the need for some of the norms. Sometimes a story helps people take this process seriously:

A team agreed to record a web map of the group brainstorming session on a whiteboard so that everyone could track how the ideas evolved. When the group finished, the leader suggested that everyone take two minutes to do a quickwrite on which ideas seemed most important or most doable. One team member raised her hand and said, "Why? Can't we just talk about it and have you circle the ones we mention?" The facilitator reminded her that the team's one Introverted member usually appreciated the moment of quiet and that everyone would benefit from clarifying their own opinion before hearing from others. The team member quickly agreed to the quickwrite.

State the norms in terms of specific behaviors. Examples might include the following:

- We will start and end on time.

- We will set clear goals for each meeting, but will change those goals if the group decides that new ones are more pressing.

- We will use written reflection time to honor Introversion and to avoid rushing to closure.

Then, ask each person to make a cue card of personal reminders to improve their collaboration skills. Sample cues might include the following:

- I'll count to five after asking any question before speaking. (Extraversion)

- I'll monitor whether our short-term decisions tie back to long-term goals. (Intuition)

- I'll remind myself that I *want* critiques of my lesson plans to improve student learning. (Feeling)

- I'll ask for a moment to think if group brainstorming starts too quickly. (Introversion)

- I'll take the role of monitoring whether our discussions stay focused on the stated goals—including checking whether the group believes the goal has rightly changed. (Judging)

Process 2: Building Collaboration Skills and Group Norms

A second skill that requires instruction and practice for adults as well as students is engaging in evidence-based discussions to build knowledge rather than share opinions. Beth remembers one training session in which she provided each group with the protocol for a text-based discussion. As she moved around the room, she noted that the members of one group had put away the article they were to be discussing and instead were sharing their opinions of why it did not apply to their school—the antithesis of what they were supposed to be doing. When Beth asked why they were not following the protocol, they said, "We know how to do that." When she prompted them to demonstrate their ability, they soon realized they had not based their discussion on the text at all. They quickly became engaged in finding the evidence the author used to draw the conclusions they disagreed with—and found the evidence to be quite solid.

Appendix C, "Reading on Student Motivation" (page 181), contains a sample article you can use to practice evidence-based discussions, as outlined in activity 5.2, "Evidence-Based Discussions." Note that we developed the article from several resources, culling out the most relevant information and conclusions so that participants can process the contents during a one-hour meeting. Or, choose a different article that relates directly to any area related to your professional development needs.

ACTIVITY 5.2 Evidence-Based Discussions

Goal: To provide practice in text-based discussions that allow for respectful processing of ideas, beliefs, and evidence to build group knowledge; to provide a model for teachers to use in establishing student-focused discussions in their classrooms

Materials: Copies of appendix C, "Reading on Student Motivation" (page 181), or another reading related to your PLC learning goals; copy the first two pages of appendix C back-to-back, and staple the actual article as a separate handout.

Directions: Ask participants to fill out the Anticipation Guide. Then, follow the Anticipation Guide Instructions on page 183 for group discussion.

Explain to participants that students struggle to build discussions around texts and evidence rather than personal opinions or personal reactions, and they also fail to listen to each other carefully enough to build on each other's ideas and construct deeper meaning together. Participants will be working with the following protocol, which they can use with their students:

1. Hand out copies of "How Do Students Get Smart?" (page 184) or another article of your choosing. Have participants read the article silently and underline two to three key sentences that they would like the group to discuss.

2. Form groups of three to five people. Designate which person in each group will go first by asking who got up latest that morning (or earliest, if tardiness is an issue).

3. Have the first person tell the group where his or her sentence can be found and then read the sentence aloud. At this point, this person makes no comments about why he or she chose the text.

4. In turn, ask each person around the group to remark about the chosen sentence. They might do any of the following:

   • Comment on a point the author might be making

   • Make a connection between the sentence and other information in the text

   • Build on something a person who spoke previously said

   • Disagree with something someone else said by pointing out contradictory evidence in the discussed text

   • Make a connection between the sentence and his or her classroom or the school

5. When everyone in the group has commented, ask the person who chose the sentence to explain why he or she chose it.

6. Continue the exercise until everyone has had a chance to share at least one sentence.

When the groups finish, ask for discussion on how the protocol honors the following:

   • Extraversion (Building thoughts in discussion)

   • Introversion (Allowing time for reflection before speaking)

   • Sensing (Working from the available text)

   • Intuition (Making connections beyond the text)

   • Thinking (Allowing room for discussion and text-based disagreement)

   • Feeling (Allowing room for agreement and uninterrupted sharing of ideas)

   • Judging (Defining a structured task with clear procedures)

   • Perceiving (Having individual freedom to choose sentences and thus influence the discussion focus)

Note that in general, because no one knows whether a sentence was chosen because the person agreed or disagreed with the statement, the discussion tends to stay respectful and focused.

Process 3: Setting a Vision

Every book on PLCs mentions a shared vision as essential. While the overall vision of PLCs is learning—adult learning that results in student learning—tailoring that vision to the unique culture and circumstances of your own school increases its usefulness.

One useful tool for setting a vision is the Problem-Solving Model, fully explained in appendix B (page 173). This model is one of our gold-standard tools for leadership, coaching, and collaboration. Whether or not your team has a balanced mix of personality types, this model provides a process to ensure that the strengths and considerations of Sensing, Intuition, Thinking, and Feeling are part of the decision-making process.

Careful attention to this model helps to avoid the syndrome of *presentism*—a term coined by Dan Lortie in 1975, referring to "overwhelming pressures on schools that kept teachers locked into short-term perspectives and unable or unwilling to envision or plan collaboratively for long-term, systemic change" (as cited in Hargreaves & Shirley, 2009, p. 2506). In an article titled "The Persistence of Presentism," Hargreaves and Shirley (2009) describe their research revealing that the tendency toward presentism in schools has grown worse in the last decade. They describe an addiction to strategies that provide quick but temporary wins at the expense of deepening teacher and student knowledge:

> Instead of building people's confidence to break out of the existing culture of presentism in teaching and to engage in the step-by-step struggle toward long-term goals, the spectacular and affirming success of the short-term strategies entrenched schools in the culture of presentism even more deeply. They became ends in themselves. Schools were not merely attracted to short-term strategies; they were addicted to them. The strategies were simple to employ, widespread, and available, they could be used right away, and they did not challenge or encourage teachers to question and revise their existing approaches to teaching and learning. (p. 2524)

The vision statement needs to incorporate the long-term vision so that teams are constantly asking whether strategies will further progress toward the real goals: engaged, lifelong learners. Activity 5.3, "A Vision for PLCs," shows how to use the problem-solving model to set a robust vision.

ACTIVITY 5.3 **A Vision for PLCs**

Goal: To develop a mission statement that focuses the work of PLCs

Materials: Flip-chart paper and markers for each group

Note: If your team has not worked with the Problem-Solving Model, consider using the "Tardiness Dilemma" practice scenario in appendix B, page 173, to help them understand the value of the process.

Directions: Ask participants to work in groups by dominant function, explained on pages 178 and 179. Or, if a small team is drafting the vision, work together but allow for reflection before discussing each prompt. Explain that you will work through the stages of the model one at a time, sharing responses after each stage.

Sensing

- What phrases, values, or other words should we emphasize to reflect our commitment to student achievement?

- What words have we seen in our readings, visits to other schools, or other sources that we might consider?

Intuition

- Which, if any, assumptions in our culture need to change? What are those assumptions? What words might help us change how we view ourselves or our students?

- What phrases might be unique to us? What are draft statement possibilities?

Thinking

- What objective criteria could we use in choosing words?

- Which phrases are the most efficient? Which will help us focus our work?

Feeling

- Which words might best motivate our students to see themselves as successful?

- Do these words match the values we want to hold?

Note: You can use the Thinking and Feeling prompts to rank the suggested vision statements. Make sure that all statements remain possibilities until the team considers both Thinking and Feeling criteria, in case the most efficient one is not the best for use with students.

Process 4: Establishing Collaboration Time

Hopefully, your PLC now has the basic tools for trust, collaborative skills and key processes (such as evidence-based discussions and a Problem-Solving Model), and a vision. These are the prerequisites for a PLC to collaboratively focus on student learning via improving instruction. With these prerequisites in place, the team can begin its real work. The next chapter focuses on tools that teams can use to make progress on each of the evidence markers of deep collaboration.

As a leader in the process, you have one other responsibility, though. In choosing PLC foci, activities, and protocols, keep asking, "Can we do it in the time we have?" Just as students deserve a viable curriculum that they can master in the time available, teachers also deserve goals and expectations that they have the time to meet. School leaders often need to pool their creativity to find that time; following are a few suggestions:

- Common team prep times are ideal if not always possible.

- Many schools ensure that all teacher meetings are PLC meetings; announcements come via email.

- Some schools set activity times that are supervised by volunteers (such as dances and field days) to release teachers for two-hour blocks.

- Other schools work with their unions to "borrow" before-school or after-school time in order to build a forty-five-minute block of team time once a week.

- Scheduling specialists can help allow for grade-level team time.

Other suggestions are available on www.nsdc.org, the National Staff Development Council website.

Reflection

1. Does your PLC implementation plan include enough time to build the following?

   - Trust

   - Collaboration skills

   - Key processes, such as norms and discussion skills

   - Vision

   - Time for collaboration

2. How will you ensure team relationships are solid enough for deep collaboration? A leadership audit? Survey? Outside help?

3. Think of a protocol for group process that you dislike. Compare it to handout 4.1, "Type Preferences and Learning Needs" (page 77), and see if you can adjust it so that it works for you. Then, consider one of your favorite protocols. Does it meet the needs of every style? If not, can you adjust it?

Handout 5.1

Collaboration Survey

	1 This is not true of our team	2 This is true for some, but not all of the team	3 Uncertain	4 Our team has addressed this	5 We act in accordance with our consensus on how to operate
Our vision for each classroom is aligned with the vision for the overall school.					
We identified barriers to collaboration and have a plan to address them.					
We exchange ideas regarding instructional materials, teaching strategies, and assessment methods.					
We give honest, tailored feedback so that each person can hear it for the purpose of improvement of practices.					
Common learning outcomes are identifiable by grade level. Our team adheres to them.					
We agreed on norms for starting a meeting as well as how to communicate with one another, problem solve, and make decisions.					

continued on next page →

page 1 of 2

	1 This is not true of our team	2 This is true for some, but not all of the team	3 Uncertain	4 Our team has addressed this	5 We act in accordance with our consensus on how to operate
We understand the implications that our personality type differences present and the strengths and needs of each collaborative style.					
We practice and use dialogue for the purpose of learning and have a sense of a shared knowledge (curriculum, assessment, decision making, and academic rigor) that we all own.					
When students are not learning in my classroom, there are agreed-upon interventions determined by the grade level teachers.					
We have agreed-upon systems of operation—for example, grading, homework policies, action plans for struggling students, rules for behavior, and common rubrics for writing—that are common across the grade level or school.					

Creating a Coaching Culture © 2010 Jane A. G. Kise and Beth Russell • solution-tree.com
Visit **go.solution-tree.com/PLCbooks** to download this page.

Handout 5.2

Learning Styles Summary

IS: Let's Be Clear on What to Do	IN: Let Me Follow My Own Star
Introversion and Sensing Requirement: Clear purpose and directions Resistance when: Personal risk seems high Result desired: Certainty of mastery Reach them through: Useful instructions, examples, and time to think	**Introversion and Intuition** Requirement: Room for imagination, uniqueness Resistance when: Objective is shallow Result desired: New possibilities Reach them through: Reflection, independent study, and creativity
ES: Let Me Do Something	**EN: Let Me Lead as I Learn**
Extraversion and Sensing Requirement: Action, hands-on Resistance when: Direct application is not clear Result desired: Immediately useful knowledge Reach them through: Learn-by-doing activities and relevant examples	**Extraversion and Intuition** Requirement: Interaction, novelty Resistance when: They're to do as they're told Result desired: Ideas for the big picture Reach them through: Debate, discussion, choices, and vision

Handout 5.3

Differentiating PLC Meetings for Learning Styles

To meet the needs of each style, consider the following:

- IS: Set clear goals and provide handouts that set expectations for learning and application.

- IN: Tie the goals to a robust theory and vision of student learning. Reference additional resources they can study.

- ES: Demonstrate the reality of how the information, teaching strategies, or other meeting content matters in their classrooms or for PLC collaboration.

- EN: Open up possibilities for what the information, skills, or strategies might mean for their team and their classrooms.

Sample Agenda for Building Awareness of Extraversion and Introversion Collaboration Needs

1. Present an agenda with goals and topics, but without strict time frames for the topics (Introversion and Sensing).

2. Give a five-minute introduction to type theory and its usefulness for adult collaboration (Introversion and Intuition).

3. Engage in an active exercise that demonstrates E-I differences, such as activity 2.1 (page 28), "Extraversion or Introversion?" (Extraversion and Sensing).

4. Explain the E-I collaboration needs in a structured way (Introversion and Sensing).

5. Complete activity 5.1, "Group Norms and Collaboration Cues" (page 90), to generate ideas for group norms (Extraversion and Intuition).

Handout 5.4

Tips for Working With Opposites

If you are an Extravert working with an Introvert:
Ask others what they are thinking but allow for reflection—maybe even a two-minute quickwrite.

Set agendas and provide thought questions, written material, or data collected for reflection before the session.

Practice paraphrasing to ensure you are listening.

Practice holding your tongue, especially if you are in charge—ten seconds can lead to a significant increase in response from others.

Slow down and reflect before deciding.

If you are an Introvert working with an Extravert:
Encourage conversations so that Extraverts can formulate their thoughts.

Press for large-group notes—flip charts or whiteboards—so that you can more easily track brainstorming or analysis.

Show enthusiasm and outward energy.

Jot down your initial thoughts and share them so that others know what you are thinking.

Ask to visit other classrooms or network with other PLCs to broaden your experiences.

If you are a Sensing type working with an Intuitive type:
Stretch yourself to think long-term (the twenty-four–month goal) while helping the team seek measurable results (the one-month goal).

Ask others how seemingly unrelated examples or information might be useful to you.

Press the team for specific, measurable goals—how will we know if we are making progress?

Tie specific practices to theories and trends in education—the big picture.

Write down your questions and save them just in case the Intuitives plan to explain the details in time.

If you are an Intuitive type working with a Sensing type:
Provide clear goals and procedures. Practice relaying direct, specific facts.

Bring ideas that have immediate classroom applications that tie changes to current or past practices.

Remember to evaluate current practices and keep what is working.

Translate theories into examples from classrooms.

Practice explaining your thinking and allow for clarifying questions.

If you are a Thinking type working with a Feeling type:
Keep track of your ratio of compliments to criticism, and seek ways to show appreciation.

Look for and acknowledge points of agreement as well as flaws.

Show how new practices help students.

Practice stepping into others' shoes to understand their viewpoints.

Remember that examples of student work and stories of student success may be more persuasive than data and theories.

If you are a Feeling type working with a Thinking type:
Remember to voice concerns and points of disagreement in healthy ways—burying conflict can make it worse.

Assume your ideas will be debated—do not take it personally.

Collect objective data to persuade and explain how strategies relate back to theories.

Be careful about the amount of meeting time spent on socializing.

Practice cause-and-effect and if/then reasoning to explain ideas.

page 1 of 2

Creating a Coaching Culture © 2010 Jane A. G. Kise and Beth Russell • solution-tree.com
Visit **go.solution-tree.com/PLCbooks** to download this page.

If you are a Judging type working with a Perceiving type:

Help to organize efficient meetings, but keep some flexibility in the schedule to allow for extended conversations.

Provide options; allow processing time before stating your own position.

Break goals into mini-goals and tasks into steps, and help with planning how to meet them.

Schedule time to revisit goals to identify whether they are the right goals and whether they need to change.

Allow flexibility in how people will carry out tasks.

If you are a Perceiving type working with a Judging type:

Work with the team on timelines for bringing closure to each process.

Be extra conscientious about timeliness.

Plan backward from group deadlines to ensure you know when you need to start.

Ask permission before changing a plan, and provide a clear reason for the change.

Remember that Perceiving types worry that people might stop trying once a goal is reached, while Judging types who reach a goal may simply set a new, related goal.

Coaching a Group Into a Collaborative Team

Before you begin reading this chapter, take a moment to reflect on the following questions:

- Identify a teaching strategy you dislike but have seen others use effectively. What keeps you from using it?

- Can you think of a meeting in which you disagreed on how an issue regarding teaching or learning was resolved, yet you didn't speak up? Why did you stay silent?

- When have you seen conflict in a school? What made it productive or unproductive?

Professional learning communities require that teachers leave behind the isolation of their individual classrooms, simultaneously leaving behind the belief that doing things "my way" is in the best interest of all students. In her book *Turning to One Another*, Margaret Wheatley describes this as a difficult imperative:

> It is very difficult to give up our certainties—our positions, our beliefs, our explanations. These help define us; they lie at the heart of our personal identity. Yet I believe we will succeed in changing this world only if we can think and work together in new ways. Curiosity is what we need. We don't have to let go of what we believe, but we do need to be curious about what someone else believes. We do need to acknowledge that their way of interpreting the world might be essential to our survival. (2002, p. 35)

Questioning your beliefs can trigger a chain reaction that might follow this process:

1. Articulate your belief so you can express it.

2. Probe where that belief came from. Experience? Expert knowledge or research? A role model?

3. Listen to others' beliefs as they explain their own positions and supporting evidence.

4. Evaluate the quality of others' evidence and arguments.

5. Consider whether a new or modified belief might better fit all the evidence.

In the preceding quote, Wheatley calls on us to cultivate this kind of curiosity around our beliefs. What might teams accomplish if they listened to each other with the goal of reevaluating what they believe to be true? That curiosity is essential to PLCs.

"Markers of a Coaching Culture for PLCs" provides eight important markers to keep in mind; in chapter 1 (page 23), you noted your team strengths and struggles with each one. Now that you have read more about coaching cultures, you might revisit the information. Do some markers deserve more or less attention?

Markers of a Coaching Culture for PLCs

Marker 1: Members welcome diversity as a tool for making better decisions and use a framework such as type to communicate more clearly and understand other viewpoints.

Marker 2: Members can ask questions, share beliefs, challenge ideas, and disagree with each other as part of their mutual commitment to adult learning and improved student achievement.

Marker 3: Sharing examples of what did not go well in classrooms becomes as natural as sharing what went well.

Marker 4: The team takes time to debate and define problems before deciding how to solve them. Team members know how to reach consensus.

Marker 5: Conflict becomes a source of renewal—members know how to handle it and use it as a context for learning and for exchanging opinions for knowledge.

Marker 6: Members are willing to admit when they do not know the answers—only then can PLCs recognize when they need outside assistance to help all students achieve.

Marker 7: Members welcome being held accountable to use what they learned and share student results with the team.

Marker 8: Members recognize and respect that there may be many paths to the same end, but they are willing to sacrifice individuality if it interferes with the needs of the group.

This chapter organizes PLC activities around the markers of a coaching culture. The process of moving from groups to collaborative teams, however, is not linear. The markers might develop in different orders, depending on team strengths and the problems a school faces. For example, one team may concentrate on Marker 2 via protocols and then move to Marker 6 to improve professional development goals for the year. Another team might work on Markers 3 and 4 together to ensure that their goals reflect problems they see in student work or in teaching strategies.

School leadership plays a major role in ensuring that the PLC activities chosen focus on the markers key to their situation. However, leadership is also responsible for:

- Providing sufficient time for PLCs to be effective, as discussed on page 113

- Modeling the welcoming of multiple perspectives

- Setting parameters and focus for the work—for example, the administrators might lay out the following:

  + Staff will establish learning goals, using agreed-upon data.

  + Everyone will . . . (for example, look at student work, construct a learning progression, engage in classroom observations, and so on).

  + Students will do more of the work, such as discuss content to construct meaning with less teacher lecture time.

- Helping staff work toward an accurate definition of rigor (see activity 6.3, "Evaluating the Rigor of Tasks," page 108)

- Introducing protocols for common activities such as looking at student work, evaluating goals, and having text-based discussions

As you read through the descriptions of the markers and their associated activities, consider which markers will have the most bearing on the current needs of your school.

Welcoming Diversity

Marker 1

Members welcome diversity as a tool for making better decisions and use a framework such as type to communicate more clearly and understand other viewpoints.

The work you do to establish a common framework pays off in "a system of shared meaning, using a 'language' that everyone understands. This both allows everyone to enter into the conversation and provides an explicit guide to action" (Andrews & Lewis, 2007, p. 144). To that end, you can use activity 6.1, "Differentiated Learning Styles" (page 106), to help team members appreciate the value of diverse viewpoints about teaching so that all students can learn. You can also use activity 2.3, "Thinking, Feeling, and Policies" (page 33), to build understanding of how different types form their positions on issues. Activity 7.4, "Discussion Model for Looking at Student Work" (page 144), builds understanding of different viewpoints and the value of diversity on a team as well.

ACTIVITY 6.1 Differentiated Learning Styles

Goal: To help teachers understand the needs of students with opposite learning styles

Materials: Flip-chart paper and markers for each group

Directions: Form groups according to learning style (IS, ES, IN, EN; see page 99). Ask members of each group to record their responses to the following questions on their paper:

- What were our favorite learning activities as students?

- How did we get in trouble at school?

Allow five to ten minutes for group discussions. Debrief by having the groups report in the following order:

- IS: Usually IS teachers' favorite activities involve structure and right answers, with little group work. They almost always say they never got in trouble at school—unless it was for pointing out mistakes in assignments or otherwise knowing more than the teacher.

- ES: The ES teachers' favorite projects are hands-on—experiments, gym, recess, and cooking class often come up. They frequently got in trouble for talking, wiggling, moving about when they were not supposed to—general nonsense rather than the schemes of the ENs.

- IN: The IN teachers' favorite projects are in-depth independent study, research, and creative writing. They often got in trouble for not following directions or refusing to do work they deemed stupid.

- EN: The EN teachers' favorite activities are large-scale simulations, debates, drama, group projects, field trips, and games. If you prompt them, you almost always uncover leadership, such as a colleague who lead a protest in the 1970s to allow girls to wear jeans to school. Occasionally, some troublesome incidents that involved "scheming" also surface. One EN reported plotting to stay in the high school all weekend (although she could not remember why she wanted to!). Another was involved in a rather elaborate bet involving the use of the principal's parking spot for a week.

After all the groups report, ask whether they see parallels with students in their classroom (if this point has not already been made). What do participants want to keep in mind as they plan lessons? Who on their team can help them remember the needs of students very different from themselves?

Asking Questions, Sharing Beliefs

Marker 2

Members can ask questions, share beliefs, challenge ideas, and disagree with each other as part of their mutual commitment to adult learning and improved student achievement.

A key part of collaboration is welcoming different points of view so that everyone can come to richer understandings of an idea or belief system. Activity 6.2, "What Is Rigor?" is an exercise we often use with teachers to build a common understanding of academic rigor, using the reading found in appendix D, "Academic Rigor Reading" (page 189). The article itself illustrates the slippery nature of a definition for rigor and provides a foundation for activity 6.3, "Evaluating the Rigor of Tasks" (page 108).

ACTIVITY 6.2 **What Is Rigor?**

Goal: To assist the team in developing a definition of rigor as well as understanding the current beliefs and biases of members

Materials: Copies of appendix D, "Academic Rigor Reading," (page 189)

Directions: Before participants read the article, ask them to do a quickwrite on the characteristics of rigor in their discipline. For elementary teachers, ask for examples of rigorous assignments.

Ask participants to read the article "What Is Rigor?" and consider the following prompts:

- Review your prereading answer. Has your thinking changed?
- Use the lens of Sensing, Intuition, Thinking, and Feeling. What connections can you draw with how people of these types might define rigor? Give evidence and build on each other's ideas.
- List the questions you have about rigor.
- Consider how you might define rigor.

By the end of activities 6.2 and 6.3, most teams agree they have more work to do in defining rigor. While some tasks are clearly rigorous and others are low-level, debates often occur around questions such as, "If our students lack prior knowledge, does that make a task rigorous or just difficult?" "Are tasks that can use procedures always low-level?" "Can a task use imagination and still be low-level?"

ACTIVITY 6.3 Evaluating the Rigor of Tasks

Goal: To build consensus regarding what makes an academic task rigorous

Materials: Flip-chart paper; copies of appendix F, "Academic Rigor Task Cards" (page 201); and activity task cards for each participant

Note: This activity works best when teachers work with tasks closely related to their own classrooms. Appendix F, "Academic Rigor Task Cards" (page 201), contains four sample tasks for each of the following: language arts, social studies, science, mathematics, and elementary level. We recommend that you add at least six more cards to each set that are tied to your school curriculum. While you can fit all the activities onto one sheet, the exercise is more engaging when the tasks are on separate cards and teachers can physically sort and re-sort them. (Go to solution-tree.com/PLCbooks to download the tasks on separate cards and to see additional tasks.)

Provide the following instructions:

- Individually, rate each of the ten content area activities for rigor as either academically rigorous (R) or low-level tasks (L).

- Tally, on flip-chart paper, how each person rated the tasks.

- As a group, agree on how to rate each task, using evidence-based discussion; record your group ratings in the final flip-chart paper column.

- For tasks you believe are rigorous, discuss how a teacher might change the task to decrease the rigor.

- For tasks you believe are low-level, discuss how a teacher might adjust the task to increase the rigor.

- Discuss whether the level of rigor is appropriate for the content or skill being taught.

- Reflect on what rigor looks like in your content area; write down your thoughts.

The tasks often reveal differences in how people with different personality types view rigor. Thinking types often view rigor as going beyond what was taught to see if students are able to construct new knowledge, while others argue that a lack of connection between what is taught and what is assessed is inherently unfair. Sensing types may view rigor as student mastery of difficult procedural tasks, even though students may be able to complete such tasks without mastering the underlying concepts. Intuitive types may view any open-ended task that allows creativity as rigorous, while others may note that the task lacks significant content. Feeling types may dislike the word *rigor* altogether (synonyms include severity, harshness, meticulousness, and inflexibility) and instead think in terms of creating tasks at which all students can succeed, with extensions for those who want more.

Sharing Struggles as Well as Successes

Marker 3

Sharing examples of what did not go well in classrooms becomes as natural as sharing what went well.

Allen (2008) summarizes well the anxiety of teachers as they begin working in PLCs:

> Sharing work and teacher assignments is fundamentally a risky business: It is personal and gets at the core of what teachers do, most often in deep privacy. Protocols create a safe space in which to share our practices; and they usually, in our experience, ensure useful and useable feedback to the teacher. (p. 105)

Again, you can use activity 7.4 (page 144) to establish a protocol for looking at student work and to build trust by using external samples. You can use a similar method to begin the work of examining lessons and assignments to improve student learning. At the elementary school level, we provide a lesson on a teacher-chosen subject. Teachers critique the lesson plan together, and then everyone uses it with their students and shares their experiences. Usually, as the teachers see how collaboration improves the results, they begin to view their PLC as a safe place for such sharing.

At the secondary school level, content-area PLC teachers often agree to try a core strategy provided by a facilitator by studying the lesson in advance, suggesting improvements, using it with students, and collaborating to improve it. Grade-level teams sometimes decide to teach the same lesson in an advisory block. Or, they all work together on a key strategy such as student-focused discussions, using the Japanese lesson study model to collaborate.

A hallmark of Japanese lesson study is concentrating on teaching a single concept or skill in depth. To gain experience with the model, one teacher uses a protocol provided by the outside facilitator and then shares the results with the PLC. The PLC members work together on improvements of the protocol and the next step for their students. Another teacher uses the second iteration, and so on. While this involves more risk than teaching the same lesson provided by an outsider, teachers are still focusing on a new technique rather than on something created internally. The protocol for critiquing assessments, given next, can be modified to use for lesson plans.

Looking at assessments can also be a productive way to increase trust, again starting with formative assessments developed by outsiders. Activity 6.4, "Looking at Assessments," provides a protocol for evaluating the whats and hows of assessment. Note that focusing the discussion is essential; too often, discussions turn to general problems in teaching and away from improving the assessment. Little (2003) found that teachers missed chances to go deeper, often did not notice when their discussions switched in focus because the purpose of their conversation was not well articulated, and took very little time to look in-depth at student work, summarizing that "the impulse to question practice resonates against the press simply to get on with it" (p. 940). In one case, high school teachers stated their purpose in looking at student work as being more consistent and improving the quality of comments they wrote on student papers. When these teachers looked at samples, no one noted that their discussion ignored the written comments. Their discussion turned to teaching evaluative writing.

Little and Horn (2007) list practices that help teachers hold more productive discussions:

- Staying focused on content knowledge and how to best convey that knowledge to students

- Referring to an extensive set of shared resources or curriculum (shared assessments fall into this category)

- Designating someone as a leader to:

    + Monitor whether the discussion stays focused

    + Ask for classroom examples

    + Ask questions regarding teaching and learning

- Making sure everyone receives encouragement to help with the leadership of the discussion

ACTIVITY 6.4 Looking at Assessments

Goal: To help teachers evaluate whether a formative assessment is appropriate and useful for enhancing learning

Materials: Copies of the assessments for each participant and the rubric or criteria to be used for grading (While groups can critique new, unused assessments, the discussions are richer when copies of student work are available.)

Directions: In no more than five minutes, have the person who prepared the assessment explain how it was used, the learning objectives it was designed to measure, and the feedback that person would like to receive on the assessment.

Sample focus questions might include the following:

- Does the assessment allow for adequate analysis of student thinking?

- Does the assessment adequately assess whether the student has mastered the learning goal? Do they align?

- Is the assessment clear? How might you have approached it as a student?

- Is the level of rigor appropriate for the content?

- Is this assessment efficient, or could we check for understanding more quickly?

- What other assessment formats might work?

Allow time for all participants to read the assessment.

Then, ask each participant to share his or her thoughts regarding the provided focus question. At this stage, the presenter takes notes rather than responding to comments. Provide sample comment stems so that the comments stay productive for the presenter. Sample stems might include the following:

- I noted that . . .

- I'm wondering why/if . . .

- I need help in understanding . . .

- Could you clarify why . . .

- Can you give an example of how a student . . .

Alternatively, ask each participant to provide one *feedback statement*—a constructive suggestion on how to modify the assessment to better align with the learning objectives.

Finally, allow the presenter to summarize what was said, ask questions, and propose possible changes. Ideally, the presenter could then use the assessment and return with samples for the PLC to discuss.

Another frequent activity is observing each other's classrooms. Because teachers with different personality types often meet instructional goals in very different ways, protocols, such as those provided in activity 6.5 (page 112), help observers refrain from misjudging activities and procedures that are unlike their own.

ACTIVITY 6.5 **Observing Each Other's Classrooms**

Goal: To make teacher observations of each other's classrooms as productive as possible for everyone by setting clear parameters

Materials: Observation sheets or copies of handout 6.1, "Peer Classroom Observation Sheet" (page 125), for each participant

Directions: Prior to the observation, meet with the teacher to set the desired learning objective for having others observe in his or her classroom. Examples might include the following:

- Level of questions asked

- Level of student involvement or engagement

- Scaffolding of ideas for struggling students

- Wait time after asking questions

- Maintenance of cognitive level of task (rigor)

- Lesson pacing

- Handling of transitions

Next, design an observation sheet, or use handout 6.1, for participants. Include the learning objective and sample comment stems to be used in the debriefing, with space for participants to organize their observations around the stems. Sample stems might include the following:

- I saw/noticed . . .

- I wondered about . . .

- I heard students say . . .

- I counted . . .

These stems are designed to keep the postconference evidence based rather than judgmental.

Then, meet with the teachers and explain the protocol to be used. Observe the entire class period or lesson being taught. Afterward, allow at least five minutes for observers to summarize their feedback, concentrating on the following items:

- What they noted about student learning as well as teaching

- Evidence-based (not judgmental or evaluative) comments

Lead a discussion of the observation, helping the group stay focused on evidence and the lens for observation that the teacher provided. Give the teacher an opportunity to respond. Then, discuss the overall process with the group, including what participants learned from the experience and what they will do differently in the future.

Defining Problems, Reaching Consensus

> ### Marker 4
>
> The team takes time to debate and define problems before deciding how to solve them. Team members know how to reach consensus.

Glaser (2005) cites the Quaker definition of consensus as "a process used to find the highest level of agreement *without* dividing the participants into factions" (p. 148). This definition allows work to continue even when a team cannot reach 100 percent agreement.

This measure of collaboration is vital as PLCs choose their areas of focus for a meeting, the month, or the year. Once again, the Problem-Solving Model is effective in considering multiple viewpoints and remaining open to alternatives. Activity 6.6, "Setting PLC Goals," provides sample questions for each step of the process and ensures that short-term goals tie to the overall vision.

ACTIVITY 6.6 Setting PLC Goals

Goal: To choose clear, measurable PLC goals tied to overall school goals and to improving student learning via adult learning

Materials: Data the PLC is expected to use and copies of the school or district goals or vision (Encourage PLC members to bring any other relevant data.)

Note: The PLC will actually work through the model twice—first to select the goal and then to determine how to reach the goal.

Directions: Have the entire group work through each step of the process together. Or, have some members analyze data in advance and bring suggested goals to the meeting. Choose two to three of the suggested questions for each part of the process, depending on your overall focus.

Sensing

- Based on our data, where do our students need the most help? Are some areas foundational to others and, therefore, should be tackled first?

- Based on your experience, what skills do students lack when they arrive in your classroom?

- What content at our grade level is most crucial for students to master for the next grade level?

continued on next page →

- What content do we struggle to teach—in what areas are we unsure that our own knowledge is sufficient?

Intuition

- What topics interest you the most as an adult learner?

- Do the suggested focus areas tie to long-term goals, or are they short-term and isolated? What are the connections?

- If students succeed, what might we see or hear?

- What would we most like to see happen in our classrooms?

Thinking

- What criteria might we use to consider the scope and resources required for each possibility?

- Are these SMART (specific, measurable, achievable, results oriented, and time-bound) goals?

- What are the possible consequences of not choosing each goal?

- What are the pros and cons of each possibility?

- Do any of the options seem most reasonable?

- Do the data support each choice?

Feeling

- Is the goal equitable?

- Does the goal match our school vision and values?

- What are our personal likes and dislikes regarding each possibility?

- How will the goal affect our students? Our classrooms?

- Did we overlook any subjective data (parent or student voices, or student motivation) that might alter our decision?

Note that activity 6.6 pulls in considerations far beyond many protocols designed to ensure data-driven instruction. Sometimes, analyzing test data reveals obvious areas for focus. At some schools, however, no such pattern emerges—the same students are behind in nearly every area, or results are uniformly satisfactory or even excellent. The questions posed in activity 6.7, "Deciding Our Data Direction" (page 115), allow for different ways to sift through the myriad of options for goals in those situations. For other schools, the questions may help identify the goal teachers are most passionate about, which—as long as they do not overlook a clearly more fundamental goal—may be key for buy-in and commitment to improving student learning.

ACTIVITY 6.7 Deciding Our Data Direction

Goal: To make use of personality type strengths and struggles with data to enhance how a particular PLC uses data

Materials: Each participant needs a copy of his or her type page from appendix A, "Descriptions of the Sixteen Types" (page 155). Also make available copies of handouts 4.2–4.5 (pages 78–81).

Directions:

1. Remind participants that while type is never destiny (their own interests or experiences may mean that how they work with data is different than others of their type), there are patterns to the data sources people trust and to their desire to analyze data. Ask each person to read the description for their type from appendix A and for their "PLC Style" (handouts 4.2–4.5).

2. Take a type inventory of the group—how many members prefer ST, SF, NF, and NT? Discuss how this distribution affects their work with data, using the following questions:

   - Do some members enjoy working with data more?

   - Does anyone enjoy organizing or summarizing the data for others?

   - Do we spend too much time with data—analyzing rather than selecting goals and working to improve student learning?

   - Do we spend too little time with data—not studying the data well enough before choosing goals?

   - Do we have the resources we need to work with data on this team, or do we need outside help?

Note: This exercise may help your team procure the assistance necessary to use data well if the answer to the last question is no. Administrators who understand type may grasp that the team's time is better used in ways other than in becoming experts at data if no one has the skills. We once worked with a group of thirteen literacy coaches who all hated data; the district coordinator quickly realized that having a data coach hand that group data summaries would be more productive than helping the group learn to analyze the numbers.

Conflict That Brings Community Renewal

Marker 5

Conflict becomes a source of renewal—members know how to handle it and use it as a context for learning and for exchanging opinions for knowledge.

Achinstein (2002), in a study of the effects of conflict on teacher collaboration, found that "conflict is not only central to community, but how teachers manage conflicts, whether they suppress or embrace their differences, defines the community borders and ultimately the potential for organizational learning and change" (p. 421). Teachers who work through conflicts build shared ideologies, rather than maintaining their own ideologies, thus staying open to changing their beliefs and growing as educators.

Few people embrace conflict. While one stereotype is that Feeling types avoid conflict most readily, type is never a box. Many people, both Thinking and Feeling types, learn how to deal with conflict after they have lived with the consequences of *not* dealing with it. Feeling *organizations,* though, often choose not to acknowledge conflict. The "function" of an organization is characterized by the emphasis within its culture. Feeling organizations tend to focus on serving others or on personal growth; elementary schools, especially, usually fit this description. Teachers often avoid conflict in the name of being nice. Using conflict to further learning requires a new mindset for many educators. Rather than nodding agreement in meetings, they need to voice concerns or differences of opinion.

The Problem-Solving Model (page 173), included in appendix B, can be invaluable in working through disagreements. The Sensing function takes people back to the facts and explains how an objective person might view the situation. The Intuitive function allows for interpretations and possible compromises, solutions, or scenarios. Then, the Thinking and Feeling functions balance out the consequences of different actions and the values involved.

However, personality types do influence how individuals view and respond to conflict. Killen and Murphy (2003) found clear patterns that involved our last two preferences: TJ, TP, FJ, and FP pairs had different concerns and definitions of closure:

- TJ types quickly look at alternatives and press for closure. They keep their emotions at bay and may seem detached. For them, decision is the end of it; they are satisfied that the conflict is resolved.

- TP types want to explore all the possible causes and options. They do not think emotions can appropriately play a role, and they may appear cold when they ignore others' emotions. They may continue to process alternatives long after others are done with the situation.

- FJ types want to keep relationships intact during and after any conflict, and work to ensure that no hurt or bitterness remains. They may settle for harmony as a sign of resolution when, in fact, the core issues remain unaddressed.

- FP types want every perspective to be heard and honored, and are invested in ensuring that different alternatives are aired. They may fail to consider logic or resist closing the issue.

Keeping these basic differences in mind can help team members avoid overreacting during disagreements.

ACTIVITY 6.8 **Productive Conflict**

Goal: To help the group recognize differences in their needs during conflict and recognize when using a protocol to resolve conflict is appropriate

Materials: Type descriptions for each person from appendix A, "Descriptions of the Sixteen Types" (page 155)

Directions: Share the preceding general information on TJ, TP, FJ, and FP conflict resolution. Ask team members to reflect on whether the information is accurate for them. How might they nuance it? Can they cite an example of a time when they responded this way at work? What was the conflict? If you conduct this exercise with a large group (more than twelve people), ask them to work in TJ, TP, FJ, and FP groups to answer the following questions (Killen & Murphy, 2003):

- How do you define conflict?
- How do you react physically and emotionally during conflict?
- How do you know if a conflict has been resolved?

Ask each person to develop a conflict manual to share with the group. This task may work best if people complete the manual outside of the PLC meeting time. Let participants know in advance that they will be sharing their statements with the team; some teams choose to create booklets for team eyes only to use as reference. Ask participants to write three to five statements for each of the following prompts:

- To me, conflict is . . .
- To work through conflict productively, I need . . .
- You can help me by . . .

continued on next page →

After participants share their manuals, discuss the following problem-solving prompts for conflict resolution. Ask group members for items they would add or remove.

Sensing

- What are the facts? Can we verify the facts and use them to justify our positions?
- How can we state our disagreement clearly?
- How does this situation relate to past discussions or disagreements?

Intuition

- What connections are there to larger issues?
- What are other ways to look at this?
- Can we interpret each other's thoughts, actions, and opinions in different ways?

Thinking

- What will happen if we don't resolve this?
- What do we need to clarify?
- Can we find objective ways to consider the issue?

Feeling

- What matters most to each of us?
- Are we serving the school vision and values?
- Who is being hurt?

Knowing When to Tap Outside Resources

> **Marker 6**
>
> Members are willing to admit when they do not know the answers—only then can PLCs recognize when they need outside assistance to help all students achieve.

Occasionally, we've heard educators overpromise on collaborative teams; they make it sound like PLCs should be able to solve all problems themselves to help all students achieve. However, the issues schools face are often huge and, as one pragmatic PLC member put it, "If we knew how to fix it, don't you think we'd have done it by now?" Sometimes, as PLCs strategize, they realize they need help.

Evidence-based discussions are an important factor in helping PLCs recognize whether they have the knowledge necessary to improve student learning or whether, in contrast, they are pooling opinions either about why students are struggling or about what will or will not work to improve student learning. Carefully using the goal-setting strategy included in activity 6.6, "Setting PLC Goals" (page 113), often unearths knowledge gaps. Another tool is collaborating on learning progressions (Popham, 2008), also called *knowledge packages* (Ma, 1999). Learning progressions help teachers recognize the piece-by-piece construction of knowledge, which may or may not be reflected in standards or in curriculum. For example, a mathematics team did not realize that learning to add fractions in which one denominator is a multiple of the other (for example, 1/4 and 1/2) was, for most students, completely separate from learning to add fractions in which the denominators have no common factors (for example, 1/3 and 1/4). Students who seemed to have mastered adding fractions fell apart when handed the latter problem. Teachers delve deeply into content knowledge when they work out the progressions for themselves.

Popham states:

> I can't provide a cookie-cutter approach to the construction of learning progressions any more than a building contractor could provide a cookie-cutter approach to the construction of houses. So much depends on what you're trying to build and the materials you have to work with. The variety of end results sought and what's available instructionally to teachers make it impossible to lay out a single design scheme. (2008, p. 32)

However, clear principles, such as those included in activity 6.9, "Building a Learning Progression," can help a PLC through the process, which is essential to the PLC goals of clarifying what students must learn and assessing whether students learned it.

ACTIVITY 6.9 Building a Learning Progression

Goal: To guide a PLC through a deep exploration of how to help students master content

Materials: Teachers might bring curriculum and other instructional materials

Note: Building a learning progression for a significant block of content can take an entire semester. Handout 6.2, "Learning Progression for Fractions" (page 126), provides an example for fractions that was also given to students to set clear learning goals.[1]

Directions:

1. Develop a thorough knowledge of the content. Identify how various topics interconnect and build on each other. The team might look at several resources before drafting a "map" of the content.

2. Identify areas in which students show misunderstandings. By looking at student work, can you determine the origin of these misunderstandings? Often, these

---

[1] Other examples are available at www.ccsso.org/publications/details.cfm?PublicationID=366.

continued on next page →

misunderstandings reflect missing steps in the progression as the material was taught to students.

Alternatively, identify areas where students "fall apart." For example, one language arts PLC noted that students reread passages of text, looking for answers when, in fact, the questions required them to infer information. The teachers then designed a lesson on how to make inferences.

3. Limit the number of items and their "grain size" to the ones for which you plan to collect evidence of learning. Too many items is as dangerous as too few. A few questions that might help limit the items include the following:

    *   What knowledge is essential for the next steps in the progression?

    *   Ask yourself, "If they haven't mastered this item, would I go back and reteach it differently?" (Popham, 2008, p. 39)

    *   Check whether you can assess progress on a particular building block. Can you isolate whether students have mastered this particular block? Can the learning be measured?

4. Work to construct an instructional sequence. Usually, you will need to revise the sequences once the teaching begins.

To find key areas in which a PLC might need outside help, discuss the following questions:

*   Does our content knowledge have holes?

*   Can we put together a learning progression?

*   Can we analyze a progression shown in curriculum materials? Do we agree with it?

*   Can we identify enduring understandings and essential questions as well as standards?

*   Do we know how to assess student mastery of the content?

*   Do we know how to engage students in authentic learning for this content?

Welcoming Mutual Accountability for Student Learning

Marker 7

Members welcome being held accountable to use what they have learned and share student results with the team.

This marker taps into whether PLCs are currently taking action as well as planning to take action. Framing the question, "How will we know if they have learned it?" in terms of action research often helps PLCs plan for measuring student learning even as they plan for teaching. You can construct a simple framework for action research by answering the following three questions:

1. What question are we trying to answer? (This should be clear from the PLC goals.)

2. What data will we collect to answer that question?

3. When will we collect the data by?

Next-action thinking—making sure that each decision includes the action step—builds this kind of accountability. PLCs that make progress on this marker constantly examine their goals to see if they can measure progress. If not, they restate the goal. When they see results, they decide if they have reached their goal or if they need to ask another question and try again, identifying new data to gather as well as a new time frame.

Diverse Paths to the Same Instructional Goals

Marker 8

Members recognize and respect that there may be many paths to the same end, but they are willing to sacrifice individuality if it interferes with the needs of the group.

Collaboration cannot mean lockstep implementation. Again, examine the type page for colleagues opposite your own type preferences and you will quickly see that many aspects of teaching simply will not look the same in every classroom. Teams, though, can agree on when they need to be consistent and where room for individuality exists. Activity 6.10, "Collaborative Unit Planning," is a lesson-planning protocol that models how flexibility can exist within consistency.

ACTIVITY 6.10 Collaborative Unit Planning

Goal: To develop a consistent unit plan that allows for some flexibility

Materials: Markers, strips of flip-chart paper, and curriculum resources

Directions: Identify in advance the standard(s) the unit will address, based on the PLC goals, and ask participants to bring related materials. Then complete the following:

1. *Enduring understanding protocol.* Provide each person with a strip of flip-chart paper and a marker. Have each person silently write his or her version of the enduring understanding

continued on next page →

for this unit—the big concept children are to take away from this unit. When everyone finishes, lay all of the paper strips on a table for everyone to read. Ask for two minutes of silence so that people can process the variations.

Comment on what is good in each statement. Provide opportunities for people to say what they would add to their own statement after seeing everyone's ideas. Then answer phrases such as the following, which are designed to help people build on the ideas of others:

- What if we combine . . .
- What's the best way to state . . .
- Can you clarify what you meant by . . .
- Can anyone help me understand . . .
- I agree and . . .
- I disagree with . . . because . . .
- Can anyone build on . . .
- Could you say more about . . .

Finally, work to reach consensus on the overall statement.

2. *Essential questions.* What questions do we want students to be able to answer at the end of the unit? Use the same process to identify the essential questions for the unit, providing several strips of paper for each teacher.

3. *Learning progression.* For this step, continue to work with moveable outlines—the strips of paper—to easily sort and combine ideas. Teachers might wish to work in groups of two or three to generate different items. Then, the larger group can pool the ideas and apply the criteria to narrow them down:

- Can we measure whether students have learned it?
- Is it essential to future learning?
- Is it core knowledge that everyone should have?

During this step, ask teachers to refer to state standards and benchmarks, including these—as appropriate—in this process. In some cases, the paper strips are based directly on benchmarks. However, some lists of benchmarks leave out key content, concepts, or skills students need to master in the overall progression.

4. *Learning activities.* Once the learning progression is set, teachers may need time to examine their resources and determine what activities they might use. Or, they may be

able to quickly pick and choose from existing curriculum. Either way, participants can complete this step orally. One person might make a table of ideas for each learning goal. To choose the activities, complete the following:

- Assess which learning style each activity meets (handout 7.1, page 151) and ensure that the unit overall has a balance of styles.

- Consider time restraints and length of the overall unit.

- Balance whose "favorite" activities are chosen.

- Identify learning modules that all students should experience in the same way and ones in which teachers can choose among activities. For example, teachers might decide that all students should conduct the same experiment so next year's teachers know that all children had the experience. However, these teachers may all choose different accompanying read-aloud books based on their own preferences.

DuFour et al. (2008) emphasize:

> Effective teaching requires considerable autonomy and discretion in the day-to-day, moment-to-moment decisions teachers make in their individual classrooms. Members of PLCs support that autonomy because they recognize scripted lessons and lockstep pacing will not develop the capacity of teachers to improve either their instruction or their schools. When, however, teachers are presented with clear evidence that particular instructional strategies consistently yield better results for students, they are expected to develop their ability to use those strategies in their classrooms. This is typically not a problem, since we have found that evidence of student learning is the most powerful motivator for teachers to change their practice. (pp. 188–189)

As one kindergarten team worked through the lesson-planning protocol for a new unit on seeds, they reached an impasse on how to grow seeds in their classrooms. Everyone had different ideas, and everyone had had varying levels of success—or disaster—with the suggestions. Finally, one person said, "Let's *not* do it the same. Then our classes can present to each other on how they grew seeds and what happened." The team quickly agreed that autonomy would not only increase student learning, but would also provide an opportunity for their young students to have a role in planning for inquiry and for sharing their results with others, perhaps even with older students. One teacher said, "Somehow this discussion skyrocketed my desire to plan more units with all of you. This is far better than how I used to teach the unit—but I can still use the activities I love." The group was well on its way to becoming a team.

Progressing Toward Effectiveness and Sustainability in Your PLC

The preceding eight markers measure whether a group is becoming a team that works together to achieve common goals and holds each other mutually accountable. Use handout 6.3 (page 127) to place yourself on each continuum regarding the eight markers. A ninth marker is each member's personal commitment to the group, often a result of their experiences:

> In the context of schooling, respect involves recognition of the important role each person plays in a child's education and the mutual dependencies that exist among various parties involved in this activity. Key in this regard is how conversation takes place within a school community. A genuine sense of listening to what each person has to say marks the basis for meaningful social interaction. In many public meetings that we observed, the communication among individuals was regulated through formal parliamentary procedures. These procedures may grant someone a right to speak but do not necessarily mean that anyone actually attends to what is said. Such exchanges are quite different from those where individuals intently listen to each other and in some fashion take others' perspectives into account in future action. Genuine conversation of this sort signals that each person's ideas have value and that the education of children requires that we work together cooperatively. (Bryk & Schneider, 2002, p. 23)

If you experience that kind of conversation in your PLC, then you have created a coaching culture. The next chapter examines a method of ensuring all students are achieving academically and becoming lifelong learners—the marker of true effectiveness of a PLC.

Reflection

1. What are the benefits to you, personally, of being part of a PLC? What do you hope to learn? How can an understanding of your learning style assist you in establishing a viable PLC and making progress toward each marker?

2. Of the eight markers described, which is most challenging to you and why? If you are a team leader, is it harder for you to coach the team toward progress on any one marker? Who might be able to help you to deepen your collaborative efforts in this area?

3. Think of a time when you were part of a collaborative team. What helped the team learn to work together? How did you realize you had become a team?

4. If you are a coach, rate the PLCs you work with on each of the continuums in handout 6.3 (page 127) and use it as a reference for marking the group progress toward deep collaboration. What goals might you set for improving the team culture? How could you measure progress and thus your effectiveness on that marker?

Handout 6.1

Peer Classroom Observation Sheet

Teacher: Class Period:

Lesson goal (as stated by teacher being observed):

Observation objective (set in collaboration with the teacher being observed):

Use the following prompts to maintain focus on factual evidence of what is happening in the classroom:

- I saw/noticed . . .

- I wondered about . . .

- I heard students say . . .

- I counted . . .

- Students told me that the lesson goal was . . . /they were learning . . .

Write a summary of your observations and questions to share with the teacher you observed.

Handout 6.2

Learning Progression for Fractions

The following list, developed by Jane and a team of teachers,[1] identifies what sixth-grade students learn about fractions. Teachers used it to structure unit plans. They also had students use it to mark their progress in mastering fractions.

1. I can give examples of how fractions are used in real life by drawing pictures or using words.

2. Fractions can describe equal parts of a whole. I can name each part as a fraction of a whole and name how many parts make a whole.

3. The bottom, or *denominator*, is the name or size of the part; the top, or *numerator*, is the number of equal-size parts of that name or size. I can use these terms.

4. I understand how to divide shapes, groups of objects, number lines, and other things into equal parts.

5. If you give me a fractional part of something, I can figure out what the whole is.

6. If I'm describing the same object, the larger the denominator, the smaller the equal part I'm describing. I can use this information to help me compare fractions and tell which one is larger or smaller.

7. I know the relative value of fractions with different denominators and can put them in order.

8. I know that the actual size of a fractional piece depends on the size of the whole.

9. I understand that fractions represent dividing things into fair, equal shares.

10. I understand that fractions can be thought of as indicating division.

11. I know how to figure out whether the value of a fraction is greater or less than $\frac{1}{2}$.

12. I understand that fractions can have different names, and I can find equivalent fractions for $\frac{1}{2}$, $\frac{1}{3}$, $\frac{1}{4}$, and others.

13. I understand that if you multiply or divide both the numerator and the denominator of a fraction by the same number, you get a fraction that is equivalent to the original fraction.

14. I understand that the value of a fraction can be greater than 1, and I can explain what an improper fraction, such as $\frac{3}{2}$, means.

15. If I divide an object into equal parts, I can use a fraction to describe each part. For example, $\frac{1}{3}$ can be read as "one of three," and $\frac{1}{6}$ can be read as "one of six."

16. I understand how to use my knowledge of equivalent fractions to build or draw objects that have fractions with different denominators.

17. I understand that in order to add two or more fractions, the fractions must have the same denominator. I know how to find a common denominator and add two fractions.

---

[1] Developed in collaboration with Anne Bartel, Sue Benhardis, Joe Chan, and Christoper Wernimont.

Handout 6.3

Noncoaching Culture or Coaching Culture?

Place your PLC on each of the continuums.

N | | | | | C

Every PLC in the school continually completes the same activities. Classrooms are expected to look the same.

Members welcome diversity as a tool for making better decisions and use a framework such as type to communicate more clearly and understand other viewpoints.

N | | | | | C

The PLC focus is on student test gains with no consideration of professional development effectiveness. Data are limited to test results and behavior.

Members can ask questions, share beliefs, challenge ideas, and disagree with each other as part of their mutual commitment to adult learning and improved student achievement.

N | | | | | C

PLC activities are restricted to reading, study, and discussion with no accountability for classroom implementation.

Sharing examples of what did not go well in classrooms becomes as natural as sharing what went well.

N | | | | | C

Educators seldom reflect upon, document, or revisit decisions.

The team takes time to debate and define problems before deciding how to solve them. They know how to reach consensus.

N | | | | | C

Teachers share superficially and avoid questioning each other's practices.

Conflict becomes a source of renewal—members know how to handle it and use it as a context for learning and for exchanging opinions for knowledge.

N | | | | | C

PLC time consists of sharing of opinions without outside resources such as books, expert information, research results, or the actions of other teams.

Members are willing to admit when they do not know the answers—only then can PLCs recognize when they need outside assistance to help all students achieve.

N | | | | | C

Attendance is sporadic. Teachers either do not find the meetings valuable, or they lack trust.

Members welcome being held accountable to use what they learned and share student results with the team.

N | | | | | C

No one can articulate the goals or purpose of the PLC.

Members recognize and respect that there may be many paths to the same end, but they are willing to sacrifice individuality if it interferes with the needs of the group.

Reflect for a moment on the information. Which term describes your team best? Circle one:

Noncoaching   Coaching

Coaching for Optimal Student Engagement and Achievement

Before you begin reading this chapter, take a moment to reflect on the following questions:

- When do you see students most engaged in classrooms?

- Was there a time during your own schooling when you felt particularly unsuccessful? In which subject? How did this affect your beliefs about your own ability in that content area?

A recent meta-analysis of studies on learning styles concluded that while students are more engaged when learning style needs are met, engagement doesn't seem to transfer to better learning outcomes, as defined by common assessments (Pashler, McDaniel, Rohrer, & Bjork, 2008). However, are test scores the only measure of the importance of engagement? Studies on students disenfranchised by school indicate otherwise:

> A recent study funded by the Bill & Melinda Gates Foundation found that poor basic skills in reading, writing and computation were not the main reason for the high dropout rate: It turns out that *will*, not *skill*, is the single most important factor. In a national survey of nearly 500 dropouts from around the country, about half of these young people said they left school because their classes were boring and not relevant to their lives or career aspirations. A majority also said that schools did not motivate them to work hard . . . 88 percent had passing grades at the time they dropped out. (Wagner, 2008, p. 114)

Jackson and Temperley (2007) remind us that the work of PLCs to improve student learning must above all be grounded in sound ethics. Those ethics include considering the viewpoints of students. At every turn, we need to fight back at directives, initiatives, or desperate moves that threaten the core ethics of education. The four "nonnegotiable principles" they identify (p. 47), along with their relationship to creating a coaching culture, are as follows:

1. *Our moral purpose.* This principle stresses the commitment to success for all children. We are all too aware that while the accountability movement heightened awareness that some student groups were being left behind, in practice the pressure to improve test scores prompted some schools to concentrate resources on the students most likely to make enough progress to test into the next level of proficiency on the state tests. Hargreaves and Shirley (2009) summarize why PLCs must fight against this trend:

   > Teachers mourned the loss of their own and their students' creativity, complained of being "very burned out," and were "tired of fighting it." Increasingly researchers are finding that success in delivering short-term targets has been temporary rather than lasting (MacBeath et al., 2007). It has been achieved at the price of long-term sustainability in lifelong learning and higher order proficiencies within a broader curriculum. Short-term gains that quickly reach a plateau have been made at the expense of continuing improvements that endure beyond an initial year or two of rising results. (p. 3)

2. *Shared leadership.* To us this means that the voices of administrators, teachers, parents, and students are all heard as we choose what and how children learn.

3. *Inquiry-based practice.* The adults within a professional learning community commit themselves to continually adding to what they know about the art and science of teaching and learning.

4. *Adherence to a model of learning.* This chapter, in particular, explores how adherence to type as a common framework can focus discussions and help teams avoid biases. Bryk (2009) states the case for finding such a model:

   > I propose a modest amendment [to the definition of PLCs]. The social organization for improvement is a professional learning community organized around a specific instructional system. . . . The instructional system details what teachers need to know about students in terms of background knowledge, skills, and interests. It involves some very specific pedagogical practices and social routines and expects automaticity in their use. Educators have a shared language about goals for students and understand how these align over time around some larger conception of student learning. Teachers also share a common evidence base about what constitutes learning. This allows them to analyze and refine the cause-and-effect logic that organizes their shared work. Finally, tying this all together is an explicit process for socializing new members into the community and for organizing ongoing social learning among all participants. (p. 600)

The Case for Type as an Education Framework

By now, most educators are well aware of the importance of considering gender, prior knowledge and skill level, cultural background, and socioeconomic status when differentiating instruction. However, while a preponderance of educators have had some exposure to type theory—perhaps taking the MBTI for self-discovery or participating in a brief teambuilding activity—few have worked with the framework deeply enough to understand the profound impact that psychological preferences have on teaching and learning, and the ease with which they can use the framework to make a positive impact.

Listen to the story of one educator, a sixth-grade mathematics teacher, who worked with us to develop interventions for students who were two to three years below grade level in fractions knowledge. For this particular intervention, we worked with all of the teachers on his team to group students by both their content knowledge and their preference for Sensing or Intuition to research the question, "Are the needs of Sensing and Intuitive students different when they are significantly below grade level?" This teacher worked with a small group of Sensing students for two weeks and then a small group of Intuitive students for the next two weeks. The groups had similar levels of content knowledge before the intervention. His report was as follows:

I was amazed at how different the S and N groups were. The biggest revelation for me came when I was teaching how to move between mixed numbers and improper fractions. The Sensing group spent four class periods working on this skill. They were excited to build the fractions with fraction strips, draw out their work on their whiteboards, and present their thinking on the interactive whiteboard. Even with this enthusiasm, though, understanding built on one day did not necessarily transfer to the next. This is why we spent four days working on this skill. Once the skill had been mastered, the Sensing students asked to end each tutoring session with a few mixed number and improper fractions problems.

It motivated me as a teacher to see how excited students got when they finally realized that math could make sense. When we started working with improper fractions and mixed numbers, these students would very confidently suggest wrong answers to the problems; they just rearranged the digits. By the end when it was making sense to them, they would think a little bit before suggesting an answer, but were almost always correct and could give a detailed explanation in front of the group.

The Intuitive students were much different. Once they understood mixed numbers and improper fractions, they were not at all interested in completing practice problems. This made it tricky to keep the group moving forward since they mastered the concepts at different times. For three days, I needed to create different types of problems for the different levels of understanding to keep everyone working. The students who needed more time with simpler problems seemed relieved that everyone was working on different problems because they did not feel like they needed to compete against the others.

The other teachers involved in the project saw similar differences in the Sensing and Intuitive groups. On more challenging word problems, the Intuitives worked longer on their own before asking for help and thrived on tutoring others once they mastered the problems. The Sensing students wanted reassurance at every step that they were on the right track. The teachers agreed,

"Yes, when students are behind, there is a difference in the instructional needs of those who prefer Sensing and Intuition." They strategized for scheduling flexibility that would allow for regrouping students who need more time to master a concept and also generated instructional strategies for times when groups needed to mix students with both preferences.

The bottom line is this: when PLCs move to answering the questions, "How will we know if students know it?" and "What will we do if they don't get it?" they need to add, "Did we consider how we communicate and how students heard us—Sensing and Intuition—when checking for understanding?" and "Will students with different preferences benefit from different interventions?"

Another way to state this is that the essential work of PLCs really includes five questions—the four outlined by DuFour et al. (2006):

1. What do our students need to learn?

2. How will we know if they learned it?

3. What will we do if they don't learn it?

4. How will we extend the learning of those who are already proficient or reach mastery?

And one more that takes type into consideration:

5. How can we engage students in learning what they need to know?

Remember that between two-thirds and three-quarters of the U.S. and Canadian populations prefer Sensing. A majority of the students in the interventions described previously preferred Sensing and responded very well to structured intervention techniques. Now imagine mixing the groups; many Intuitive students typically react to boredom in their regular classrooms by either withdrawing (Introverts) or acting out (Extraverts). Without the filter of type, a PLC might conclude, "Students need structured interventions, but we may need to isolate students with behavior problems to engage in the practice they need." Or the PLC might blame the student in some other way rather than reevaluate the one-size-fits-all approach.

Type Biases in Education

Again, most educators are not deeply aware of type and, therefore, are unable to use it to check for biases in their beliefs, practices, and decisions. Here is what we know about the impact of those biases in education: type demonstrates a measurable bias in our measures of ability.

Consider the following:

*   Intuitive students perform better on almost all standardized tests. For example, 82 percent of the National Merit Scholarships go to Intuitive students even though those

students make up only 25–30 percent of the population. A 140-point "Intuitive gap" exists on the Preliminary SAT (PSAT), with a 250-point gap between the top-three personality types in score and the bottom-three types. The test favors their innate style of guessing (Wilkes, 2004).

- Tests of giftedness and creativity often select Intuition over Sensing rather than measuring some difference in ability (Robinson, 1994). For example, checklists that identify giftedness often list "Boredom with repetitive tasks." Our experiences with the fractions intervention clearly shows that Intuitive students are bored by repetition even if they are behind their peers—what if this definition of giftedness causes PLCs to emphasize repetitive tasks for all nongifted students? Conversely, many high-achieving Sensing students like repetition because they compete against themselves to increase speed or efficiency at those tasks—will their gifts go unrecognized or, worse, will they become frustrated by a seemingly endless stream of new learning when they yearn to focus their expertise?

- Teachers create assessments that match their own type preferences, potentially putting their opposites at a disadvantage (Murphy, 1992).

- Recall from chapter 1 that type preferences influence the subject areas and instructional practices teachers choose (Hammer, 1996). Further, a majority of elementary school teachers prefer Sensing and Judging. Therefore, the preferred methods in many disciplines are biased against students with other learning styles. Think of the implications for content-area PLCs!

- Multiple studies, confirmed in our own work at many schools, show that students who prefer Sensing and Perceiving are vastly overrepresented in alternative schools and other programs for at-risk students (Fouts, 2000; Hart, 1991; Kise & Russell, 2000). Further, these same types are vastly underrepresented among teachers. One might surmise that Sensing and Perceiving types hated school and avoid it as a profession. This means that their ideas of how students learn are largely absent from the educational debates, perpetuating the problem.

We conducted a differentiation workshop for about one hundred members of a district's curriculum and instruction department. When we led participants in the "Living Type Table" exercise, in which people end up on type-alike groups, only one person stood in a Sensing/Perceiving space. Approximately 80 percent of the group filled the Intuitive/Feeling space. When Jane mentioned that around 90 percent of the students in alternative schools prefer Sensing/Perceiving, the one SP remarked, "That makes so much sense, based on my school days." The room fell silent. Finally, one person remarked, "What this really shows is that our district doesn't have the voices in the room that can help us reach the students we are failing."

To summarize, type can be an essential PLC tool for examining whether the content, teaching strategies, assessments, and interventions teachers choose have inherent biases.

Differentiation Through Personality Types: A Framework for Instruction, Assessment, and Classroom Management (Kise, 2007) lays out how to use type to differentiate instruction, assessment, and classroom management for interests, skill level, and culture. Type thus becomes a powerful tool for ensuring all students have equitable access to learning.

For classroom management, consider the different impact of classroom rules and structures on students with different preferences. We tell teachers, "If you don't plan instruction so that Extraverted students have opportunities to move and interact, they will move and interact when you least want them to!" Consider the primary grade student who struggles to complete seatwork. Is the child ADD, disobedient, immature, or merely an Extraverted and Perceiving student who could use an extra period of recess to gain energy for mental exercises? In fact, Naperville High School in Illinois found that struggling students showed more progress in mathematics when they took an extra hour of physical education rather than an extra hour of mathematics (Richardson, 2009).

For culture differentiation, type provides a bridge of understanding, especially in districts in which a myriad of cultures merge. In Minneapolis and St. Paul, our hometowns, students have more than ninety different first languages—it is unrealistic to think that teachers will understand the nuances of so many cultures, even though they need to grasp as much as they can about students in their own classrooms. With type, they can begin the work of differentiating for culture by considering archetypal factors. *Archetypes* describe what a culture values, in contrast to *stereotypes,* which are sweeping generalizations other groups make about behavior. For example, the Native American educators we work with describe their culture as more Introverted than Extraverted, thus opposite the archetype for the United States in general and the French Canadian culture. See "What Engages Students in Learning" (page 138) for a story on how understanding archetypes helped the teachers motivate their students.

Changing What It Means to Teach

Even how we define good teaching can show type biases. In many classrooms, teacher-directed learning is still the norm—lectures, seatwork, and instruction that focus on mastering prescribed content. Yet the real world of businesses, higher education, and entrepreneurial enterprise is demanding 21st century skills—teamwork, problem solving, higher-level thinking, and so on.

Frequently, teachers wonder if those activities really involve teaching and might say things like, "This isn't a good day to observe my classroom. I won't really be teaching. The students are doing group work." They need help in understanding that facilitating learning may mean less focus on the teachers; however, ensuring that learning takes place through activities like group work is just as labor intensive.

This traditional view of teacher-directed learning seems to have an archetype of Introversion, Sensing, and Judging, with its emphasis on students as receivers of knowledge, content, and set schedules and outcomes. And in fact, more than 50 percent of teachers do prefer Sensing and Judging. Consider how Elmore (2004) describes the current consensus on teaching:

> **Most teachers tend to think of knowledge as discrete bits of information about a particular subject and of student learning as the acquisition of this information through processes of repetition, memorization, and regular testing of recall. . . . The teacher, who is generally the center of attention in the classroom, initiates most of the talk and orchestrates most of the interaction in the classroom around brief factual questions, if there is any discussion at all. (pp. 8–9)**

Discussions with Sensing and Judging teachers often reveal a basic discomfort with open-ended questions, discussions, and group work because they lose control over the teaching process. Unless these teachers learn the art of controlling these processes, they are inherently uncomfortable with them.

Now think about how using type language to describe teacher strengths and struggles with moving toward 21st century skills classrooms might reframe the problems Elmore sees with changing schools:

> **Clearly getting more students to learn at higher levels has to entail some change in both the way students are taught and in the proportion of teachers who are teaching in ways that cause students to master higher-level skills and knowledge. It is possible, of course, that some piece of the problem of the distribution of learning can be solved by simply getting more teachers to teach more demanding academic content, even in boring and unengaging ways, to a broader population of students. But at some level it seems implausible that the large proportions of students presently disengaged from learning academic content at high levels of understanding will suddenly become more engaged if traditional teaching practices in the modal U.S. classroom remain the norm. (2004, p. 14)**

We are really asking classrooms to change from Sensing/Judging to Intuition/Perceiving to reach students, making student engagement as core to the work of PLCs as the other essential questions. We cannot sacrifice the long-term goal of engaging all students in rigor that leads to lifelong learning to the short-term goals of yearly test-score gains.

The next section reveals how type can help PLCs avoid biases in decisions about what to teach and how it will be taught and assessed.

"What Do Our Students Need to Know?" and Type

If who we are is how we teach—if our beliefs and practices reflect our personality types, as mounting evidence demonstrates—then our PLC becomes a check on those biases. Our colleagues can help us analyze whether a practice is really best practice or a reflection of how *we* learn best.

First, however, PLCs need to examine their own type distribution. Is distribution balanced, or might group decisions reflect inherent type biases? Activity 6.1, "Differentiated Learning Styles," on page 106 often helps teams pinpoint holes in their ideas about effective teaching or their perceptions of students. Handout 7.1, "Learning Styles, Favorite Activities, and Motivating Words" (page 151), can also serve as a check to whether one style is emphasized over another.

Then, as PLCs develop unit plans, identify learning progressions, and choose resources, those possible biases serve as criteria. Following are some examples of the effectiveness of this.

Identifying Teacher Biases That Impede Content Mastery

A majority of teachers on a middle school mathematics team that we worked with preferred Sensing. They identified three-digit multiplication problems as a core skill and began working on an intervention to ensure that all students mastered this skill, using it as a test for whether students were ready for prealgebra. The intervention consisted of teaching a procedure that helped keep place values straight, followed by practice problems. When students completed a certain percentage of the problems correctly, they exited the intervention.

We introduced Ma's (1999) research on teacher understanding of this concept, which compares how Chinese teachers and U.S. teachers approach mathematics. The Chinese teachers reported that they had "never seen students struggle with three-digit multiplication." Instead, they spent more time on two-digit multiplication and the concept of composing and decomposing numbers (often referred to as *regrouping*). With this information, the PLC rethought their learning progression to emphasize the meaning of place value for two-digit multiplication, rather than procedures for three-digit multiplication.

Identifying PLC Biases in Curriculum Emphasis

A state language arts standard read that students would be able to read, analyze, and understand a wide variety of fiction, poetry, and nonfiction texts. The language arts PLC, of which every member preferred Intuition, focused on fiction and poetry for their unit plans on both reading and writing. They informed the other content-based PLCs, "Nonfiction is covered in science and social studies. No one else covers fiction, so we need to place our emphasis there."

Later, in studying how type affects the materials students prefer to read (Kise, 2007), the PLC discovered that Sensing types are often motivated by nonfiction—and that typical science and social studies textbooks lack the essays, memoirs, and theme-based information that these students crave. Instead, the textbooks were generally summaries of facts—resources rather than texts to analyze and interact with. The language arts PLC reconsidered where they could include nonfiction.

Identifying Biases for Mastering Facts Versus Mastering Processes

A sweeping generalization that contains an essential truth is that Sensing types emphasize memorization while Intuitive types see very little that is worth memorizing. See if you can spot the type biases in the following scenario:

A history teacher explains his Advanced Placement course at a parent meeting: "Ninety percent of the course will be lecture. I assign approximately five pages of text each night, and I expect every student to be able to answer questions based on that text. The assignments reflect the rigor of the text; few students can handle larger chunks. For the 20-point quizzes given every Wednesday, a score of 10 earns a C. Mastery of history takes hard work."

The quizzes actually measured mastery of facts. Very little in the course reflected the rigorous work of historians—researching cause and effect, culling out key information, unearthing voices, analyzing the different impacts of catalytic events in different cultures, and so on. Yes, students needed to commit a certain body of information to memory in preparation for the standardized Advanced Placement tests, but the fact that the average score was 50 percent on the weekly quizzes most likely indicated that much of the knowledge assessed fell short of being enduring in nature.

An Intuitive teacher might make the opposite mistake—for example, teaching students to explore and compare differences in historical circumstances leading up to various revolutions around the world yet failing to provide an essential timeline approach that grounds students in the flow of history, which is necessary for that Advanced Placement test!

Together, PLCs can find the happy medium by working together to determine, "What in the core knowledge of our content area should students memorize?" Math facts are a prime example since math becomes far more enjoyable when "six times seven" is automatic rather than a laborious process. However, many Intuitive teachers admit avoiding the "drill and kill" that brings this mastery because of their own dislike of repetitive tasks. In contrast, many Sensing teachers overestimate what must be memorized, forgetting that the information we have is ever expanding, meaning that students need to learn where to find facts.

In science, core knowledge might include the symbols for many elements, eventually easing working with formulas in organic chemistry, but not the atomic weight of each element. In language arts, teachers may over- or underemphasize the facts of a story in comparison to helping students find themes and connections.

ACTIVITY 7.1 Essential Facts for Our Content Area

Goal: To balance student learning of essential content and essential processes

Materials: Core standards identified for each grade level; curriculum maps and/or unit assessments as handouts for each participant; and strips of paper, such as adding machine tape

Directions: Ask each person to review the materials and identify which items he or she believes are essential content that students should memorize or be able to use automatically (such as sentence structures) and which involve nonessential content. (If meeting time is limited, focus on a few standards or unit plans). Then, ask participants to write a description of each piece of essential content on a paper strip. Criteria may include the following:

- Will future learning be easier if this is committed to memory?

- How easily can students find the information in the future?

- Is the information specific to the way we teach this unit? In other words, might we substitute a different book, period in history, science concept, or math idea and cover the same standard?

- What will happen if students don't master this content?

- Does my preference for Sensing or Intuition in any way create a bias for how I look at this?

Discuss the suggested content on each paper strip, using the protocol for evidence-based discussions. Ask teachers to justify their reasoning for how they would classify the material. When the group reaches consensus, post the paper strip on the wall or whiteboard under one of two categories: "Content to be mastered" or "Content students might use while mastering core processes."

After all of the standards are categorized, ask the group to do a quickwrite on the final product. Is it free from any type biases the group might have? Are there any action steps needed regarding changing our "power standards" or the emphasis in any of the units? Ask participants to share any thoughts they believe are significant with the group.

"What Engages Students in Learning?" and Type

Once PLCs have determined what students will learn, they can collaborate to determine what will engage students while they learn. Read how one teacher transitioned students from passive to active learning:

A middle school history teacher struggled to get her students to master writing thesis statements. They were planning their National History Day projects and kept writing out topics such as, "I'm going to study Martin Luther King," or "I'm going to study the 1923 lynching in Duluth." Students stared at the worksheet the teacher had designed to help them turn those topics into theses and said, "Show us how. Tell us what to write."

Finally, the teacher said to the class, "George Bush was the greatest president our country ever had." A furious debate quickly ensued. "That's bogus." "No it isn't—he's no-nonsense." As student voices escalated, the teacher finally called the class back to attention. "My statement was a thesis. You all presented arguments in favor of it or opposed to it. That's what History Day is all about. You take a position and find evidence to defend it."

The teacher said, "That day, I realized that almost all of my students prefer Introversion and Sensing—we're a magnet school for Native American students, and their traditional way to learn is through listening and watching. After the 'presidential debate' incident, I pointed to my big poster of learning styles and told them, 'You're asking me to make History Day a Sensing project, but it requires Intuition. I can't tell you exactly what to do—you get to explore, make connections, and decide for yourselves what is important. You're feeling uncomfortable because it's a stretch, but you can do it.' They got it and dove in, once they knew why the whole thing seemed so hard to them." No student from that high-poverty school had ever made it to the District History Day competition before; that year, five students competed at the state level.

When teachers use type for lesson planning, it works as a framework for motivating students in so many ways:

- At the most fundamental level, type taps into the energy and information students need to learn.

- Teachers can use type to help students realize when school activities use their strengths or where they have to stretch—and then provide skill development paths.

- Type helps teachers design choices that appeal to everyone. One of our teachers remarked, "I've always given choices, but type showed me that the choices still all appealed to *me* and not to my students with the opposite style!"

- Type provides tools that help students become independent learners, recognizing different needs in time management, project planning, and work styles.

Further, to begin using type for differentiation is a two-step process. First, plan for how you would normally teach the subject, and second, adjust the plan for students with the opposite learning styles. Done—you have planned something for everyone. For example, if you prefer Introversion and

Sensing, you have already partially met the needs of those who prefer Introversion and Intuition, as well as those with Extraversion and Sensing. Add Extraversion and Intuition to your initial plan, and no one is left out. Handout 7.1 (page 151) provides a planning grid to get you started and can be used with activity 7.2, "Differentiated Learning Lesson." This brief lesson planning activity often demystifies the process of using type in planning. Many teachers tape copies of handout 7.1 on their desks and use the motivating words to quickly adjust assignments or add an alternative question. Think about it—are you more comfortable "making" or "creating"? Simple word substitutions actually motivate students to engage in an assignment.

The debriefing process also reinforces how PLC members can serve as resources to their opposites by clarifying directions, improving choices, and finding new materials.

ACTIVITY 7.2 Differentiated Learning Lesson

Goal: To give PLC members a brief, introductory experience in planning based on type

Materials: Appendix F, "Academic Rigor Task Cards" (page 201), and copies of handout 7.1, "Learning Styles, Favorite Activities, and Motivating Words" (page 151)

Directions: Ask participants to work in groups of two or three to do the followings steps:

1. Choose one of the task cards.

2. Work through the following three-step differentiation process:

   a. Identify the lesson goal—consider what you want the students to learn.

   b. Start as usual—consider whether the task as currently stated favors one of the four learning styles.

   c. Adjust for the opposite style—you might also add activities for the other two quadrants, if appropriate.

3. Use handout 7.1 to generate formative assessment ideas.

4. On flip-chart paper, record your main lesson-plan ideas for each of the learning styles. Be ready to give a two-minute explanation of your lesson plan to the other groups.

   After each group explains their lesson, ask other participants to comment on the ideas suggested for their own learning styles. Do they seem appropriate? Would any changes make them better or more motivating?

Using Type to Evaluate Student Experience

Data on how students actually experience school can also be key information for PLCs to consider as they work to motivate all students. PLCs can collect this data in three main ways—for a school, for a department on a specific topic, or for a student—in each case taking care to ensure that teachers see the process as informational, not evaluative. The data on a single student might be used to show a "typical" day for a secondary student on a particular team or grade level or to develop intervention strategies for a given student. When we observe classrooms in this way, we inform teachers that we will only be sharing data in the aggregate—all math classrooms, all seventh-grade classrooms, or all the classes for one secondary student's schedule, for example. They can see the results for their own classroom if they wish.

At an elementary school, teachers might decide to look for patterns in reading instruction to identify any type biases. A middle school language arts PLC might want to see similar data. An observer would visit each classroom, keeping a running record of instruction. Handout 7.2, "A Sample Running Record of Classroom Observation" (page 152), shows a running record of an eighth-grade classroom engaged in a vocabulary activity. During the class, the observer should (1) take notes on teacher moves and student responses—the more detail the observer records, the more information is available for analysis and for providing examples to any teacher who requests feedback—and (2) record the time spent on each task as well as categories for transition and for time off task—sometimes these provide the biggest clues for analyzing student engagement. At this particular school, we decided that if 80 percent or more of the students were on task, the class was on task, reflecting the high level of students who were consistently cited for behavior problems. Each school needs to define this level for themselves.

After the class, the observer can use the observation notes and handout 7.1 to categorize the activities by learning style. We often bring laptops and record our observations directly into spreadsheets so the software can do the calculations and graph results for us, showing the percentage of time spent on certain tasks, activities, or cognitive levels. Figure 7.1 (page 142) shows the aggregate graph for a middle school we worked with. The data sparked a new goal: increasing student time on task.

See handout 7.1, "Learning Styles, Favorite Activities, and Motivating Words" (page 151), for sample activities included in each of the learning style categories.

When the professional development team at this school saw the aggregate chart, they also decided that they needed to revisit the subject of student-centered discussion, an Extraverted and Intuitive activity. Even though teachers had shown understanding during PLC meetings on how to implement it in their classrooms, the chart indicated that such discussion was not happening frequently. The running record shown in handout 7.2 was completed *after* the second round of professional

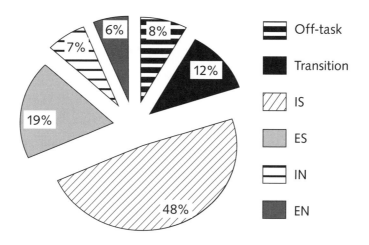

Figure 7.1: Schoolwide aggregate graph of running record results.

development, in which each content-area PLC designed a discussion task (see activity 3.2, page 58) and discussed methods of improvement after every teacher tried it with his or her students.

At a middle school, interdisciplinary teams might decide to observe how students spend an entire day. An observer follows a given student's schedule, completing running records for each class. In some instances, only observing core classes allows for better focus on how the child experiences academics, since an hour of physical education class can inflate the amount of Extraversion/Sensing activity. Sometimes this reveals that nearly every class involves seatwork—or that small-group work was featured in every class with very little Introverted and Intuitive self-management of learning.

Occasionally, a team decides to follow a particular student who seems to be struggling or who performs unevenly. McLaughlin and Talbert (2006) describe one such observation:

> The consultant also used intensive focus on one student learner in the class as a springboard to help teachers rethink their instruction. . . . He had found some success in the math class, but struggled in other subjects . . . she shared her observation that Miguel became quickly bored with basic, repetitive tasks but thrived when engaged in higher-order problem-solving and discussing strategies in all subjects. (p. 53)

Through the lens of type, a PLC might hypothesize that this student prefers Intuition, as did the math intervention children who dodged repetitive tasks. Teachers could then consider adding choices or changing activities in their classrooms to better meet the needs of this child and other Intuitive students—as well as build Sensing students' confidence so that all have access to a rigorous curriculum.

"How Will We Know If They Know It?" and Type

Focusing on learning progressions and knowledge packages (see activity 6.9, "Building a Learning Progression," page 119) often provides PLCs with a more helpful picture of whether, and exactly how, a student falls short of mastery. Using the right kinds of assessments provides feedback to quickly change instruction—more quickly than common written assessments, as important as those may be.

Checking for Biases in the Assessments Used

PLC members can help each other avoid biases in how they assess for mastery and also improve the efficiency of those assessments. Handout 7.3, "Formative Assessments and Learning Styles" (page 153), shows how most of the assessments used for the fractions learning progression (see handout 6.2, "Learning Progression for Fractions," page 126) fit within the learning styles.

ACTIVITY 7.3 Differentiated Formative Assessments

Goal: To help PLCs implement efficient and unbiased formative assessments

Materials: Copies of handout 7.3, "Formative Assessments and Learning Styles" (page 153)

Directions: Ask participants to review handout 7.3. Let them know that they can switch many of the activities to other quadrants by changing from oral to written responses, or by making the activity more or less open ended (Sensing versus Intuition). Use the following prompts for discussion:

- Which of these activities have you used in your classroom? Give examples of similar assessments in your content area.
- Of the activities you haven't used, which would you consider? Why?
- Which activities wouldn't you consider? Why not? Does your hesitation reflect your own learning style to any degree?
- Which of these activities are efficient ways to assess for learning? How quickly would you know whether students have mastered content?
- Which activities allow for instant adjustment in instruction?
- When would you want to use written assessments rather than some of the activity-based assessments given here?
- What concerns do you have about any of these forms of assessment?
- What would you add to the chart? Give examples.

Checking for Biases in How We Mark Assessments

If we are not careful, our own learning styles can keep us from correctly assessing whether students "get it." Many Intuitives report that they got low scores on repetitive tasks because of careless mistakes, so worksheet drills or detailed science lab reports did not always reflect what they learned. We designed the student work sample problem provided in appendix E, "Student Work Samples" (page 195), so that we could quickly discern the difference between lack of understanding and careless mistakes. Jane's preference for Intuition keeps her on the lookout for this—her own careless mistakes with diagramming sentences in seventh grade disqualified her for enrichment-group book discussions.

The importance of this is paramount when you are using assessments to determine which students need more help. Sometimes, telling students, "This is your chance to show us what you know and whether you need more help" is sufficient warning to Intuitives to do their best work. Other times they do not hear what you say—those students are usually the ones who ask questions you answered five minutes ago.

As your group works through activity 7.4, "Discussion Model for Looking at Student Work," monitor the depth of conversation. Coburn and Russell (2008) point out that deep conversations concentrate on the following topics:

- Pedagogical principles underlying instructional approaches

- Nature of students' thinking

- Underlying concepts students need to complete the task

- Understanding of mathematical concepts

When these topics are present, the conversation is focused on how students learn content and what teachers can do to ensure that all students learn.

ACTIVITY 7.4 Discussion Model for Looking at Student Work

Goal: To provide a focused method for examining student work in order to meet the goals of the group or the individual sharing the work

Materials: Appendix E, "Student Work Samples" (page 195), can be used the first time a group uses this protocol. Often, once the group experiences how using the protocol increases knowledge about student learning, their fear of sharing work from their own classrooms greatly decreases.

Directions: Explain that the lens for this discussion will be hypothesizing about students' ability to articulate their thinking and their solution. Other topics could be the rigor of the assignment or the teaching methods used before giving the assessment, but the group needs to negotiate the topic in advance to focus the discussion.

Ask participants to examine the student work samples silently for a few minutes and then choose one to work on to report to the group. Participants should use the following questions to examine the work:

- How would you rank the student's ability to explain his or her thinking? Score them based on the following rubric:

  1. Student explanation does not show mastery of concepts.

  2. Student explains thinking used but without clear mathematical language. Examples include "1/3 equals 2/6" rather than equivalent fractions. Or, "I had to find a number that divides by 3 and 4" rather than common denominator. Or, the explanation details a procedure but does not demonstrate concept mastery.

  3. Student clearly articulates his or her thinking process and mathematics concepts. He or she uses clear, accurate mathematical language such as numerator, denominator, and equivalent fractions.

- What questions might you use to help the student clarify his or her thinking?

- If the work seems to show a careless mistake, what evidence shows possible understanding of the key concept?

- If the work seems to show misunderstanding, what specific concept does the student not understand? How is this evident from the work sample? What might have happened during the instructional process to cause this misunderstanding?

- Could the task be better designed to clarify the difference between careless mistakes and misunderstanding? How?

"What Will We Do If They Don't Get It?" and Type

The preceding math intervention story highlights how important it is to consider type when designing interventions. A few other considerations are also well worth investigating.

Time Considerations and How Students Learn

We frequently show a film of a boy constructing a figure that is one-quarter red and three-quarters yellow. He begins to draw a figure that will end up being one-eighth red. He looks at the problem again and says, "Now I'm starting to get it." He flips the paper over and draws a new rectangle, dividing it into thirds. "I need a new piece of paper," he says as he grabs a fresh piece.

This time, he draws a new rectangle, draws another rectangle inside it that equals one-quarter of the whole shape, adds cross marks to show the fourths, and colors in the squares. Teachers who view the film quickly grasp that this child, who prefers Extraversion and Sensing, learns by purposeful trial and error. He makes sense of the problem by fitting it to reality. Usually, though, a teacher remarks, "I generally stop children like that after their second mistake so they don't get frustrated. I'm not actually helping them, am I?"

Another teacher will add, "Maybe not, but we don't have time for students to try so many different ways." The room usually quickly realizes what has just been said: schools do not allow time for some students to learn.

A basic premise of the principle that effort, not innate talent, creates ability is that students can learn if given expert instruction, time, and support. The danger is that teachers rush to procedures or memorization rather than letting students like this child develop the concept mastery that comes from learning in his or her own style.

One way that PLCs can collaborate to prevent this bias is to constantly review intervention materials, and how they are being used, to ensure that the goal is long-term mastery that students will long remember beyond a test, versus short-term procedural knowledge that students, especially Sensing students, will forget if they cannot tie it to a mastered big idea.

Biases in Reading Interventions

Another bias to be careful of involves students who struggle in reading. Because Sensing students in general hate to guess, they enjoy practicing tasks they can master—reading a text aloud with familiar words more than once, memorizing basic vocabulary sight words, and so on. Intuitive students actually engage at higher levels when asked to memorize words like *isosceles* rather than *ice* even when they struggle to read.

In oral reading, mistakes usually take different forms as well. Sensing students may not want to guess the pronunciation of new words. They pause, ask for teacher assistance, or perhaps start the sentence over as if hoping a running leap will help them recognize the word. Fluency may improve if they are able to glance through a passage before tackling the task.

Intuitives usually happily invent their own pronunciations or even unknowingly substitute words they know for written ones they do not know. Sometimes, they will note from context that their substitution was incorrect and back up to correct themselves.

When PLCs have both Sensing and Intuitive members, sharing stories of their own school successes and struggles can go a long way toward helping teachers help students with the opposite preferences.

"How Will We Extend Learning?" and Type

Finally, type can help teachers challenge students who "get it" the first time. While all kinds of resources on differentiated instruction tackle this issue, the following type-based "big four" strategies work in many disciplines so that all students have access to a rigorous curriculum, whether their pathway to mastery is shorter or longer.

Choices

Choice is a key motivator for students and adults—and teachers can embed choices that differ by personality type and complexity in many, many units. Table 7.1 shows choices a teacher gave for final projects on books students read on utopias and dystopias. Note that the teacher had already differentiated for reading ability by allowing students to choose literature circles based on the book in which they were most interested, from a list of books that differed in length, theme complexity, and reading level. Students also previewed a few pages to ensure they were comfortable with the text.

Table 7.1: Final Project Choices for Utopia/Dystopia Unit

Introversion and Sensing	Introversion and Intuition
Create a test for the book you read. The test should contain ten true/false questions, five multiple-choice questions, and one short-answer question. Provide the answers.	Rewrite the ending of your book. What do you wish would have happened? Start by copying a few lines from the story to "begin" your ending. Then, write the rest of the book as if you were the author. Or, write an additional scene for the book that could have happened but didn't—either during the story or after the book ends.
Complete a timeline for your book. Include important events from the beginning, middle, and end of the story. For each event, provide a drawing or picture, describe what happened in two to three sentences, and describe why the event is important to the story.	Rewrite a key scene from the book as a drama, providing dialogue for the characters. List the setting and character descriptions, and include stage directions.
Make a shoebox diorama of the climax from the book you read. Include at least five objects in the diorama, as well as a background. Write a paragraph that describes the scene to post next to your diorama.	Create a tourist's pamphlet or a PowerPoint "tour" of the utopia or dystopia of your book. What will tourists see? What rules do they need to follow? Summarize the culture.
Write a letter to the author of your book. Give your overall opinion of the book, describe what you liked and disliked, which character you liked best and why, and what you learned. Ask questions about what happened or describe any ways you would change the book.	Create a picture book or video, or use PowerPoint, to retell the story for someone in first or second grade. For videos, turn in an outline of the script.

continued on next page →

Extraversion and Sensing	Extraversion and Intuition
Make an audio or video recording of an interview with a character from your book. Come up with at least ten questions and have the character answer them. Turn in a brief written outline of the questions and answers. Partners who ask the questions can receive extra credit.	Create a recorded monologue (audio or video) of one of the characters of your book. In the monologue, you should discuss the character's experiences, feelings, attitudes, and reactions to the culture and events in the book. Turn in an outline of your monologue.
Assemble a "Hall of Fame, Hall of Shame" poster for the main characters in your book. Draw each character or find a magazine picture. Designate which "Hall" you would assign them to. Under each picture, write down your reasons, with evidence from the story, to support your placement.	Design a game to help players understand what it would be like to live in the culture written about in your book.
Draw a storyboard (comic strip) version of your story from beginning to end, illustrating at least ten major scenes or events. Use dialogue quoted directly from the story or thoughts of the characters.	With a partner, create a newspaper that reports on the final scenes in your book. Articles could include interviews with key characters, editorials or letters to the editor, political cartoons, eyewitness reports, crossword puzzles, or articles that report on story events. These articles must accurately reflect the events of the story.
In a group of no more than four, write a script based on one scene from the book. Videotape the scene. Turn in a copy of the script. It need not have stage and action directions, but the videotape should show evidence of careful rehearsal and thought.	Design a project (poem, sculpture, short video, model, diorama, pop-up book, labeled diagram, and so on) that illustrates a theme of your book. Then, write a full paragraph to answer each of the following questions: • What lesson does the author want readers to learn by the end of the story? • What about the theme is most meaningful to you in your own life? • How does one of the characters grow or change with respect to this theme?

Project-Based Learning

A second great way for PLCs to incorporate "extensions" into a unit plan are projects such as science fair investigations, History Day research, inventing, preparing for speeches, and other rigorous assignments that can easily be designed to tap into student interests. Most students naturally gravitate toward project scopes that match their current ability level—and final product choices can further differentiate for type. Take National History Day, for example. Students can write an in-depth investigation (Introversion and Intuition), create a succinct display (Sensing), or work in a group on a performance (Extraversion and Intuition) or media presentation. Teacher attention is directed toward scaffolding the project for students who need more help in planning, investigating, or otherwise executing the project.

Assignment Menus

Another key strategy is building a menu of learning activities. Nunley (2006) calls this a *layered curriculum* that provides choices based on the complexity of the student's thought process. Students receive a menu for three levels of a curriculum, with points assigned to each task. Students then select from the items until they reach a given number of points. The layers are as follows:

- C Level—Students gather information; choices might include reading, researching, listening to lectures, or completing worksheets.

- B Level—Students apply or manipulate that information; choices might include experimenting, applying the information to a previous situation, writing a story based on the information, or creating an art project.

- A Level—Students critically evaluate an issue related to the information; choices might include investigating open-ended problems, applying learning to current events, resolving decision dilemmas, or creating new knowledge in the area.

How this differs from many tiered assignments is that *all* students complete items from Level A, B, and C. Those who struggle see that even if their Level A choice will be a stretch, they can get a C on the overall unit by completing the Level C assignments—so what they do on the Level A choice is "gravy" for their grade. Intuitive students know from the start by perusing the Level A choices how they will use the information they gather in Level C. Sensing students benefit from the certainty of the process.

Student-Centered Discussions

Reread handout 7.2 (page 152). This discussion took place in a classroom in which only about half the students were at grade level, yet all were engaged in the discussion. The clear structure and directions prepared the Sensing students to make the inferences the assignment required. The Intuitive students enjoyed the chance for word play and the lack of "right answer" emphasis. The more that PLC members can collaborate to increase the incidence of high-level, student-centered discussions in their classroom, the more they allow all students, regardless of reading or math skill level, access to a rigorous curriculum. Activity 5.2, "Evidence-Based Discussions" (page 92), can be modified for use with students to help them focus on text.

Using Type in PLCs: An Equity Strategy

Our goal for PLCs is to ensure that *all* students succeed regardless of where they begin regarding their background, learning style, culture, or gender. Keeping type in mind as PLCs plan instruction, assessment, and intervention helps us avoid biases and keeps us moving toward the overall vision of every student as a motivated, achieving, lifelong learner.

Reflection

1. Where do you recognize yourself in this chapter? Answer the following questions based on your choice:

    •   As a learner. Can you think of times in school where your own learning style put you at a disadvantage? At an advantage? What were the results?

    •   As a teacher. What biases do you need to keep in mind? Which colleagues can you use as a resource?

2. Summarize how using type assists in the goal of equity in education. How might you explain this concept to your PLC?

Handout 7.1

Learning Styles, Favorite Activities, and Motivating Words

Introversion and Sensing	Introversion and Intuition
Motivating activities: Labs Demonstrations Read and think processes Timelines Hands-on manipulatives Programmed learning Computer-assisted learning Direct instruction Clear writing assignments **Motivating words:** read, identify, list, label, name, notice, observe, apply, analyze, graph, examine, work, prepare, do, organize, complete, answer, listen	**Motivating activities:** Reading Research Imaginative or open-ended processes Writing assignments Self-paced tutorials Brain twisters Independent study Independent projects **Motivating words:** read, think, consider, design, evaluate, clarify, speculate, dream, envision, paraphrase, brainstorm, create, elaborate, illustrate, write, reflect, chew on, make connections, compare, contrast, compose
Extraversion and Sensing	**Extraversion and Intuition**
Motivating activities: Videos Group projects Contests Games Skits Songs Physical activities Class reports Hands-on manipulatives **Motivating words:** build, show, assemble, tell, discover, make, demonstrate, figure out, touch, design, suggest, solve, choose, construct, examine, explore, discuss	**Motivating activities:** Problem solving Improvisations, drama, role-play Discussions and debates Experimentation Group projects Working with ideas Field trips Self-instruction Developing models **Motivating words:** create, discover, pretend, design, develop, discuss, synthesize, collaborate, find a new . . . , generate, visualize, evaluate, problem solve, experiment, invent, hypothesize

Source: Kise (2007, p. 48)

Handout 7.2

A Sample Running Record of Classroom Observation

Class: Eighth-Grade English, 31 students

Start Time	End Time	Activity Description	Instructional Minutes					
			Off-Task	Trans-ition	IS	ES	IN	EN
12:04	12:05	Teacher chit-chats with class, laughter		1				
12:05	12:17	Context clues. "Good readers make guesses about word meanings in a millisecond. From that, what do you think context clues are?" "Words around the words?" Silent time to look at example on board. *The misogynist avoided women, did not speak with them or touch them.* "Any guesses?" Students guessed *loser, gay, abstinent, sexist,* and *"womophobic."* Students were asked to clarify their answers, explain more, both by the teacher and by other students. The class agreed, for example, that a gay person did not necessarily avoid women. The student who made up the word *womophobic* was told to spell it. The class then brainstormed parts of the words and possible meanings. One pointed out that the misogynist could be female. No context clue prevented that possibility. Class members said that was good thinking. The teacher gave the dictionary definition and the class agreed that *womophobic* was the closest guess. The teacher then used word parts to show the word for man-hater, misandrist.				2		10
12:17	12:19	Joking about words	1					
12:19	12:22	Instructions for group work on vocabulary for the Vonnegut story they will read. "Go through these words as a group. Identify the part of speech and then look for context clues and word parts. Agree on what you think it means. No one gets a dictionary until you have worked through the process. No silly guesses. And no sluffers, waiting to get the answers."			3			
12:22	12:23	All-class discussion about first word				1		
12:23	12:26	Clarifying questions				3		
12:26	12:40	Individual and group work on context clues					5	9
			1	1	3	6	5	19

Handout 7.3

Formative Assessments and Learning Styles

Introversion and Sensing	Introversion and Intuition
Quickwrite: Write about one way you use fractions. We will quickly share answers. **Task:** To keep your work private, work behind an upright three-ring binder building the following shapes with color tiles. Let's all start with making one that is $\frac{1}{4}$ red, $\frac{3}{4}$ blue. When you've made a shape, raise your hand and I will check it, ask you to explain how your shape fits the problem and provide new tasks ($\frac{1}{2}$ red, $\frac{1}{4}$ blue, $\frac{1}{4}$ green, and so on). **Fingers up:** Let's see if this activity is helping. If you think you really understand how to change improper fractions into mixed numbers, hold up five fingers. If you don't get it, put up zero fingers. If you're somewhere in between, hold up the number that shows how close you are to getting it. **Roll 2 game:** Roll the fractions dice (dice where each face displays a different fraction) and add the two fractions together ($\frac{1}{6} + \frac{4}{6}$). Then, record the equation and your answer on your whiteboard. Repeat at least five times.	**Whiteboard problem:** Draw a circle. Divide it into two equal parts. Now divide one of those parts into two equal parts. To the side, write the fraction name that describes one of the smaller pieces. Explain your answer. **Task:** Make a number line about eighths and label the parts. Also, label a segment that doesn't start at 0 that equals $\frac{3}{8}$. Show where $\frac{10}{8}$ would be. **Task:** Divide your paper into four quadrants. In each quadrant, draw a picture that shows eighths. Clearly mark $\frac{5}{8}$. Only one picture can show a geometric shape. **Quickwrite:** All of you agreed that sharing half a candy bar with another person would be fair—until you saw that the candy bars were different sizes. Explain using math language why sharing candy bars of different sizes is not fair.
Extraversion and Sensing	**Extraversion and Intuition**
Whiteboard problem: If you had 16 cupcakes and wanted to frost $\frac{1}{4}$ of them with red frosting and $\frac{3}{4}$ with green frosting, how many would be red? How many would be pink? **Whiteboard problem:** Use unit bars to show $2\frac{1}{3}$. Rewrite the number as an improper fraction. **Movement activity:** Stand in front of me. Move left if the number I call out is greater than $\frac{1}{2}$. Move right if it is less than $\frac{1}{2}$. Stay put if it equals $\frac{1}{2}$. Don't just move with your friends, because you may be asked to explain how you know!	**Group activity:** You have a set of flash cards with different fractions on them. Work together to rank them from lowest to highest. Be ready to justify your answers. **Group activity:** Create a word problem that involves adding fractions with different denominators. Solve it. Be ready to explain both your answer and why the problem and solution reflect a real-life use of fractions. **Group activity:** With a partner, choose any shape except the hexagon from the pattern blocks. Trace the shape at the top of your paper. If your shape equals $\frac{1}{2}$, what would the whole shape look like? Draw that shape. Do the same for $\frac{1}{3}, \frac{1}{4}, \frac{1}{6}$. If your shape equals 2, what does 1 look like?

APPENDIX A

Descriptions of the Sixteen Types

ISTJ

General Strengths: ISTJs are consistent, hardworking, stable, and sensible educators. They excel at structuring routines and improving what works. They are decisive and dependable, and expect others to be the same.

Value to the PLC	How to Show ISTJs Their Value as PLC Members
Using norms and protocols to help the group be well planned, organized, and on task Cutting through peripheral data with laser-like focus on what will bring results Leading the setting of SMART goals; aligning work to meet goals Mulling relentlessly over problems or issues until solutions emerge	Recognize past and present contributions Acknowledge deep commitment—that they do what they say they will do when they say they will do it Arrive on time, ready to work Answer their questions; address their concerns
Approach to Data	**Approach to Accountability**
Organize data efficiently, develop or improve protocols, and enjoy the process Focus on numerical facts and details Make clear connections between data and standards Use data to close the gap between what students know and what they need to know	Want to be held accountable for clear learning targets with no hidden surprises Align standards, assignments, assessments, and PLC work to help adults help students Make learning goals paramount Use past practice to help guide future work
Pragmatic PLC Activity Preferences	**Communication Style**
Modeling by other teachers; demonstrations directly related to students and content area Reviewing student work samples and developing grading rubrics Engaging in focused action research Receiving implementation details and clear expectations	Prefer to reflect before responding; may not speak until they have a plan Take a businesslike approach in meetings Use a sequential, detailed approach May seem inflexible if no one meets their information needs
What Causes Distress or Discouragement	**Strategies for Relieving Stress**
Others' disregard for protocols, procedures, or checklists, leading to inefficiencies Hard work that does not produce results—they may begin to believe that it does not matter what they do or say	Talk with colleagues about alternative explanations and solutions for student difficulties Work with a colleague to try something new and creative with students that still has a clear learning goal

An ISTJ might say: "I'm willing to work within a PLC if the rest of the group works as hard as I do. Let's be clear about our purpose, our goals, and how we'll know if we reach them. Please know that often my questions reflect my need for clarity about why a proposed change will be better than the present. I'll support it 100 percent if your answers truly support the change."

ISTP

General Strengths: ISTPs bring a wealth of problem-solving knowledge from their own experiences and interests. Their objective, straightforward approach helps them adapt to unexpected circumstances, take risks, and stay flexible.

Value to the PLC	How to Show ISTPs Their Value as PLC Members
Keeping the focus practical and relevant Spotting "red tape" and devising ethical shortcuts Finding logical, efficient ways to get things done Troubleshooting by drawing on prior experiences and storehouses of knowledge	Make room for independence as they seek solutions Honor time frames and objectives; keep meeting time productive and worthwhile Respect silence—it may mean they are still analyzing alternatives Recognize individual contributions

Approach to Data	Approach to Accountability
Stress the use of objective, timely data May enjoy organizing and prioritizing data for PLC use Generate ideas for quick, easy-to-use formative assessments Expect to receive data in useful formats that allow for efficient analysis and decision making	Expect mutual accountability—receiving resources needed to reach goals Want real-time feedback on whether students are making progress Improvise and meet the needs of the moment that support clear long-term goals Need clear expectations for how success will be measured as well as any restrictions on autonomy

Pragmatic PLC Activity Preferences	Communication Style
PLC activities with immediate classroom applications Examining student work to improve task and assessment efficiency and consistency Chances to see or experience lessons or strategies Focused agendas, goals, and conversations	Prefer communication through actions more than words May prefer protocols that provide for reflection or structured brainstorming Emphasize facts, sequential planning, and details Prefer a businesslike approach to meetings and communications

What Causes Distress or Discouragement	Strategies for Relieving Stress
Wasting time in meetings Ignoring logical ideas for improving processes Allowing emotions (theirs or others) to get out of control	Carve out time for your favorite solitary activity, no matter how busy you are Clarify your values—what is most important to you—to stay focused

An ISTP might say: "I hate wasting time, energy, and other limited resources. Show me how our collaboration is improving the efficiency of our efforts toward helping all students succeed. Then give me time to make them even more efficient. You'll find I'm a bit of a walking encyclopedia of past successes that can benefit our new ideas for the future."

ESTP

General Strengths: ESTPs bring a practical, here-and-now orientation to every endeavor. They work to solve immediate problems and make things more efficient while at the same time adding fun and excitement to everyday tasks.

Value to the PLC	How to Show ESTPs Their Value as PLC Members
Focusing on immediate needs and making the most of available resources Being open to new ideas and strategies; pushing to not make decisions too soon Improvising when plans or circumstances change Focusing on facts and truth and asking questions that clarify expectations, tasks, and goals	Recognize their efficiency in getting work done—and join in following through Focus on practical, logical solutions rather than on processing theories Give weight to precedents and prior experiences, not just research Join with them in making learning fun—for adults and for students
Approach to Data	**Approach to Accountability**
Use data to identify practical goals and push them forward Need to see the immediate use of data activities—a logical, practical approach Prefer summaries that highlight relevant numbers so they do not bog down in details Can be persuaded by concrete results from classrooms similar to their own	Recognize a sense of urgency once it is made clear Drive for consistency—grading rubrics, team expectations and policies, and so on Work to identify practical steps to help all students succeed Prefer to tell it like it is—no sugarcoating or excuses for student performance
Pragmatic PLC Activity Preferences	**Communication Style**
Experiencing a practice and then discussing its merits Observing and discussing model lessons they can use immediately Discussing film clips to better understand instructional strategies Developing formative assessments other than pencil-and-paper assessments	Prefer concrete, sequential discussion of events and ideas Drive for accuracy and practicality Question to resolve practical details and implement new practices Maintain focus on solving problems and troubleshooting
What Causes Distress or Discouragement	**Strategies for Relieving Stress**
Anything irrelevant to their own classrooms, especially lengthy, theoretical discussions Overly structured schedules or plans that do not provide immediate results	Pursue favorite activities even if you do not feel you have time for them Find at least one creative outlet that uses your imagination—coaching, planning a remodeling project, or helping students launch a new extracurricular activity

An ESTP might say: "I'll be a willing participant if my PLC gives me practical tools to use in my classroom right away that will help students learn. Show me what to do, answer my questions, let me try it, and if it works I'll come up with improvements and multiple ways to use it. Skip the theories; give me the bottom line."

ESTJ

General Strengths: ESTJs work hard to get results, promoting action through efficient procedures and structures. They focus on facts and reality while at the same time drawing on past experience and traditions to avoid mistakes.

Value to the PLC	How to Show ESTJs Their Value as PLC Members
Focusing on high standards and data to meet goals Organizing the work environment and procedures for efficiency and results Dealing with emotions by evaluating them in terms of solving the problem at hand Anticipating problems, spotting flaws, and planning to correct them in advance	Acknowledge their logical suggestions for how to proceed Recognize that their drive for structure also means they are willing to take responsibility Work with them to clarify goals, timelines, expectations, and roles Note that their plans and schedules often allow teams to have fun along the way
Approach to Data	**Approach to Accountability**
Need objective, proven data sources Work to find efficient ways to use data and stick to them Desire partnering to frame new data questions and ways to probe more deeply Search for new data when workable decisions are not feasible with existing data	Appreciate the structure and uniformity of standards and data-driven decisions Want clear expectations and goals for all students Focus on any process that accurately assesses whether students have learned Value recognition (both positive and negative) of adult and student progress
Pragmatic PLC Activity Preferences	**Communication Style**
Setting clear goals and the path to reach them Learning from real classrooms through modeling, observation, or film clips Action research—choosing a strategy, evaluating results, and improving it Efficiency in readings, discussion, data analysis, and so on	Prefer direct, realistic, matter-of-fact, efficient communication Focus on how to improve results Prefer detailed instructions to reduce chances for error or implementation difficulties Seek clarity and accuracy via a businesslike approach
What Causes Distress or Discouragement	**Strategies for Relieving Stress**
Failing to bring the desired results despite executing an excellent plan Having the incompetence of others reflect on their performance	Engage in physical activities, perhaps with a social component Search for a solution that may prevent the stressful situation from recurring

An ESTJ might say: "I'm driven to get things done. I don't always have to be in charge, but I want to make sure our efforts produce results. Endless processing of new ideas, with no progress on a plan, shuts me down. I'll listen, organize, and reframe group input into a logical framework if we agree on a time frame for making a choice and moving to action."

ISFJ

General Strengths: ISFJs are consistent, duty bound, and loyal. They take on the administrative aspects of group efforts while working to ensure that every person feels valued; they achieve results through positive relationships.

Value to the PLC	How to Show ISFJs Their Value as PLC Members
Working behind the scenes on practical matters as team players	Follow through on details and commitments so that they have time for their creative style
Following through; honoring commitments	Keep the focus of teamwork on helping students learn
Using creativity to improve good processes and employ them in multiple ways	Acknowledge their hard work and dedication in the classroom
Modeling cooperation and consideration of team members	Welcome the people-oriented perspective they bring to decisions
Approach to Data	**Approach to Accountability**
Use data to set work priorities	Want clear expectations for work and for how the PLC will be evaluated
Work to help others understand how data-driven decisions impact people	Work to establish and communicate a clear plan based on student needs
Prefer to use multiple data sources, especially from students they know	Seek hands-on, concrete ways to improve student achievement
Often help organize PLC data for efficient analysis if they are comfortable with numbers	Feel personally responsible for the success of each student
Supportive PLC Activity Preferences	**Communication Style**
Learning by doing in PLC activities	Usually listen well; others may need to ask for their opinions
Seeing how strategies work through observations or modeling	Often communicate their wishes or opinions indirectly
Collaborating on lesson plans from initial design to improvement via looking at student work	May desire protocols that allow time for reflection, questions, and respect
Emphasizing student engagement while planning and evaluating strategies	Focus on harmony, mutual support, and sincerity
What Causes Distress or Discouragement	**Strategies for Relieving Stress**
Taking on more than their fair share of the work when others fail to follow through	Insist that others take on responsibilities, perhaps by talking through boundaries with an objective person
A lack of harmony in PLC interactions or failure to provide clear direction for improving student achievement	Find at least one creative pursuit such as writing, quilting, art, or woodworking

An ISFJ might say: "Although my natural strengths are handling details and following through, don't leave me stranded with all the work that involves. I'll do it all rather than let the group fail, yet that robs me of using my creativity to improve the things that are working well. Working together to add structure to implementing big strategies helps me gain confidence to bring the innovations to my own classroom."

ISFP

General Strengths: ISFPs prefer to work behind the scenes to meet others' needs, foster harmony, and uphold group values. They model compassion and gentleness, preferring to win cooperation through example.

Value to the PLC	How to Show ISFPs Their Value as PLC Members
Putting a face on data, such as the needs of individual students Reminding others of our mission, values, and traditions Helping quietly; providing direct and personal care Adding flexibility to rules and processes	Quietly acknowledge the many practical tasks they accomplish Help them in creating a harmonious, respectful atmosphere Listen to their thoughts on solving immediate, concrete problems Recognize that people are more important than goals or policies
Approach to Data	**Approach to Accountability**
Enjoy analysis and digging into the details—unless math anxiety is present Want clear connections between spending time with data and helping individual students Prefer formative assessment and assignment results to standardized tests Look to include data on the whole child	Focus on what they can do personally to improve student achievement Appreciate vision and leadership toward implementing rigor and a thinking curriculum Hope to influence each child to strive for success Prefer clear goals but flexibility in how goals are met
Supportive PLC Activity Preferences	**Communication Style**
Co-teaching to learn through experiences and to receive immediate feedback A clear PLC focus—limiting the initiatives undertaken at any given moment Collaborating to develop or improve lessons Analyzing results of their own students' recent work	Often prefer to communicate by example, not through words Benefit from protocols that allow for reflection and ensure that all can be heard Concentrate on concrete realities, practical matters, and details May not voice dissenting opinions unless asked by people they trust
What Causes Distress or Discouragement	**Strategies for Relieving Stress**
Conflict that has become a personal attack rather than a dispute about how things will be done Rules or structures that become too restrictive, to the detriment of people	Pull back from meeting others' needs; work with an objective person to set boundaries Interact with the natural world—outdoor activities, gardening, playing with animals

An ISFP might say: "My natural tendency is to go unnoticed in a group, but my students are too important to me; I need to be heard. Give me time to process as we collaborate to set goals and choose strategies. I'll be thinking of the needs of each student and how to ensure they feel valued. When I do speak up, listen carefully. My input reflects a need to influence our overall values and goals."

ESFP

General Strengths: ESFPs add fun and friendship even as they strive to provide personal help to those within their circle of influence. Their easygoing approach to tasks lets them adapt in the moment to unexpected circumstances.

Value to the PLC	How to Show ESFPs Their Value as PLC Members
Providing energy, enthusiasm, and warmth for each encounter Linking people, resources, and practical information to the tasks at hand Focusing on pragmatic, immediate solutions to present problems Reacting quickly when trouble brews; flexibility	Acknowledge that teams are most effective when they enjoy their time together Accept each person as they are—feelings, strengths, values, and worries Be patient—their questions reflect their eagerness to do things right Allow for autonomy, choices, and flexibility in meeting the goals
Approach to Data	**Approach to Accountability**
Motivated to change via insights from their own grade books, formative assessments Appreciate receiving organized data to reduce distraction of too many details Look for evidence that the changes they make motivate students to work harder Interested in data on student attitudes, motivations, and self-efficacy	Strive to see the whole child succeed by emphasizing relationships and caring Seek instructions, details, and support for major instructional changes Thrive when leadership recognizes progress even as they seek improvement Feel personally responsible for the students they serve
Supportive PLC Activity Preferences	**Communication Style**
Modeling and co-teaching; learning through collaboration Planning collaborative lessons and applying strategies in multiple ways Engaging in learn-by-doing activities for text-based discussion, rating task rigor, and so on Focusing on implementation of one or two PLC strategies or ideas at a time	Prefer positive, humorous, enthusiastic communicators May avoid responses that could lead to conflict View experiences as relevant information for decisions Communicate sequentially and incorporate details
What Causes Distress or Discouragement	**Strategies for Relieving Stress**
Tight deadlines, too much structure, and loss of fun in the present moment Speculation, long-range planning, and creative problem solving without concrete application	Find an outlet such as music, crafts, art, or writing to enjoy your own form of creativity Experiment with structured time for health's sake such as exercise, sleep, or family time

An ESFP might say: "Our time together helps me refocus on the broader strategies that lead to student success rather than the day-in, day-out needs of my own students. My frequent questions come from trying to understand how to make new ways work with my own students—please answer them by detailing the information that will help us make the strategies work within our own unique strengths."

ESFJ

General Strengths: ESFJs promote group harmony while at the same time organizing events and initiatives efficiently and predictably. They work to meet others' needs, provide support, and foster cooperation.

Value to the PLC	How to Show ESFJs Their Value as PLC Members
Structuring, organizing, clarifying purpose Focusing on what matters to individuals and teams Plan how to meet the academic, physical, social, and emotional needs of others Handling logistics smoothly with procedures and rules, as necessary, for success	Acknowledge and support their efforts toward group harmony and effective processes Understand that their first concern in decisions is the impact on community Know that a little negative feedback goes a long way Keep sight of traditions and what really works when initiating change
Approach to Data	**Approach to Accountability**
Use data to determine how to help others May enjoy organizing the numbers, depending on their affinity for math Need to see data connected directly to students they currently teach Encourage use of grading rubrics and other tools to establish equity among classrooms	Constantly seek ways to meet the unique needs of each child Advocate for proven protocols, policies, or structures that bring student success Keep the focus on community values and the needs of each person Strive for success of the whole child, not just academic success
Supportive PLC Activity Preferences	**Communication Style**
Studying exemplary lessons, then adapting techniques in multiple, creative ways Observing peers; modeling to learn how a strategy works Examining student work to improve assignments and assessments Covering implementation details, including social aspects of learning	View conversation as opportunity to build relationships and gather opinions Process ideas out loud as they form them and enjoy conversing about them Provide information to prompt action rather than telling people what to do Focus on the positive, but may ignore potential sources of conflict
What Causes Distress or Discouragement	**Strategies for Relieving Stress**
Unappreciated hard work; drained physical and emotional reserves Handling conflict, negative feedback on efforts or ideas, or critical colleagues	Talk through difficult situations with a logical person to seek new perspectives on causes and implications Take care of yourself with a healthy diet, exercise, sleep, and time with friends

An ESFJ might say: "I can keep us organized, on track, and results oriented. I need to know we value each other as individuals and take each other's needs seriously. I do wear my heart on my sleeve because my strengths and hopes are meeting everyone's needs—my colleagues, my students, and my family. I welcome ways to stay objective about my role in student success."

INFJ

General Strengths: INFJs see what ought to be and work to inspire others to catch the vision. Often motivated to help others reach their full potential, they take creative approaches to resolve complex issues that are important to people.

Value to the PLC	How to Show INFJs Their Value as PLC Members
Encouraging others to make a common vision reality Providing creative, future-oriented ideas focused on helping others grow Working independently, managing time and priorities Synthesizing various possibilities to solve complex problems	Set goals within a big-picture framework to create engaged, lifelong learners Join in meaningful activities that promote growth and progress toward goals Work with them to process ideas with a drive toward identified actions Respect each person; allow independence in meeting team goals
Approach to Data	**Approach to Accountability**
Seek comprehensive yet efficient data sources to improve student learning Push to make data accessible and timely Emphasize data that are helpful in assisting individual students Drive for qualitative information to foster student motivation and whole-child focus	Concentrate on values, creativity, and possibilities to help all students Keep the focus on developing student thinking, creativity, and motivation Work to instill in others the belief that all children can learn Design environments and tasks that increase student and teacher confidence
Collegial PLC Activity Preferences	**Communication Style**
Creating and improving lessons and teaching strategies (for instance, Japanese lesson study model) Strategizing for academic interventions Developing and facilitating new PLC activities Studying independently and researching new ideas for teaching and learning	Inspire through ideas, quiet enthusiasm At their best when topics for discussion are set in advance, giving time for reflection Use a big-picture perspective of nonnegotiable items if all students are to succeed Work to bridge differences, synthesize information, and move others forward
What Causes Distress or Discouragement	**Strategies for Relieving Stress**
Systems that treat teachers or students as interchangeable parts; expectations for lockstep implementation Policies or systems that ignore differences in student strengths, needs, and learning styles	Find some alone time before, during, or after school Choose one detail-oriented activity that allows your Intuition to rest—examples are data entry, counted cross stitch, or filing student work

An INFJ might say: "I'll gladly join in the work of PLCs if we can keep in mind that student motivation is just as important as student achievement. I want data that track whether students like school—and enough flexibility in my classroom to ensure that they enjoy the process of meeting learning goals."

INFP

General Strengths: INFPs work to uphold group harmony, values, and ethics. They work tirelessly on the efforts they believe in, focusing on what is compassionate and caring.

Value to the PLC	How to Show INFPs Their Value as PLC Members
Upholding values and ideals by working for them Recognizing the uniqueness of each adult and child Insisting on reflection, especially on unintended consequences, before decisions Building a vision of what can be achieved	Take their unique perspectives seriously Remember that team decisions may impact how children view themselves Balance team efforts between tasks and relationships with each other Give them time to work independently so they have energy for group interactions
Approach to Data	**Approach to Accountability**
May view the spark in a child's eye as the most important indicator of achievement Prefer organized, useful data and may get involved in finding and streamlining sources Motivated by formative assessments to change instruction to help each child Interested in holistic data that shows growth in the whole child	Believe deeply in creating environments in which every child can succeed Frustrated when accountability measures threaten classroom creativity Seek in-depth strategies that resulted in systemic change at similar schools Wary of one-size-fits-all ideas
Collegial PLC Activity Preferences	**Communication Style**
Independent study or work before collaboration Peer coaching and mentoring Case study or lesson study for in-depth learning Exploring multiple strategies and models before setting plans	Persuade through values, emotions, and strength of ideas Appreciate protocols that allow for reflection, formulating thoughts Find too much interaction draining Often use stories or images to convey ideas
What Causes Distress or Discouragement	**Strategies for Relieving Stress**
Taking a stand, based on ideals, that is then ignored or belittled Watching others engage in political maneuvering, act hypocritically, or compromise values	Talk with an objective, trusted friend to find a different, more realistic perspective or logical way to proceed Pursue beading or woodworking that requires logical planning, or find an enjoyable mental puzzle such as chess or Sudoku

An INFP might say: "I view every strategy through the lens of its impact on all students. Will it help those who are ahead of grade level? Behind? Struggling to learn English? Struggling to get three square meals a day? Struggling to find personal meaning in the curriculum? It isn't that I need to be unique if I seem resistant to a strategy; it's that I know all of my students are unique, and I want to create paths for each one to succeed."

ENFP

General Strengths: ENFPs bring energy, enthusiasm, and a wealth of ideas and resources to a group. They inspire others to try innovative strategies while at the same time helping them realize their full potential.

Value to the PLC	How to Show ENFPs Their Value as PLC Members
Modeling strong collaboration skills through facilitation of sharing and valuing input of others Making connections among members, various efforts, and outside resources Building enthusiasm and belief for meeting the needs of all students Believing that collaboration will bring better results than any one person's individual effort	Listen carefully, acknowledge their contributions, and build off each other's ideas Keep team goals, not a given protocol or rule, as top priority Focus on possibilities and problem solving, not barriers, while working to help all students succeed Share their enthusiasm for changes and for maintaining momentum
Approach to Data	**Approach to Accountability**
Need data to be contextual, balanced, and from multiple sources Work to integrate other data in spite of national emphasis on test scores Include personal data about each student, focusing on the whole child Appreciate receiving data summaries organized into useful formats	Support accountability to ensure all students are learning Feel personally responsible for student outcomes Go beyond expectations to assist students Constantly search for better ideas and reject complacency even when results are good
Collegial PLC Activity Preferences	**Communication Style**
Brainstorming to plan and improve lesson plans and teaching strategies Creating chances for students to think deeply while expressing creativity Leading professional development Engaging in peer observations and peer coaching	Focus on the big ideas and on human potential Enthusiastically promote change; may leave details to others Uphold values, group harmony, and impact on people Influence by incorporating the ideas of others
What Causes Distress or Discouragement	**Strategies for Relieving Stress**
Too many details and activities; goals or protocols that detract from natural group progress or strengths Losing sight—as a team—of the big picture, goals, or relationships	Make physical health a priority—exercise, a healthy diet, and sleep Reserve time for relationships, including time with someone who can help balance perspectives

An ENFP might say: "I believe we can do it all and do it well. We can get students excited about learning and motivate them to succeed not just as test takers but as lifelong learners. I'll keep bringing new strategies and ideas until we find what works. I automatically see connections among our efforts, but welcome help in focusing them."

ENFJ

General Strengths: ENFJs motivate others to work together to achieve goals and uphold community values. They see relationships as key to success and are often involved in encouraging and mentoring those around them.

Value to the PLC	How to Show ENFJs Their Value as PLC Members
Facilitating group harmony and respect for all members Maintaining focus on PLC vision, mission, and values Drawing out the best in each teacher and student via modeling and mentoring Communicating vision and ideas in ways that inspire others	Value and make use of team diversity of strengths and perspectives Remember that for them, relationships and harmony come first—it's all about people Respect efforts to keep things positive; celebrate successes and contributions See PLC work as an opportunity for personal growth and learning
Approach to Data	**Approach to Accountability**
Less interested in working with the numbers than in working to improve them Would rather work from summaries of data than delve into all the details Need to include evidence of student engagement, motivation May benefit from putting a "face" on data by analyzing results via a few key children they know	Focus on ensuring success for the whole child, not just academics Work tirelessly to reach each child they serve Fight against strategies that make children feel labeled or otherwise violate core values Take a collective, community approach to helping all students achieve
Collegial PLC Activity Preferences	**Communication Style**
Mentoring or being coached by like-minded souls Collegial lesson planning and improvement Leading or providing input to PLC activities and professional development Focusing on key strategies for student success such as student-centered learning	Connect emotionally with others Listen well and seek to understand other viewpoints More comfortable delivering positive rather than tough messages Gain cooperation through enthusiasm, warmth, and focus on vision
What Causes Distress or Discouragement	**Strategies for Relieving Stress**
Contentious situations, especially if they feel responsible for resolution Violation of core values	Review the situation with an impartial third party to gain perspective on what is not under your control Pursue self-care by meeting with friends and by setting boundaries on responsibilities

An ENFJ might say: "My top two priorities for the community are ensuring everyone feels valued and ensuring our solutions uphold our overarching value of success for every adult and every child. How we treat each other and whether we all enjoy our time together thus become as important as sifting through data and strategies to help students learn."

INTJ

General Strengths: INTJs seek to shift paradigms to enact effective change. They strive for deep understanding of issues and solutions, charting a course to effective implementation through logical planning.

Value to the PLC	How to Show INTJs Their Value as PLC Members
Identifying the big picture for change and plotting a course to get there Leading complex decisions by conceptualizing, clarifying, and communicating to shift paradigms Thinking and acting independent of the status quo Striving to have a positive impact on the future	Pay serious attention to the long-range plans they suggest, while keeping short-term ideas consistent with the big goals Listen to their observations and challenges—it is how they improve ideas Allow for independent work—they need to own goals to care about them Trust their processes toward clear, good decisions
Approach to Data	**Approach to Accountability**
Love using data as the basis for logical, robust decisions Develop strategies to quickly cull out the most useful numbers and systematize analysis Create new assessments or surveys if available data cannot answer questions Prefer objective data but are open to subjective data if collection can be efficient	Hold themselves and everyone else to high intellectual standards View accountability from a systemic level and are concerned with whether the entire school or building is succeeding Work to identify key leverage points for sustainable change Seek continuous improvement in their own classrooms and welcome results-oriented suggestions
Intellectual PLC Activity Preferences	**Communication Style**
Setting ambitious goals and planning and acting to meet them Using data and research to make decisions about instruction Fine-tuning assessments for useful data on what students have and have not mastered Having intellectual discussions focused on informing decisions or practice	Use systems thinking; synthesize and organize ideas Straightforward; focused on strategies or solutions Speak from a prepared, well-formed position, sometimes misinterpreted as arrogance Emphasize unconventional perspectives
What Causes Distress or Discouragement	**Strategies for Relieving Stress**
Failure of careful plans due to unforeseeable circumstances Too much time spent in Extraversion or working with details; arbitrary deadlines	Take time for a project that you can control—garden planning, organizing supplies, and so on Use the senses—exercise, cook, paint, play music; find a reason to laugh

An INTJ might say: "The more audacious the goal, the more engaged I get in planning to bring it to reality. Once we set our sights, don't mistake my single-mindedness for arrogance—I honestly *see* what we need to do to get there. Question me with solid facts or alternatives, and my ears are wide open."

INTP

General Strengths: INTPs thrive on conceptualizing solutions to complex problems and analyzing situations and the theories or models that might provide insights. Their high expectations work to motivate others toward excellence.

Value to the PLC	How to Show INTPs Their Value as PLC Members
Unearthing possibilities and analyzing their merit Developing or applying models and theories Finding errors of logic and long-term consequences of decisions Providing in-depth knowledge and analysis	Allow time for them to thoroughly evaluate options by checking research and theory Do not get defensive at questions—the answers help them clarify mental models Clarify team principles and welcome reminders to uphold them Know that they do not start with a favorite solution—their goal is to find the optimal one
Approach to Data	**Approach to Accountability**
Work to find new questions to ask and better ways to organize data May work independently, delving into data outside of PLC time and sharing results Seldom take numbers at face value; search for factors that might influence data Identify key factors to track for true continuous improvement	Thrive when high standards are the expectation for all Often focus on big strategies rather than day-to-day routines for students Fight against short-term strategies that do not provide for long-term gains Press others to think deeply and focus on systemic factors to improve student achievement
Intellectual PLC Activity Preferences	**Communication Style**
Engaging in independent study and then using PLC meetings to share and apply learning Concentrating in depth on key goals Developing useful tools to measure and improve student learning Strategizing to systemically help students who need more time to learn	Often communicate best in writing by logically expressing their thinking in depth Wait to share until their position is fully formed and they are ready to articulate it Make use of intellect in precise communication of ideas View debate as a healthy forum to improve solutions and strategies
What Causes Distress or Discouragement	**Strategies for Relieving Stress**
Arbitrary or illogical leadership of initiatives, especially if given no voice Emotions allowed to overshadow group purpose and people who fail to listen to reason	Develop a matrix of what others view as important; if empathetic communication would influence them, practice it Spend time with people you care about—preferably at home or other quiet places

An INTP might say: "Every idea benefits from being analyzed from multiple perspectives. I don't pass opinions until I've done that, so humor my questions as I work to compare new ideas to past successes and failures, to the models with which I'm familiar, and to the research I enjoy analyzing in the same thorough way."

ENTP

General Strengths: ENTPs embrace new ideas, motivating others to join in large-scale initiatives for effective change. They are resourceful in solving complex problems and thrive on taking risks to meet challenges proactively.

Value to the PLC	How to Show ENTPs Their Value as PLC Members
Having boundless energy for initiatives they help articulate Showing resourcefulness at finding solutions in which others see only barriers Synthesizing diverse models and approaches to creatively solve problems Meeting challenges proactively	Never assume something cannot be done View team discussions as paths to clear thinking, not as contentious debates Encourage them to take the reasoned risks they propose Allow for individuality as the team strives toward common goals

Approach to Data	Approach to Accountability
More interested in overall trends than detailed analysis Will question data protocols and seek better methods and deeper insights More concerned with critical thinking than the skills standardized tests assess Prefer to receive data summaries along with possible interpretations for use in decisions	Maintain a big-picture focus on frameworks or principles resulting in student achievement Push students for intellectual growth Seek new resources or community partners to improve student success Work to have students take responsibility for their own academic growth

Intellectual PLC Activity Preferences	Communication Style
Applying models and theories to teaching and learning Big-picture planning for rigorous curriculum and in-depth units of study Taking on the leadership role or voice in the PLC Developing expertise in theories or reform proposals key to PLC success	Focus on the big picture of models, theories, and ideas Enjoy intellectual banter and debate Influence others through strength of ideas and personal confidence Seek give and take as well as a critique of opinions, ideas, and possibilities

What Causes Distress or Discouragement	Strategies for Relieving Stress
Too much structure, detailed procedures, or lockstep implementation expectations Refusal to give up even if all options seem closed	Recount the facts of the situation to determine what limits exist Seek balance—time in nature, sleep, a healthy diet, and exercise

An ENTP might say: "PLCs are the perfect environment for the strategic brainstorming I enjoy so much. My ideas may not seem realistic, but at one time neither did landing on the moon. I want to shoot for the stars, but you can help me stay grounded in how to get there so that we make real progress at every step of the journey."

ENTJ

General Strengths: ENTJs mobilize others to meet strategic goals. They thrive on tackling seemingly impossible tasks and organizing systems and structures to solve problems that arise.

Value to the PLC	How to Show ENTJs Their Value as PLC Members
Organizing the PLC to tackle complex problems head-on Finding flaws as a pathway to improvement Pursuing knowledge of both practical strategies and theories Keeping focus on making decisions, setting goals, and measuring progress	Join with them in critiquing options so the team makes the best possible choices Acknowledge their objective, fair-minded viewpoint Keep collaboration efficient and effective and strive to meet goals Take their analysis not as criticism, but as an effort to improve each strategy and idea
Approach to Data	**Approach to Accountability**
Work to establish systems for deep, efficient data analysis Focus on objective data that can be used to measure outcomes Use logical, analytical strengths to probe for the big picture the data present Prefer hard over soft data	Will lead the charge, driving for results in their own classrooms without delay Hold self and others to high standards and visionary goals Constantly strive for better outcomes Take a tough-minded stance, expecting everyone to overcome obstacles to student success
Intellectual PLC Activity Preferences	**Communication Style**
Leading professional development activities Engaging in debate over strategies, lesson plans, and appropriate rules and rubrics Designing common assessments and devising new formative assessment techniques Sifting through expert knowledge and research-based strategies	Direct, efficient, and analytical; impatient with prolonged discussions Keep conversations task-oriented and focused in the interest of time Tend to be direct with feedback, both positive and negative May communicate in terms of models and strategic pathways
What Causes Distress or Discouragement	**Strategies for Relieving Stress**
Feeling powerless to influence decisions or results Situations in which truths, principles, or competencies are disregarded and emotions run high	Talk with a trusted person to identify personal emotions and new possibilities Reflect on the impact of goals, activities, or communication on others—how to develop buy-in or ownership by all

An ENTJ might say: "I'm a team player, but I will take over if I see we aren't making progress toward the goal of student achievement for all. If I'm questioning your ideas, it's because I think they have merit and want to work with you to make them the best they can be. I often can clearly see the steps we need to take to get to our goals."

APPENDIX B

Problem-Solving Model

The framework of personality type provides an excellent, balanced process for the following:

- Making decisions

- Solving problems

- Resolving conflict

Individuals and teams can use this process to include the strengths and key input from each of the functions: facts and history (Sensing); possibilities (Intuition), logical ramifications of each option (Thinking), and community values and commitment (Feeling).

Without a guided process, most people spend too much or too little time on one aspect of decision making. For example, when we use "The Tardiness Dilemma" scenario (page 174) with teams to illustrate the process, the dominant Intuitives in the room jump right to new consequences or ways to motivate students to come to class on time without defining the real problem. Often, decisions are made based on Thinking criteria (cost, schedules, and efficiencies) with almost no attention paid to Feeling criteria (who is committed or how various individuals might be affected). Or, a group goes with the solution that seems obvious without taking enough Intuitive time to generate other options.

For teams to use the model effectively, they need to (1) see evidence of the team blind spots and how the model helps members compensate, and (2) practice. At first, the steps can be time-consuming because people with different preferences may disagree about whether the correct input is being given at various stages (we have had dominant Sensing types reject whole lists of "facts" generated by dominant Intuitives because they were really hunches or extrapolations from the data). Therefore, we suggest the following process.

Step 1: Practice Problem

"The Tardiness Dilemma" scenario on page 174 works well for groups to practice problem solving. Group experiences with a sample scenario usually provide sufficient evidence that the time spent on using the model is worthwhile. You can use a real-life dilemma as well. Handout B.1, "Problem-Solving Model" (page 177), contains nine different prompt questions for each stage of the process. Choose two to three of the most relevant prompts for the situation.

Begin by asking individuals to identify their dominant function, using handout B.2 on page 178, and then form groups by dominant function. Provide each group with four pieces of flip-chart paper and a marker. Ask them to write *Sensing* at the top of one paper, *Intuition* on the second, *Thinking* on the third, and *Feeling* on the last.

The Tardiness Dilemma

Read the following scenario to the team:

Teachers at a secondary school examined attendance data and noticed a sharp rise in student tardiness during the previous school year. There were few changes to the demographics of the student body, but a significant percentage of teachers were new to the building that year. Some teachers believe that PLCs should focus on reducing tardiness for the coming year.

Ask every group to concentrate on the Sensing prompts for five minutes. For the "Tardiness Dilemma," the Sensing prompts are as follows:

- What are the facts of the situation?

- How is the problem best defined?

Ask the Sensing group to report first because this is their strength. Usually, their lists are short and accurate; the short dilemma contains few facts. For contrast, have the Intuitive group go next and ask the Sensing types to determine the quality of their list. Intuitives usually proceed directly to possible solutions. Or, their lists are full of assumptions that they do not realize they're making. Then ask the Feeling and Thinking groups to report, again allowing the Sensing group to comment on items they do not view as factual. Feeling types often present opinions as facts. Usually, the facts of the Thinking group are quite accurate.

Then move to the Intuition step. Again, ask all groups to work on the same prompts, this time writing their ideas on the paper marked *Intuition*:

- What are possible ways to solve this dilemma?

- Is this problem analogous to other situations you can think of? Does the analogy provide new ways of thinking of solutions?

This time, have the Intuitive group report first since possibilities are their strength, and then the Sensing group as this step is the hardest for them. Intuitive groups usually generate the most options; they latch onto a theme such as, "Oh, we need to motivate students; we could . . ." Sensing types usually generate the fewest options unless they have a clear problem definition; their analogy is usually focused and practical. Thinking types might put forth one solution and stop, sure that it is the best. Feeling types often generate ideas about involving students in the process ("Let's get a focus group of frequently tardy students. What would motivate them to get to class on time?").

Continue in the same fashion with the Thinking function. The group now has a list of possibilities. How will members decide which is best? Use the following prompts:

- What criteria should we use in making the decision?

- What precedents might we be setting?

Let the Thinking group report first. They usually generate clear criteria: cost, counselor time, and so on. Intuitive and Feeling types often struggle to think of criteria; they frequently ask for examples. Sensing types may not generate as many as the Thinking types but will usually have one or two that are objective.

The last step uses the Feeling function. Remind your team that no matter what solution seemed the best using Thinking criteria, they are now to reconsider the list using Feeling criteria. Sometimes, the best Thinking choice is eliminated completely once they apply the Feeling criteria. Use the following prompts:

- How do the proposed solutions fit with community values?

- Do we have buy-in to the proposed solutions? Will the staff carry out what we decide?

Often, the Feeling group reports a process for gaining group consensus, even suggesting that students or teachers be polled. Thinking types may discount this step if they've provided logical criteria and struggle to come up with other ways to judge the options. Sensing types may struggle with so much processing time and just want to take action. Intuitive types often talk about motivating the team by appealing to the mission statement—they may talk about persuasion rather than building consensus.

Step 2: Work on a Real Problem

In preparing to focus on a real problem, choose two to three prompts for each step of the process from handout B.1 (page 177).

Once your team has learned to use the model, the whole group can work on the process simultaneously. Ask the dominant function members to assess whether a step is complete; for example, the dominant Sensing types on the team would bring closure to the Sensing step.

However, remember that when a type preference is a clear majority, team members with the opposite preference may mask their opinions. Make sure that you seek out the minority opinion. You might do so in any of the following ways:

- Consider allowing two to three minutes of reflection at each stage of the process so that Introverted team members have a chance to form their thoughts (announcing the topic in advance of the meeting can help them prepare).

- Use the dominant group process described in the "Tardiness Dilemma" example. While this takes more time, the groups often do a better job of contributing through their strengths when working alone.

- Formalize the process of checking the reactions of the team members with preferences least like the "team type," perhaps providing extra time for them to prepare a response.

This book provides several examples of how to use this model, including the following:

- Setting a vision, page 94

- Setting PLC goals, page 113

- Discussing conflict, page 117

Handout B.1

Problem-Solving Model

Sensing

- How can we best define the problem?

- What are the facts? Who? What? When? Where? Why?

- Which facts are verifiable? (By a clock, a budget, test results, survey, and so on)

- How did we get into this situation?

- What have you or others done to resolve this or similar problems?

- What already exists and works?

- What has already been tried or done? By whom?

- How would a nonbiased individual view the situation?

- What resources are available?

Thinking

- What objective criteria need to be satisfied?

- What is the practicality of each alternative?

- What are the pros and cons of each possibility?

- What are the logical consequences of the options?

- What are the costs of each alternative?

- What is the most reasonable course of action?

- Would this option apply equally and fairly to everyone?

- What are the consequences of not deciding and acting?

- What impact would pursuing each option have on other priorities?

Intuition

- What are the connections to larger issues or other people?

- What other ways are there to look at this?

- What are the possible solutions or ways to approach the problem?

- What insights and hunches do you have?

- What is this problem analogous to?

- What other directions can be explored?

- What would be other possibilities if there were no restrictions?

- What do the data imply?

- What theories address this kind of problem?

Feeling

- What is the "fit" with personal and organizational values?

- How will the outcome affect the people, process, or organization?

- How will each option contribute to harmony and positive interactions?

- What are the underlying values involved in each choice?

- What are your personal reactions (likes and dislikes) to each alternative?

- How will others respond?

- Who is committed to carrying out the solution?

- How will people be supported if this decision is made?

- How will this affect my own priorities?

Handout B.2

Order in Which the Four Functions Develop

D: dominant function   T: third or tertiary function

A: auxiliary function   I: inferior function

ISTJ	ISFJ	INFJ	INTJ
D: Sensing A: Thinking T: Feeling I: Intuition	D: Sensing A: Feeling T: Thinking I: Intuition	D: Intuition A: Feeling T: Thinking I: Sensing	D: Intuition A: Thinking T: Feeling I: Sensing
ISTP	**ISFP**	**INFP**	**INTP**
D: Thinking A: Sensing T: Intuition I: Feeling	D: Feeling A: Sensing T: Intuition I: Thinking	D: Feeling A: Intuition T: Sensing I: Thinking	D: Thinking A: Intuition T: Sensing I: Feeling
ESTP	**ESFP**	**ENFP**	**ENTP**
D: Sensing A: Thinking T: Feeling I: Intuition	D: Sensing A: Feeling T: Thinking I: Intuition	D: Intuition A: Feeling T: Thinking I: Sensing	D: Intuition A: Thinking T: Feeling I: Sensing
ESTJ	**ESFJ**	**ENFJ**	**ENTJ**
D: Thinking A: Sensing T: Intuition I: Feeling	D: Feeling A: Sensing T: Intuition I: Thinking	D: Feeling A: Intuition T: Sensing I: Thinking	D: Thinking A: Intuition T: Sensing I: Feeling

In the chart, the preference, or function, listed immediately following the four-letter type code is referred to as the *dominant* function. For example, for ISTJ, Sensing is the *dominant* function. Find your own dominant function and think back to childhood. How would adults who knew you best have described you?

- Dominant Sensing types often agree that they were known as sensible or matter-of-fact children.

page 1 of 2

- Dominant Intuitive types were often viewed as imaginative children (or as daydreamers).

- Dominant Thinking types were often known for asking questions, wondering "Why?" and "How?"

- Dominant Feeling types were often seen as empathetic children, aware of the feelings of others and concerned that everyone be included.

Now look at the next function in the list, which is the *A*, for *auxiliary*, function. If the dominant function describes how you take in information (Sensing or Intuition), then the auxiliary function balances this with your preferred method for making decisions (Thinking or Feeling). If the dominant function describes how you make decisions, the auxiliary function describes how you take in information. As you develop your first two preferences, you gain balance between these two processes.

Further, if you prefer Extraversion, you use that dominant function in the outer world—when you are acting and interacting with others. If you prefer Introversion, you use that dominant function in the inner world—when you have chances for reflection. We use our second, or auxiliary, function in the opposite world. To use our second functions—to ensure we are both taking in information and coming to closure—means we all need time alone and time with others, which is a key realization for all educators.

APPENDIX C

Reading on Student Motivation

Anticipation Guide

What Do You Know About Student Motivation?

Write an *A* in the blank if you *agree* with a statement. Write a *D* in the blank if you *disagree* with a statement.

_____ **1.** Artists are born, not made.

_____ **2.** Part of our genetic makeup is our intellectual capacity—how smart we are.

_____ **3.** One of the differences between advanced students and those who are at or below grade level is the speed with which they learn.

_____ **4.** Teachers behave differently toward students they believe are smart and students they believe have a limited learning capacity.

_____ **5.** Students who believe they are unintelligent direct attention away from their inadequacy by either boasting about possessions or other talents, or attempting to play by different rules.

_____ **6.** Students who develop good problem-solving strategies continue to use and improve them while working on increasingly more difficult tasks.

_____ **7.** If students believe that they can master tasks if they try hard enough, they continue working on a problem despite repeated failure.

_____ **8.** Student performance is affected by whether tasks emphasize performance or learning.

_____ **9.** Students who believe that their academic ability is fixed have little interest in pursuing challenging tasks for fear of showing inadequacy, even if they are capable of succeeding on them.

_____ **10.** Students have a natural tendency to either pursue tasks with low risk for failure or ones that have a higher risk for failure but bring about new learnings.

_____ **11.** Many students believe that if they have to work hard at a task, they must not be very smart.

Anticipation Guide Instructions

Goal: To help students access prior knowledge, work as a group to pool knowledge, justify conclusions, and generate hypotheses

Directions:

1. For a given text excerpt, article, or short story, generate several declarative statements. For middle grades, eight to ten statements is a good number; for the primary grades, you might use fewer statements.

2. Ask students to read through the statements individually, marking whether they agree or disagree.

3. In groups, ask students to share information and debate ideas. You can moderate the discussion, but should not give hints or state whether you agree or disagree.

4. Ask students to read the text to get more information.

5. Direct students to review and revise the statements and discuss how their thinking has changed.

Type Connections:

Thinking students love to debate and provide support for their views. This exercise also provides important practice in these skills for Feeling students.

This exercise also gives Extraverted students a chance to process out loud the information they will be reading for, making it easier for them to engage in the more Introverted activity of reading.

Sensing students and Intuitive students will probably bring different kinds of prior knowledge to bear on the statements. Intuitive students may go more with hunches and connections instead of facts they've read or gathered through sources such as television or other coursework. Sensing students may hesitate to take a position without clear facts. Using the language of Sensing and Intuition could be helpful as students discuss and compare their ideas.

How Do Students Get Smart?

Can you draw? Most of us will clearly answer *yes* or *no* to that question. We've learned that artistic ability is something you either have or haven't got. Yet Betty Edwards, an art teacher in New York, succeeds in teaching all of her clients to draw. What is startling is that she can look at your first attempts and determine how old you were when you quit trying to draw. Either someone told you that you weren't very good at it, or you learned that drawing was not a valued skill for schoolwork, so you stopped working at it. Effort, plus expert instruction, creates artistic ability (Schwartz, 1995).

Are you smart? Can you get smarter?

For centuries, school systems in the United States have operated on the assumption that the answer to the latter question is *no*. At an early age, students judge which of their peers are smart or not so smart by the way they are grouped, the tasks and leadership roles they are given, and the patterns in how teachers call on them. They echo the adults in their lives who say things like, "I'm not good at math," "I can't give speeches," or "I just can't sit still with a book."

When we talked with at-risk students about how they differ from students who get good grades (notice we did not say smarter), they told us the following:

- They get to keep learning new things. We're stuck with the same old.
- Teachers pay more attention to them.
- They blurt the answers so fast we don't have a chance.
- They don't even try, and they get As.
- They've been a teacher's pet at some time.
- I don't learn. I watch.
- By the time I'm ready, all the good answers are taken.

Paraphrase their comments. In a nutshell, "Smart students learn effortlessly and get to do all kinds of interesting things. It takes me more time, so I must be dumb. If I learned fast, teachers would like me more."

Is smart all about being fast? Thomas Edison would be shocked to hear that, since it took him over two years, three thousand theories, and six thousand tries before he developed a commercially viable light bulb. (Incidentally, Edison, who had hearing problems and was bored by rote memorization, was labeled a misfit and dropped out of school at age twelve.)

page 1 of 5

The students we spoke with internalized that they were not cut out to be good students. And students live up to expectations—their own and those of their teachers. The frightening result of assuming that "smart" is something innate is that teachers actually change how they treat students when they are told how "smart" or "dumb" the students are. Feinberg (2004) reports:

> One study at Columbia University took two groups of college students and asked them to act as teachers. In the first group, subjects were told that intelligence was fixed and innate; the second was told that intelligence could be cultivated. "What we saw bowled us over," said Carol Dweck, the Ransford Professor of Psychology at Columbia. "The fixed intelligence group really humored their underachievers, complimenting them as much as possible to make them feel good." But the teachers with the malleable intelligence mindset did something quite different. Instead of praising the children at every turn, Dweck found that teachers started meeting with the students, trying to diagnose what went wrong. "They felt it was worth thinking up every possible way to help that child improve." (p. 4)

Up until now, school structures in the United States have thus reinforced that students are or are not smart. So-called smart students are given challenging curricula, and teachers expect good results. Other students are given lower-level work without being taught to think and reason. Their lack of ability to do so is then cited as evidence that they cannot learn at higher levels. Low expectations mean they never received rigorous instruction. But what if intelligence isn't fixed?

Resnick (1999) summarizes how research in cognitive science and social psychology is merging to provide an entirely different way of looking at intelligence. Cognitive science concludes, "Intelligence is the habit of persistently trying to understand things and make them function better. . . . Intelligence is knowing what one does (and doesn't) know, seeking information and organizing that information so that it makes sense and can be remembered" (p. 2). Think how different this is from the comments of the at-risk adolescents who believed that smart meant instantaneous knowing!

Whether students think intelligence is innate or that effort creates ability actually changes how they tackle tasks. Dweck and Leggett (1988) studied changes in the cognition, affect, and behavior of children as they moved from tasks they could easily succeed on to those that were far more difficult. They noted two patterns: mastery oriented and helpless. If anything, the helpless children were slightly more proficient at the tasks everyone could do easily. However, when the work grew difficult, they did the following:

- Quickly attributed their failures to personal deficits in intelligence, memory, or problem-solving ability

- Complained of being bored, hating the task, or having anxiety even though they'd enjoyed the first tasks

- Made comments unrelated to the tasks (more than two-thirds of them), such as altering the rules, or bragging about sports or how much money they had, apparently wanting to otherwise feel successful

- Lapsed into ineffective problem-solving methods instead of continuing with the mature, useful strategies they'd used on the easier problems

In contrast, the mastery group:

- Verbalized to themselves such comments as, "I'll have to keep trying" or "This one takes more concentration"—they viewed the problems as challenges to master.

- Made optimistic statements (two-thirds of them), such as "I did it before, I can do it again," or "I'm almost there."

- Stayed positive and enjoyed the challenge

- Increased the complexity of the strategies they tried even if they failed to solve the very last problems

In other words, the students who think that effort creates ability keep putting in effort. Those who believe that ability is fixed see no point in trying. The good news is that teachers can create classroom atmospheres in which students learn that effort creates ability. Saphier (2005, p. 97) chronicles the beliefs that need to change, as shown in the following table.

In an ability-based atmosphere . . .	In an "effort creates ability" atmosphere . . .
Mistakes are a sign of weakness.	Mistakes help us learn.
Speed counts—faster equals smarter.	Care, perseverance, and craftsmanship count.
Good students do it by themselves.	Good students need help and a lot of feedback.
Inborn intelligence is the main determinant of success.	Effort and effective strategies are the main determinants of success.
Only the bright few can achieve at a high level.	Everyone is capable of high achievement.

The good news is that students can be taught to put in the kind of effort that creates ability. Saphier (2005) suggests focusing on the following with students, based on a model developed by Jeff Howard of The Efficacy Institute (www.efficacy.org):

- Do students understand the *time* and effort required for quality work?

- Are students able to *focus* on work? What skills could we help them develop in this area?

page 3 of 5

- Are students *resourceful* when they need help? Do they know where to go and who to ask?

- What *strategies* do they have for academic tasks?

- Do they seek and accept *feedback?* Do they use it to improve their performance?

- Are they *committed* to trying hard?

Being willing to try may be the hallmark of those who know that effort creates ability, but that hard work must pay off. Teachers need to design tasks so that students succeed. That success then embeds the belief "If I work hard, I can do it."

In the popular book *Outliers: The Story of Success,* Malcolm Gladwell (2008) probes how effort, ability, and culture interact to produce greatness. In fact in most endeavors, hard work is more important than talent. He documents how seven thousand more hours of practice differentiates piano virtuosos from piano teachers. Breakout musical groups like the Beatles put in ten thousand hours of practice before anyone heard of them. Bill Gates, founder of Microsoft, had logged more hours of programming by the age of fifteen than most professionals and eventually dropped out of Harvard to start his own company.

Gladwell devotes a chapter to learning mathematics, describing how cultures differ in their attitudes toward math. In some cultures, such as the United States, the prevailing attitude is that you either are or are not good at math. In others, including most Asian cultures, the prevailing attitude is that anyone can learn math if they work hard.

He cites the work of Alan Schoenfeld, a professor at Berkeley, who through filming students found that math is not so much ability as attitude. Students mastered mathematics concepts if they were willing to try. Gladwell (2008) summarizes:

> Schoenfeld attempts to teach his students that success is a function of persistence and doggedness and the willingness to work hard for twenty minutes to make sense of something that most people would give up on after thirty seconds. [Get students to persevere] in a classroom, and give them the space and time to explore mathematics for themselves, and you could go a long way. (p. 246)

He compares this attitude to cultures around the world. Many Asian cultures are grounded in rice patty farming; farmers there say, "No one who can rise before dawn 360 days a year fails to make his family rich." Growing rice takes almost three times the effort of corn or wheat, where fields sit dormant for months. Machinery is no substitute for manual labor in that delicate environment, yet the labor brings a direct return of higher yields. Effort is worth it.

An interesting correlation exists when one looks at performance on the Trends in International Mathematics and Science Study (TIMSS) test. Countries with students who have the patience to fill out the 120-question general information before the mathematics questions are the ones with the highest scores on the test. Gladwell (2008) summarizes:

> Think about this another way. Imagine that every year, there was a Math Olympics in some fabulous city in the world. And every country in the world sent its own team of one thousand eighth graders . . . we could predict precisely the order in which every country would finish in the Math Olympics without asking them a single math question. All we would have to do is give them some task measuring how hard they were willing to work. (p. 248)

In other words, effort creates ability. Every goal worth pursuing (for example, career, relationships, or moral strivings) at some point poses risks or perceived barriers. Our students need to believe that "Smart isn't something you are, but something you get," if they are to be successful in and out of the classroom.

References

Dweck, C. S., & Leggett, E. L. (1988). A social-cognitive approach to motivation and personality. *Psychological Review, 95*(2), 256–273.

Feinberg, C. (2004, Spring). The possible dream: A nation of proficient schoolchildren. *Ed. Magazine.* Accessed at www.efficacy.org/Resources/TheEfficacyLibrary/tabid/227/Default.aspx on October 24, 2009.

Gladwell, M. (2008). *Outliers: The story of success.* New York: Little, Brown and Company.

Resnick, L. B. (1999). Making America smarter. *Education Week Century Series, 18*(40), 38–40. Accessed at www.edweek.org/ew/vol-18/40resnick.h18 on August 27, 2009.

Saphier, J. (2005). Masters of motivation. In R. DuFour, R. Eaker, & R. DuFour (Eds.), *On common ground: The power of professional learning communities* (pp. 85–113). Bloomington, IN: Solution Tree Press.

Saphier, J., Haley-Speca, M. A., & Gower, R. (2007). *The skillful teacher: Building your teaching skills.* Acton, MA: Research for Better Teaching.

Schwartz, T. (1995). *What really matters: Searching for wisdom in America.* New York: Bantam Books.

APPENDIX D

Academic Rigor Reading

What Is Rigor?

Compare the following two sets of history questions from standardized examinations. If you teach courses that prepare students for these tests, how might instruction be the same or different for the questions on the left? On the right? What texts might you need? Would there be differences in course scope and sequence? Which requires more rigorous instruction?

Write an essay to answer one question from each grouping of questions.	Answer two prompts, each chosen from a different topic (the test provides six topics with five prompts each for a total of thirty questions to choose from—see the following examples). The prompts must be answered with reference to events and developments in the twentieth century.
Group 1 **1.** Analyze the impact of the rise of militarism and the Second World War on the lives of European women. In your answer, consider the period 1930–1950. **2.** Considering the period 1953–1991, analyze the problems within the Soviet Union that contributed to the eventual collapse of the Soviet system. **3.** Analyze the problems and opportunities associated with the rapid urbanization of western Europe in the nineteenth century. **Group 2** **1.** Analyze the factors that prevented the development of a unified German state in the sixteenth and seventeenth centuries. **2.** Britain and France were engaged in a geopolitical and economic rivalry during the eighteenth century. Identify the factors that contributed to this rivalry and assess the results for both countries over the period 1689–1789. **3.** Identify the grievances of the groups that made up the Third Estate in France on the eve of the French Revolution and analyze the extent to which one of these groups was able to address its grievances in the period 1789–1799. (A final section of this test asked students to analyze short quotes from a dozen primary sources to write an essay on a culture's view of child raising.) *Source: The College Board (2007)*	**Topic 1: Causes, practices, and effects of war** **1.** Account for either the defeat of the Central powers in the First World War or the Axis powers in the Second World War. **2.** To what extent do you agree with the view that war accelerates social change? **3.** Evaluate the contribution made toward the war effort by civilians on both the home front and the battle front in two wars, each chosen from a different region. **4.** Compare and contrast the reasons for, and impact of, foreign involvement in two of the following: Russian Civil War, Spanish Civil War, or Chinese Civil War. **5.** Peace settlements create conditions for new conflicts. With reference to at least two settlements, explain the extent to which you agree with this statement. **Topic 2: Nationalist and independence movements, decolonization, and challenges facing new states** **Topic 3: The rise and rule of single-party states** **Topic 4: Peace and cooperation: international organizations and multiparty states** **Topic 5: The cold war** **Topic 6: The state and its relationship with religion and with minorities** *Source: IB Diploma Programme (2005)*

page 1 of 4

Is there a difference between the two tests? What is rigor?

In an *Education Week* article titled "Rigor on Trial," Tony Wagner (2006) described his experiences with a group of school principals who met to develop a rubric for assessing academic rigor at all levels. Together they visited classrooms, individually ranking them for rigor and then discussing their results. No one agreed. Educators do not have a common understanding of what rigor means. The group Wagner worked with decided that rigor ties to the abilities students need *after* they graduate. How does our society define an educated adult? What education helps us become good citizens and successful workers? Advanced math classes? Advanced Placement classes? Wagner (2006) reports:

> Here's what we discovered: rigor has less to do with how demanding the material the teacher covers is than with what competencies students master as a result of the lesson. We agreed on this because in our journey, our "rigor rubric" changed from teacher-centered observations to a set of questions we asked students. In classrooms, we chose students at random and asked,
>
> 1. What is the purpose of this lesson?
>
> 2. Why is this important to learn?
>
> 3. In what ways are you challenged to think in this lesson?
>
> 4. How will you apply or communicate what you've learned?
>
> 5. How will you know how good your work is and how you can improve it?
>
> 6. Do you feel respected by other students in this class?
>
> 7. Do you feel respected by the teacher in this class?
>
> Discussing these questions with students let us see all the courses we'd observed in a new light, especially the Advanced Placement classes. In virtually all the AP classes we visited, teachers were covering more academic content at a faster pace. But the primary competency students were being asked to master was memorizing copious amounts of information for the test. Teachers' questions to students tended to be almost entirely related to factual recall. By our measures, not a single one of the AP classes we saw was sufficiently rigorous to prepare students for work, citizenship, and continuous learning in today's world. (p. 28)

Look back at the test question examples (page 1). The ones on the left came from Advanced Placement tests. What is the relationship between these questions and the teaching methods Wagner saw? What competencies will be mastered? Will students be prepared to do the work of historians, the work that college requires, and the work that employers will hire them to do?

Following up on his experiences in defining rigor, Wagner (2008) researched what corporate executives were really looking for in graduates. One told him, "We can teach the technical stuff. But for employees to solve problems or to learn new things, they have to know what questions to ask. And we can't teach them how to ask good questions—how to think. The ability to ask

page 2 of 4

the right questions is the single most important skill" (p. 2). Other executives added the abilities to engage in good discussions and critical thinking.

Karen Bruett, a high-level executive at Dell Computer Corporation, paints a succinct picture of what is expected of graduates:

> Work is no longer defined by your specialty; it's defined by the task or problem you and your team are trying to solve or the end goal you want to accomplish. Teams have to figure out the best way to get there—the solution is not prescribed. And so the biggest challenge for our front-line employees is having the critical-thinking and problem-solving skills they need to be effective in their teams—because nobody is there telling them exactly what to do. They have to figure it out. (as cited in Wagner, 2008, p. 14)

In other words, our students need to be able to work in teams, gather information (which will not be handed to them), determine what is important, and choose among alternatives they themselves generate. Students need to be able to think in order to face the rigorous demands of the workforce. They need to be lifelong learners.

Barth (2005) describes how he came upon a group of senior honors students who had finished all their final exams. They were dumping all of their notes and books into a flaming trash can, celebrating that they wouldn't need them anymore. He pondered how these students were at risk of leaving school with little likelihood of lifelong learning:

> I once saw an estimate that 50 years ago students graduated from high school knowing 75% of what they would need to know for the rest of their lives—in the workplace, in their families, and for life in general. The estimate today is that graduates of our schools leave knowing perhaps 3% of what they will need to know in the future. And yet they leave school today knowing far more than they did 50 years ago. (p. 117)

In other words, the rigor needed in the real world is discovering what you need to know and then learning it. Barth (2005) concludes:

> Clearly the most basic graduation requirement, then, is that our students leave each grade and each school imbued with the qualities, dispositions, and capacities of insatiable, lifelong learners. The students who do will acquire that 98% yet to come and will thrive. Those who burn their books will be relegated to the periphery of the 21st Century. (pp. 117–118)

Plaut (2009) expands the usual notion of literacy associated with standardized tests to also include students' abilities to analyze sources, examine issues from alternative perspectives, understand whose perspectives are missing, and take a stand. Plaut works with others who consider literacy a civil right, with students having a right to an education that provides the following:

- Active *engagement* with content worthy of sustained attention
- Thorough *thinking* about that content

- Deep *understanding* of key concepts in core content
- Increased *independence* through skills they can use to make meaning of current and future content and contexts
- Access to *relevant* knowledge
- *Power* to participate in a democracy—to interact with, influence, and transform their world (pp. 2–3)

In science, this kind of literacy involves forming hypotheses and following through on inquiry. In mathematics, it involves complex, nonalgorithmic thinking with no predictable or rehearsed approach; students need to explore and understand mathematical concepts and the connections among them (Stein, Smith, Henningsen, & Silver, 2009).

What is rigor? Wagner (2006) asks if academic tasks ready students to sit on a jury. Are you satisfied that your students could analyze arguments, sift through evidence, understand when witnesses provide facts or opinions, balance justice and mercy, and communicate clearly? Take a look at curriculum with that goal in mind, or the needs expressed by corporate executives, as you work to define rigor in your content area.

References

Barth, R. S. (2005). Turning book burners into lifelong learners. In R. DuFour, R. Eaker, & R. DuFour (Eds.), *On common ground: The power of professional learning communities* (pp. 115–133). Bloomington, IN: Solution Tree Press.

The College Board. (2007). *AP European history free-response questions.* New York: Author. Accessed at http://apcentral.collegeboard.com/apc/members/exam/exam_questions/2085.html#name07 on October 23, 2009.

International Baccalaureate Diploma Programme. (2005). *History higher level and standard level: Paper 2.* Accessed at www.ibo.org/diploma/curriculum/examples/samplepapers/documents/gp3_historyhlsl2.pdf on October 24, 2009.

Plaut, S. (Ed.). (2009). *The right to literacy in secondary schools: Creating a culture of thinking.* New York: Teachers College Press.

Stein, M. K., Smith, M. S., Henningsen, M. A., & Silver, E. A. (2009). *Implementing standards-based mathematics instruction: A casebook for professional development* (2nd ed.). New York: Teachers College Press.

Wagner, T. (2006). Rigor on trial. *Education Week, 25*(18), 28–29.

Wagner, T. (2008). *The global achievement gap: Why even our best schools don't teach the new survival skills our children need—and what we can do about it.* New York: Basic Books.

APPENDIX E

Student Work Samples

A Baking Problem

You are making cookies. The recipe says to combine $\frac{1}{2}$ cup butter with $\frac{3}{4}$ cups chocolate chips and $\frac{3}{8}$ cups butterscotch chips. Here are some questions.

1. When these ingredients are mixed together, how many cups of cookie dough will you have? Show your work. Explain your thinking.

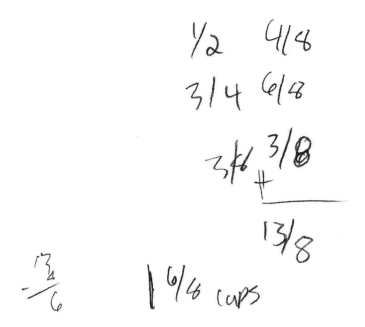

A Baking Problem

You are making cookies. The recipe says to combine $\frac{1}{2}$ cup butter with $\frac{3}{4}$ cups chocolate chips and $\frac{3}{8}$ cups butterscotch chips. Here are some questions.

1. When these ingredients are mixed together, how many cups of cookie dough will you have? Show your work. Explain your thinking.

$$\frac{1}{2} + \frac{3}{4} + \frac{3}{8} = \frac{13}{8} \quad 1\frac{5}{8}$$

you will have $1\frac{5}{8}$ cups of cookie dough.

A Baking Problem

You are making cookies. The recipe says to combine ½ cup butter with ¾ cups chocolate chips and ⅜ cups butterscotch chips. Here are some questions.

1. When these ingredients are mixed together, how many cups of cookie dough will you have? Show your work. Explain your thinking.

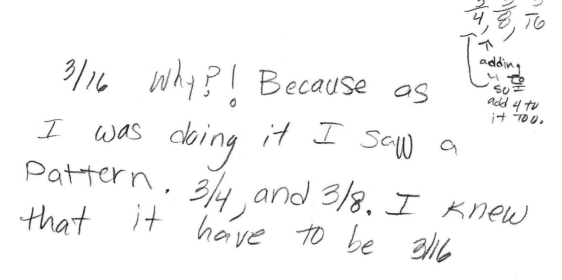

3/16 Why?! Because as I was doing it I saw a pattern. 3/4 and 3/8. I knew that it have to be 3/16

A Baking Problem

You are making cookies. The recipe says to combine ½ cup butter with ¾ cups chocolate chips and ⅜ cups butterscotch chips. Here are some questions.

1. When these ingredients are mixed together, how many cups of cookie dough will you have? Show your work. Explain your thinking.

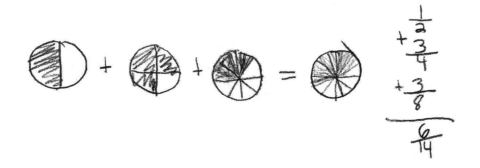

page 2 of 4

A Baking Problem

You are making cookies. The recipe says to combine ½ cup butter with ¾ cups chocolate chips and ⅜ cups butterscotch chips. Here are some questions.

1. When these ingredients are mixed together, how many cups of cookie dough will you have? Show your work. Explain your thinking.

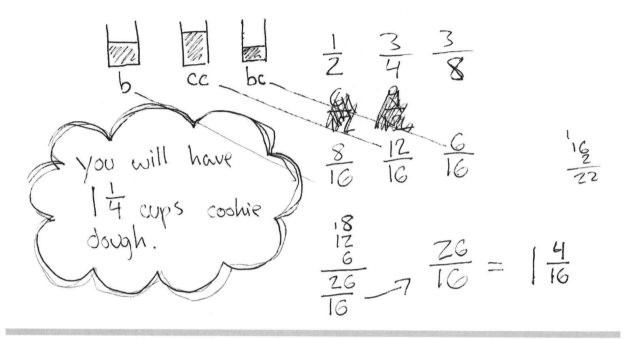

A Baking Problem

You are making cookies. The recipe says to combine ½ cup butter with ¾ cups chocolate chips and ⅜ cups butterscotch chips. Here are some questions.

1. When these ingredients are mixed together, how many cups of cookie dough will you have? Show your work. Explain your thinking.

A Baking Problem

You are making cookies. The recipe says to combine $\frac{1}{2}$ cup butter with $\frac{3}{4}$ cups chocolate chips and $\frac{3}{8}$ cups butterscotch chips. Here are some questions.

1. When these ingredients are mixed together, how many cups of cookie dough will you have? Show your work. Explain your thinking.

$$\frac{1}{2} + \frac{3}{4} + \frac{3}{8}$$

$$\frac{4}{8} + \frac{6}{8} + \frac{3}{8} = \frac{13}{8} = 1\frac{5}{8} \text{ cups of dough}$$

To add fractions you have to have a common denominator, so I converted each fraction and added them. I converted my answer to a mixed number.

A Baking Problem

You are making cookies. The recipe says to combine $\frac{1}{2}$ cup butter with $\frac{3}{4}$ cups chocolate chips and $\frac{3}{8}$ cups butterscotch chips. Here are some questions.

1. When these ingredients are mixed together, how many cups of cookie dough will you have? Show your work. Explain your thinking.

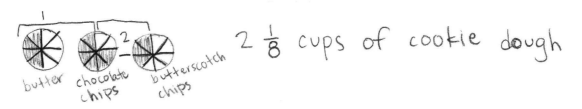

butter   chocolate   butterscotch
          chips   chips

$2\frac{1}{8}$ cups of cookie dough

Reduce to eighths.

page 4 of 4

APPENDIX F

Academic Rigor Task Cards

Activity 6.3, page 108, is designed to help team members develop common beliefs about what constitutes rigor in academic tasks. Rigor is often confused with tasks that are difficult for students because of lack of prior knowledge, but which in fact may not require higher-level thinking to complete. Without a common understanding of rigor among teachers, students in different classrooms may receive tasks with very different cognitive demands—and high-level tasks are necessary for students to learn to perform at high levels. Thus a common understanding of rigor is key to answering the questions, "What do our students need to learn?" and "How will we know if they've learned it?"

The following are sample academic rigor task cards for language arts, social studies, science, mathematics, and elementary-level PLCs. Note that while the first four content area cards are middle school–level tasks, the cards work well for high school PLCs as well; more advanced tasks often focus the discussion on what is hard for the teachers in the group rather than what is rigorous. Teachers need to work with about ten tasks together to develop a common understanding of rigor. Use the examples here and add at least six more from your own curriculum, or use the additional tasks provided at **solution-tree.com/PLCbooks**.

References

Santulli, T. V. A. (2006). Using simulations in the mathematics classroom. *Mathematics Teacher, 100*(4), 258–263.

Language Arts

1. _____ Review the notes you took in class today and the reading you just completed. Locate important points, words, or phrases. Identify each one by placing a sticker, dot, or star near it.

2. _____ Allies are people who stand up for someone else when they face injustice.

   a. Make a list of times when you have experienced injustice or been discriminated against.

   b. Choose one incident and write a narrative about it. Include a description of the scene, the people involved, and the dialogue. You might also include your own feelings and how the incident changed you.

   c. After you finish writing your narrative, analyze whether you had an ally:

      + Did someone stand up for you? If so, how did this affect the incident? Rewrite the ending as if the person had not been your ally.

      + If you had no ally, who could have stood up for you? Rewrite the ending of your narrative as if the person had been your ally.

3. _____ Make a 20 Questions–style "Who Am I?" game about mythical characters. Your clues can include details of the character's adventures, family, personal details, accomplishments, and so on.

4. _____ (The teacher identifies a key decision the main character in a book made. For example, in *Romeo and Juliet* the lovers decide to pretend that Juliet is dead.) What happened as a result of that decision? Brainstorm at least three alternative solutions the character(s) could have pursued. Determine the criteria he or she might have used to choose among the options. Then, write a short paper describing (1) each of the alternatives you came up with, (2) which one you believe was the best alternative and why, and (3) what might have happened in the story if the character had chosen that option.

Social Studies

1. _____ Work with a partner. Use the textbook and assigned video to identify the most important events of the Industrial Revolution. In the three-column grid provided, list the important events in the first column. To fill in the second column, watch television news programs to look for current events similar to the events you identified in the Industrial Revolution. In the third column, explain how the two are alike. Class presentation: Each person will show a news clip to the class and explain how the event was like an event in the Industrial Revolution.

2. _____ Evaluate the topographical map of an imaginary country you have been given. Where would be the best place to establish a settlement? Justify your placement based on what you have studied about the factors that influence where people live such as food, shelter, transportation, and defense.

3. _____ Design interview questions for a key person in a current news story. Your questions should cover not only important issues and events in the story, but also new developments of your own creation. With a classmate, role-play your interview on audiotape or videotape.

4. _____ (Each student in this class has printed off a biographical entry on the historical figure they are studying from the same online biography source.) Work together to produce a chart that analyzes the length of each entry as well as the cultural, gender, and ethnic characteristics of each subject. What patterns do you see? Do the lengths of the entries correlate with any of the characteristics of the subjects? What hypotheses might you draw about the people who developed this online source?

Science

1. _____ Review the information given to you about frogs and toads. Create a graphic organizer that compares and contrasts these two amphibians.

2. _____ Design your own insect. Construct a model or sketch of the insect. Then write a field guide entry that includes the following:

- Common name
- Scientific name
- Physical features
- Life span

- Eating habits
- Habitat
- Characteristics that make it an insect

3. _____ Create a drawing to show how you classify or organize your clothes, free-time activities, toys, books, or DVDs.

4. _____ In this experiment, you will make predictions about evaporation and compare them to actual results.

- Take three pie plates. Fill as follows:
    + Pan 1: $\frac{1}{4}$ cup water
    + Pan 2: $\frac{1}{4}$ cup water and three cups soil
    + Pan 3: $\frac{1}{4}$ cup water and a five-inch square of black felt
- Place the three pans in the sun.
- Make predictions. How long will it take for the water to evaporate from each pan? Why?
- Record how much water is left in each pan at one-hour intervals.
- Make a chart that compares your predictions to the actual results. Give reasons for any discrepancies.

Mathematics

1. Chandra won a drama scholarship worth $1,000 to study in New York City. A roundtrip plane ticket is $320 while a train ticket is $140. Once in New York, she can take acting classes at $60 per day or rehearse with an acting troupe as an extra in a production of *Grease* at $40 per day, with some instruction. Chandra's food and other expenses are fixed at $45 per day. If she does not plan to spend any money other than the scholarship, what are *all* choices of travel and instruction plans she could afford to make? Explain which option you think Chandra should select and why.

2. Use the following set of numbers (2, 3, 4, 7) to write eleven separate equations that equal 0, 1, 2, 3, 4, 5, 6, 7, 8, 9, and 10, respectively. You may use any operation we have studied, but you must use all four numbers in the set *and* use each operation only once within each equation. If you do not think you can write an equation equal to one of the numbers, explain how you came to that conclusion.

3. To help solve a national overpopulation problem, the government of a country rules that each family must stop having children as soon as they have one son. After a while, some families will have only one boy, some will have two girls and one boy, some will have three girls and one boy, and so on. Also, some families will only have girls because they give up trying for a son. Would girls tend to outnumber boys in this country? What do you expect the ratio of boys to girls will be? (Santulli, 2006)

4. A basketball player calculated her statistics on her own goal shooting. Over eleven games, her mean (average) score was 6, the median was 7, and the mode was 8. What might her scores be in each of the games?

✂ ·

Elementary Level

1. _____ Create a baseball card for an insect of your choice. Give your insect a nickname to identify a specific characteristic (for example, "Hairy" or "Skitter"). Include stats on your insect for the back of the card, including its size and other physical features.

2. _____ Retell a folktale or fairy tale from the villain's perspective. Share your story by creating a comic strip.

3. _____ Work with a group to put together a newspaper that covers historical events portrayed in the book you read. Articles could include interviews (from key characters to people on the street), obituaries, weather reports for key episodes, editorials on controversial points, political cartoons, eyewitness reports, crossword puzzles, letters from key figures, and so on. *Note: These must be historically accurate. Use other sources if necessary to support your statements.*

4. _____ (First grade) Our grocery store sells hot dog buns in packages of ten. I like whole wheat buns, but I think that my guests for dinner like white buns. I didn't want to buy two packages—that would be twenty buns, and we'd have to eat way too many hot dogs! I asked the grocer why he didn't make packages with some white and some wheat buns. He said there would be so many ways to make them—like one white and nine wheat, or five white and five wheat, and so on—that he got confused just thinking about it and simply made all the packages the same! Do you think we could figure out all the different combinations?

✂ ·

Glossary of Key Concepts and Terms

academic confidence: Students' belief in their ability to learn when they put forth effort and receive adequate support.

academic rigor: Curriculum and strategies that engage students in using higher-order thinking skills and developing a deep understanding of and ability to use relevant content worthy of sustained attention.

accountability: To establish action-oriented goals and objectives regarding adult learning that will improve student learning, and then to hold people responsible for meeting those goals.

action orientation: PLC acknowledgment that people learn by doing. They target what they need to learn to change their classrooms, determine how to best learn it (through lesson study, coaching, outside resources, reading, and so on), and apply what they are learning in their classrooms.

coaching: The art of guiding valuable people from where they are to where they want to be. Instructional coaching helps teachers meet the needs of all students.

coaching culture: A learning community where people understand and honor their colleagues' strengths, beliefs, and struggles with teaching and learning. Teams have a common language for discussion and strive to meet the needs of each member while collaborating to improve student learning.

collaboration, deep or Level III: Teaching team engagement in deep discussions about teaching and learning, serving as resources to each other in developing curriculum and lessons. Together, members unearth assumptions, gain from each other's natural strengths, share strategies and ideas, and discover what is possible in the classroom (Kise, 2006).

collective responsibility: Responsibility for the learning of all students, not just those with whom educators have direct contact.

common framework: A language for discussing teaching and learning that is nonjudgmental, strengths-based, can describe which learning styles a practice will reach, works across cultures and for all ages, and provides bridges among varying professional development efforts (Kise, 2006).

consensus: The highest level of agreement *without* dividing participants into factions (Glaser, 2005).

constructive use of differences: Acknowledgment of very different strengths, beliefs, and experiences of others and recognition that those differences are assets for effective collaboration.

differentiated coaching: The act of providing information, support, and other resources tailored to the needs of individual teachers when they are asked to change their classrooms (Kise, 2006).

differentiation: Tailoring of instruction to meet individual learners' needs, styles, and interests.

enduring understanding: The big ideas that students are to master during a unit of study. What concepts should become part of their core knowledge long after the details are forgotten? (Wiggins & McTighe, 1998)

equity in education: Access for all students, regardless of background, interests, learning style, and other forms of diversity, to a rigorous education that will prepare them to be successful citizens in our democracy.

essential questions: Questions that pose dilemmas, point to core ideas in a discipline, ask that knowledge be examined, and can be applied across curriculum in multiple ways. They reveal the complexity of content knowledge (Wiggins & McTighe, 1998).

evidence-based or text-based discussions: Agreement to restrict comments, ideas, or opinions to those based on and supported by the text participants have read together, or to make explicit connections with other texts or examples.

Extraversion (E): A preference for gaining energy from activities and/or interactions with other people. The psychological opposite of Introversion.

Feeling (F): A preference for coming to judgments through consideration of the impact of each alternative on the people involved and on values. The psychological opposite of Thinking.

group think: A condition that arises when groups are too cohesive or wish to minimize conflict, and therefore fail to consider alternative lines of thought or introduce information outside the group's comfort zone. This can lead to poor, unbalanced decisions (Janis, 1972).

Introversion (I): A preference for gaining energy from time spent in solitude and reflection or an in-depth activity. The psychological opposite of Extraversion.

Intuition (N): A preference for gathering information through hunches, connections, and analogies before working with details or experience. The psychological opposite of Sensing.

Japanese lesson study: A model developed by Japanese teachers in which teachers collaboratively choose a learning goal, research methods for teaching, plan the lesson, teach and observe the lesson, critique the results, revise, and reteach in a cycle of action research.

Judging (J): A preference for planning, sticking to the plan, and coming to closure. The psychological opposite of Perceiving.

learning progression: A sequenced set of subskills and bodies of enabling knowledge for students to master before they will be able to master subsequent curriculum goals (Popham, 2008). Also called knowledge packages (Ma, 1999).

learning styles: Patterns and variations in the ways students best gather, process, master, and apply information.

levels of questions: Costa's (2001) model of three different kinds of questions and their relevant rigor. Level 1 questions check for knowledge. Level 2 questions require inference, generalizing, combining information, or making decisions based on the information. Level 3 questions go beyond the text, asking for evaluation, synthesis, application, or speculation.

loose/tight leadership: The act of setting clear goals while allowing for multiple pathways or individual approaches to meeting those goals (Peters & Waterman, 1982).

Myers-Briggs Type Indicator® (MBTI): A self-reporting psychological instrument that helps people identify their four-letter type code, which gives them access to countless resources for applying the theory of personality type. An ethical interpretation includes learning about the theory, self-selecting one's four type preferences, receiving MBTI results, and then determining one's own best-fit type with the help of a certified practitioner.

Perceiving (P): A preference for staying open to more information and the needs of the moment. The psychological opposite of Judging.

personality type: A theory, developed by Carl Jung and expanded by Katharine Briggs and Isabel Myers, of normal differences in how normal people gain energy, gather information, make decisions, and approach life and work.

presentism: An attitude concentrating on short-term perspectives and gains, in which overwhelming outside pressures prevent educators from concentrating on collaborative planning and teaming for long-term, systemic change (Lortie, 1975; Hargreaves & Shirley, 2009).

problem-solving or "Z" model: A tool for making decisions or resolving conflict that ensures that the strengths and key considerations of Sensing, Intuition, Thinking, and Feeling are used, leading to balance and thorough results.

professional development: A comprehensive, sustained, and intensive approach to improving teachers' and principals' effectiveness in raising student achievement. It fosters collective responsibility for improved student performance, is job-embedded, ongoing, and may be supported by outside resources such as workshops or technical consultants (NSDC, 2009).

professional learning community (PLC): A group of educators committed to working collaboratively in ongoing processes of collective inquiry and action research to achieve better results for the students they serve. Professional learning communities operate under the assumption that the key to improved learning for students is continuous job-embedded learning for educators (DuFour et al., 2005).

protocol: A specified process that helps a group meet a predetermined observation, discussion, or decision goal. Well-designed protocols meet the needs of various learning and processing styles.

relational trust: The belief that colleagues have one another's best interest in mind, will adhere to norms for confidentiality, and will constructively help evaluate beliefs and practices without bias.

results orientation: A focus on the outcomes that PLC activities produce. Members determine in advance how they hope to improve student learning, plan how to measure improvements, and keep, revise, or change practices depending on results.

Sensing (S): A preference for gathering information through the five senses and through past experience before discerning themes or drawing conclusions. The psychological opposite of Intuition.

shared leadership: The acknowledgment that no one has all the strengths or the time to carry out all the vital roles of school leadership, nor does sustainable change happen when one person tries to do so. Leaders share leadership by calling on those around them to use their own strengths.

shared practice: The act of observing colleagues' classrooms, welcoming critiques and suggestions for improving lessons, examining the work of colleagues for evidence of learning, and openly sharing both the positive and frustrating classroom events and results.

SMART goals: Goals that are specific, measurable, achievable, results oriented, and time bound (O'Neill & Conzemius, 2005).

student-focused or student-centered discussions: Conversations in which teachers take a facilitative rather than directive role. Students take responsibility for voicing ideas and hypotheses, building on each other's thoughts, raising questions to improve every student's understanding, and drawing conclusions.

sustainable PLC: A PLC that continues to effectively focus on improving student achievement for years, whether leadership and membership are stable or not.

teambuilding: A facilitated process, by a team's leaders or outside facilitators, that helps members understand and appreciate one another's strengths while developing effective practices for goal-setting, communication, decision making, and other key team processes.

Thinking (T): A preference for coming to judgments through logic and objective reasoning and using if/then and pro/con tools for analysis. The psychological opposite of Feeling.

type development: The theory that holds that while we are born with eight innate personality preferences (four pairs), we favor one style, although over time we develop skills with all four pairs of preferences. We never become equally adept at using them all, but mature people have conscious control over their preferences and can choose behaviors that match situations.

References and Resources

Achinstein, B. (2002). Conflict amid community: The micropolitics of teacher collaboration. *Teachers College Record, 104*(3), 421–455.

Alcock, M. A., Murphy, E. A., & Ryan, P. M. (2000, Summer). *Researching connections: Developing personality preferences, electrophysiological brain patterns, teaching and learning strategies.* Unpublished manuscript. Keller, TX: Consortium for Type Development.

Allen, D. (2008). *Coaching whole school change: Lessons in practice from a small high school.* New York: Teachers College Press.

Andrews, D., & Lewis, M. (2007). Transforming practice from within: The power of the professional learning community. In L. Stoll & K. S. Louis, *Professional learning communities: Divergence, depth and dilemmas* (pp. 132–147). New York: Open University Press.

Barth, R. S. (2005). Turning book burners into lifelong learners. In R. DuFour, R. Eaker, & R. DuFour (Eds.), *On common ground: The power of professional learning communities* (pp. 115–133). Bloomington, IN: Solution Tree Press.

Bolam, R., McMahon, A., Stoll, L., Thomas, S., & Wallace, M. (2005). *Creating and sustaining effective professional learning communities* (Research Brief No. RB637). London: Department for Education and Skills.

Brown, J., & Isaacs, D. (1994). Merging the best of two worlds: The core processes of organizations as communities. In P. M. Senge, R. Ross, B. Smith, C. Roberts, & A. Kleiner (Eds.), *The fifth discipline fieldbook: Strategies and tools for building a learning organization* (pp. 508–517). New York: Broadway Business.

Bryk, A. S. (2009). Support a science of performance improvement. *Phi Delta Kappan, 90,* 592–595.

Bryk, A. S., & Schneider, B. (2002). *Trust in schools: A core resource for improvement.* New York: Russell Sage Foundation.

Coburn, C., & Russell, J. (2008). Getting the most out of professional learning communities and coaching: Promoting interactions that support instructional improvement. *University of Pittsburgh Learning Policy Brief, 1*(3), 1–5. Accessed at www.learningpolicycenter.org/data/briefs/LPC%20Brief_June%202008_Final.pdf on May 18, 2009.

The College Board. (2007). *AP European history free-response questions.* New York: Author. Accessed at http://apcentral.collegeboard.com/apc/members/exam/exam_questions/2085.html#name07 on October 23, 2009.

Cooper, M. (1988). Whose culture is it anyway? In A. Lieberman (Ed.), *Building a professional culture in schools* (pp. 342–367). New York: Teachers College Press.

Costa, A. L. (Ed.). (2001). *Developing minds: A resource book for teaching thinking* (3rd ed.). Alexandria, VA: Association for Supervision and Curriculum Development.

DuFour, R., DuFour, R., & Eaker, R. (2008). *Revisiting professional learning communities at work: New insights for improving schools.* Bloomington, IN: Solution Tree Press.

DuFour, R., DuFour, R., Eaker, R., & Many, T. (2006). *Learning by doing: A handbook for professional learning communities at work.* Bloomington, IN: Solution Tree Press.

DuFour, R., Eaker, R., & DuFour, R. (Eds.). (2005). *On common ground: The power of professional learning communities.* Bloomington, IN: Solution Tree Press.

DuFour, R., & Marzano, R. J. (2009). High-leverage strategies for principal leadership. *Educational Leadership, 66*(5), 62–68.

Dweck, C. S., & Leggett, E. L. (1988). A social-cognitive approach to motivation and personality. *Psychological Review, 95*(2), 256–273.

Elias, M. J. (2008). From model implementation to sustainability: A multisite study of pathways to excellence in social-emotional learning and related school programs. In A. M. Blankstein, P. D. Houston, & R. W. Cole, *Sustaining professional learning communities* (pp. 59–96). Thousand Oaks, CA: Corwin Press.

Elmore, R. F. (2004). *School reform from the inside out: Policy, practice, and performance.* Cambridge, MA: Harvard Education Press.

Feinberg, C. (2004). The possible dream: A nation of proficient schoolchildren. *Ed. Magazine.* Accessed at www.efficacy.org/Resources/TheEfficacyLibrary/tabid/227/Default .aspx on October 24, 2009.

Fitzgerald, C. (1997). The MBTI and leadership development. In C. Fitzgerald & L. Kirby (Eds.), *Developing leaders: Research and applications in psychological type and leadership development* (pp. 33–39). Palo Alto, CA: Davies-Black.

Fouts, B. M. (2000). Psychological types, learning styles and type of intelligences of successful students in alternative and traditional high school. *Proceedings of Center for Applications of Psychological Type Fourth Biennial Education Conference* (pp. 87–97). Gainesville, FL: Center for Applications of Psychological Type.

Gladwell, M. (2008). *Outliers: The story of success.* New York: Little, Brown and Company.

Glaser, J. (2005). *Leading through collaboration: Guiding groups to productive solutions.* Thousand Oaks, CA: Corwin Press.

Grossman, P., Wineburg, S., & Woolworth, S. (2001). Toward a theory of teacher community. *Teachers College Record, 103*, 942–1012.

Gunn, J. H., & King, M. B. (2003). Trouble in paradise: Power, conflict, and community in an interdisciplinary teaching team. *Urban Education, 38*, 173–195.

Hammer, A. L. (Ed.). (1996). *MBTI applications: A decade of research on the Myers-Briggs Type Indicator.* Palo Alto, CA: Consulting Psychologists Press.

Hargreaves, A. (1994). *Changing teachers, changing times: Teachers' work and culture in the postmodern age.* London: Cassell.

Hargreaves, A. (2002). Teaching and betrayal. *Teachers and teaching: Theory and practice, 8*, 394–407.

Hargreaves, A. (2007). The challenge of sustainability in professional learning communities. In L. Stoll & K. S. Louis (Eds.), *Professional learning communities: Divergence, depth, and dilemmas* (pp. 181–195). New York: Open University Press.

Hargreaves, A., & Fink, D. (2004). The seven principles of sustainable leadership. *Educational Leadership, 61*(7), 8–13. Accessed at www.ascd.org/publications/educational_leadership/apr04/vol61/num07/The_Seven_Principles_of_Sustainable_Leadership.aspx on February 25, 2009.

Hargreaves, A., & Shirley, D. (2009). The persistence of presentism. *Teachers College Record, 111*, 2505–2534. Accessed at www.tcrecord.org/content.asp?contentid=15438 on June 18, 2009.

Hart, H. (1991). Psychological types of students attending a high school credit remediation program for students at risk of not graduating. *Journal of Psychological Type, 22*, 48–51.

Hord, S. M. (Ed.). (2004). *Learning together, leading together: Changing schools through professional learning communities.* New York: Teachers College Press.

Hord, S. M., Meehan, M. L., Orletsky, S., & Sattes, B. (1999). Assessing a school staff as a community of professional learners. *Issues . . . About Change, 7*(1). Accessed at www.sedl.org/pubs/catalog/items/cha37.html on November 3, 2009.

Hord, S. M., & Sommers, W. A. (2008). *Leading professional learning communities: Voices from research and practice.* Thousand Oaks, CA: Corwin Press.

Huffman, J. B., & Jacobson, A. L. (2003). Perceptions of professional learning communities. *International Journal of Leadership in Education, 6*(3), 239–250.

International Baccalaureate Diploma Programme. (2005). *History higher level and standard level: Paper 2.* Accessed at www.ibo.org/diploma/curriculum/examples/samplepapers/documents/gp3_historyhlsl2.pdf on October 24, 2009.

Jackson, D., & Temperley, J. (2007). From professional learning community to networked learning community: Lateral capacity building for system learning. In L. Stoll & K. S. Louis, *Professional learning communities: Divergence, depth and dilemmas* (pp. 45–62). New York: Open University Press.

Janis, I. L. (1972). *Victims of groupthink.* Boston: Houghton Mifflin.

Joyce, B. (2004). How are professional learning communities created? History has a few messages. *Phi Delta Kappan, 86,* 76–83.

Killen, D., & Murphy, D. (2003). *Introduction to type and conflict.* Palo Alto, CA: Consulting Psychologists Press.

Kise, J. A. G. (2006). *Differentiated coaching: A framework for helping teachers change.* Thousand Oaks, CA: Corwin Press.

Kise, J. A. G. (2007). *Differentiation through personality types: A framework for instruction, assessment, and classroom management.* Thousand Oaks, CA: Corwin Press.

Kise, J. A. G., & Russell, B. (2000). [The psychological types of students identified by teachers as at risk, either academically or behaviorally]. Unpublished raw data.

Kise, J. A. G., & Russell, B. (2008). *Differentiated school leadership: Effective collaboration, communication, and change through personality type.* Thousand Oaks, CA: Corwin Press.

Kruse, S. D., & Louis, K. S. (2007). Developing collective understanding over time: Reflections on building professional community. In L. Stoll & K. S. Louis, *Professional learning communities: Divergence, depth and dilemmas* (pp. 106–118). New York: Open University Press.

Little, J. W. (1990). The persistence of privacy: Autonomy and initiative in teachers' professional relations. *Teachers College Record, 91,* 509–536.

Little, J. W. (2003). Inside teacher community: Representations of classroom practice. *Teachers College Record, 105,* 913–945.

Little, J. W., & Horn, I. S. (2007). "Normalizing" problems of practice: Converting routine conversation into a resource for learning in professional communities. In L. Stoll & K. S. Louis, *Professional learning communities: Divergence, depth and dilemmas* (pp. 79–91). New York: Open University Press.

Lortie, D. C. (1975). *Schoolteacher: A sociological study.* Chicago: University of Chicago Press.

Ma, L. (1999). *Knowing and teaching elementary mathematics: Teachers' understanding of fundamental mathematics in China and the United States.* Mahwah, NJ: Lawrence Erlbaum.

Macdaid, G. P., McCaulley, M. H., & Kainz, R. I. (1991). *Myers-Briggs Type Indicator atlas of type tables.* Gainesville, FL: Center for Applications of Psychological Type.

Marzano, R. J., Waters, T., & McNulty, B. A. (2005). *School leadership that works: From research to results.* Alexandria, VA: Association for Supervision and Curriculum Development.

McLaughlin, M. W., & Talbert, J. E. (2006). *Building school-based teacher learning communities: Professional strategies to improve student achievement.* New York: Teachers College Press.

Mohr, N., & Dichter, A. (2001). *Stages of team development: Lessons from the struggles of site-based management.* Providence, RI: Annenberg Institute for School Reform.

Murphy, E. (1992). *The developing child: Using Jungian type to understand children.* Palo Alto, CA: Davies-Black.

Murphy, E. (2007, July 12). *Exploring the video expression of type as type develops.* Paper presented at the XVII Biennial Conference of the Association for Psychological Type International, Baltimore, MD.

Myers, I. B., McCaulley, M. H., Quenk, N. L., & Hammer, A. L. (1998). *MBTI manual: A guide to the development and use of the Myers-Briggs Type Indicator* (3rd ed.). Palo Alto, CA: Consulting Psychologists Press.

National Staff Development Council. (2009). *NSDC's standards for staff development.* Accessed at http://www.nsdc.org/standards/index.cfm on November 20, 2009.

Nunley, K. F. (2006). *Differentiating the high school classroom: Solution strategies for 18 common obstacles.* Thousand Oaks, CA: Corwin Press.

O'Neill, J., & Conzemius, A. (2005). *The power of SMART goals: Using goals to improve student learning.* Bloomington, IN: Solution Tree Press.

Pashler, H., McDaniel, M., Rohrer, D., & Bjork, R. (2008). Learning styles: Concepts and evidence. *Psychological Science in the Public Interest, 9,* 105–119.

Payne, D., & VanSant, S. (2009). *Great minds don't think alike! Success for students through the application of psychological type in schools.* Gainesville, FL: Center for Applications of Psychological Type.

Pearman, R. R. (2001). Section 3: Style of leadership. In L. V. Berens, S. A. Cooper, L. K. Ernst, C. R. Martin, S. Myers, D. Nardi, et al., *Quick guide to the 16 personality types in organizations: Understanding differences in the workplace* (pp. 6–37). Huntington Beach, CA: Telos.

Pearson, P. D., & Gallagher, M. C. (1983). The instruction of reading comprehension. *Contemporary Educational Psychology, 8,* 317–344.

Peck, M. S. (1987). *The different drum: Community-making and peace.* New York: Simon and Schuster.

Peters, T., & Waterman, R. (1982). *In search of excellence: Lessons from America's best-run companies.* New York: HarperCollins.

Plaut, S. (Ed.). (2009). *The right to literacy in secondary schools: Creating a culture of thinking.* New York: Teachers College Press.

Popham, W. J. (2008). *Transformative assessment.* Alexandria, VA: Association for Supervision and Curriculum Development.

Reeves, D. B. (2006). *The learning leader: How to focus school improvement for better results.* Alexandria, VA: Association for Supervision and Curriculum Development.

Reichstetter, R. (2006). *Defining a professional learning community: A literature review* (Evaluation and Research Department Report No. 06.05). Raleigh, NC: Wake County Public School System.

Resnick, L. B. (1999). Making America smarter. *Education Week Century Series, 18*(40), 38–40. Accessed at http://ifl.lrdc.pitt.edu/ifl/media/pdf/MakingAmericaSmarter.pdf on August 27, 2009.

Resnick, L. B., & Hall, M. W. (1998). Learning organizations for sustainable education reform. *Daedalus, 127*(4), 89–118.

Richardson, V. (2009). Get fit, get smart: Along with physical strength, a little exercise helps kids build brain power. *Edutopia, 9*(3), 16–17.

Robinson, D. C. (1994). Use of type with the 1990 United States Academic Decathlon program. In *Proceedings: Orchestrating Educational Change in the 90's—The Role of Psychological Type* (pp. 35–41). Gainesville, FL: Center for Applications of Psychological Type.

Sagie, A. (1997). Leader direction and employee participation in decision making: Contradictory or compatible practices? *Applied Psychology: An International Review, 46,* 387–415.

Santulli, T. V. A. (2006). Using simulations in the mathematics classroom. *Mathematics Teacher, 100*(4), 258–263.

Saphier, J. (2005). Masters of motivation. In R. DuFour, R. Eaker, & R. DuFour (Eds.), *On common ground: The power of professional learning communities* (pp. 85–113). Bloomington, IN: Solution Tree Press.

Saphier, J., Haley-Speca, M. A., & Gower, R. (2007). *The skillful teacher: Building your teaching skills.* Acton, MA: Research for Better Teaching.

Schwartz, T. (1995). *What really matters: Searching for wisdom in America.* New York: Bantam Books.

Snyder, K. J., Acker-Hocevar, M., & Snyder, K. M. (1996). Principals speak out on changing school work cultures. *Journal of Staff Development, 17*(1), 14–19.

Sparks, D. (2006). Appeal to the heart as well as the head. *Tools for Schools for a Dynamic Community of Learners and Leaders, 9*(4), 1–2.

Stein, M. K., Smith, M. S., Henningsen, M. A., & Silver, E. A. (2009). *Implementing standards-based mathematics instruction: A casebook for professional development* (2nd ed.). New York: Teachers College Press.

Stoll, L., & Louis, K. S. (2007). *Professional learning communities: Divergence, depth and dilemmas.* New York: Open University Press.

Tallevi, L. (1997). The S-N balance in learning. *Bulletin of Psychological Type, 20*(1), 36–38.

Toole, J., & Louis, K. S. (2002). The role of professional learning communities in international education. In K. Leithwood & P. Hallinger (Eds.), *The second international handbook of educational leadership* (pp. 245–279). Dordrecht, The Netherlands: Kluwer.

Wagner, T. (2006). Rigor on trial. *Education Week, 25*(18), 28–29.

Wagner, T. (2008). *The global achievement gap: Why even our best schools don't teach the new survival skills our children need—and what we can do about it.* New York: Basic Books.

Wheatley, M. J. (2002). *Turning to one another: Simple conversations to restore hope to the future.* San Francisco: Berrett-Koehler.

Wiggins, G., & McTighe, J. (1998). *Understanding by design.* Alexandria, VA: Association for Supervision and Curriculum Development.

Wilkes, J. W. (2004, July 21–25). *Why do intuitives have an advantage on both aptitude and achievement tests?* Paper presented at the International Conference of the Association for Psychological Type International, Toronto, Canada.

Index

Learning by Doing
A Handbook for Professional Learning Communities at Work™
Richard DuFour, Rebecca DuFour, Robert Eaker, and Thomas Many
The second edition of *Learning by Doing* is an action guide for closing the knowing-doing gap and transforming schools into PLCs. It also includes seven major additions that equip educators with essential tools for confronting challenges.
BKF416

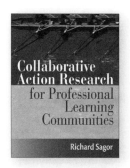

Collaborative Action Research for Professional Learning Communities
Richard Sagor
Become disciplined and deliberative with data as you design and implement program improvements to enhance student learning with the five habits of inquiry in this book. Detailed steps walk you through how to develop each habit in your own school system.
BKF354

Differentiated Professional Development in a Professional Learning Community
Linda Bowgren and Kathryn Sever
If differentiated instruction works for students, why not apply it to teacher learning? A practical guide for designing school or district professional development plans, this book explains a three-step model that is core to the differentiation process.
BKF275

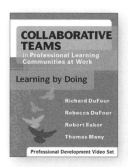

Collaborative Teams in Professional Learning Communities at Work™
Learning by Doing
Richard DuFour, Rebecca DuFour, Robert Eaker, and Thomas Many
This video shows exactly what collaborative teams do. Aligned with the best-selling book *Learning by Doing*, it features unscripted footage of collaboration in action. Learn how teams organize, interact, and find time to meet; what products they produce; and more.
DVF023

Solution Tree | Press  *a division of* Solution Tree

Visit solution-tree.com or call 800.733.6786 to order.